DOCUMENTARY DISPLAY

Nonfictions is dedicated to expanding and deepening
the range of contemporary documentary studies.
It aims to engage in the theoretical conversation
about documentaries, open new areas of scholarship,
and recover lost or marginalised histories.

General Editor, Professor Brian Winston

Other titles in the *Nonfictions* series

Direct Cinema: Observational Documentary and the Politics of the Sixties
by Dave Saunders

Projecting Migration: Transcultural Documentary Practice
edited by Alan Grossman and Àine O'Brien

The Image and the Witness: Trauma, Memory and Visual Culture
Edited by Frances Guerin and Roger Hallas

Vision On: Film, Television and the Arts in Britain
by John Wyver

Building Bridges: The Cinema of Jean Rouch
edited by Joram ten Brink

Films of Fact: A History of Science in Documentary Films and Television
by Timothy Boon

Forthcoming titles in the *Nonfictions* series

*Chávez: The Revolution Will Not Be Televised
– A Case Study in Politics and the Media*
by Rod Stoneman

Playing to the Camera: Musicians and Musical Performance in Documentary Cinema
by Thomas Cohen

DOCUMENTARY DISPLAY

RE-VIEWING NONFICTION FILM AND VIDEO

KEITH BEATTIE

WALLFLOWER PRESS
LONDON & NEW YORK

First published in Great Britain in 2008 by
Wallflower Press
6 Market Place, London W1W 8AF
www.wallflowerpress.co.uk

A catalogue record for this book is available from the British Library

ISBN 978-1-905674-72-5 (pbk)
ISBN 978-1-905674-73-2 (hbk)

Book design by Elsa Mathern

Printed by Replika Press Pvt Ltd, India

contents

To the memory of my father

... the most diverse and unexpected possibilities

– Jean Painlevé

acknowledgements

Re-viewing and revising the field of documentary film involved a lengthy process which benefited from the support of a number of friends and colleagues. Dr Julie Ann Smith patiently listened to my ideas and offered invaluable comments on the arguments presented here. For this support and encouragement, and myriad other reasons, thank you, again thank you, and always thank you...

I am grateful to Professor Roger Bell of the University of New South Wales for introducing me to documentary film and for providing me with a firm foundation in my academic endeavours. The research conducted by Professor John Corner of Liverpool University has constantly reminded me of the vibrancy of the field of documentary representation. I am also indebted to the critical writings of Professor Brian Winston on documentary film and television, Professor Bill Nichols on documentary film and Dr Jane Roscoe on documentary television. Associate Professor Adrian Martin's encouragement of a progressive film culture must be acknowledged. Professor Sam Girgus of Vanderbilt University offered extremely generous comments on my earlier work on documentary.

The project benefited from access to various archival sources and over the years I have welcomed the opportunity to watch films at the Australian Centre for the Moving Image, Melbourne; the Australian National Film and Sound Archive, Canberra; Anthology Film Archives, New York; the Pacific Film Archive, Berkeley; and the Centre Georges Pompidou, Paris.

Certain material in this book originally appeared in substantially different forms in the following refereed journals: *Continuum: Journal of Media and Cultural Studies* (November 2001), the *Australasian Journal of American Studies* (December 2004) and *Screening the Past* (December 2006). A section of chapter 5 was presented during the *On the Beach* conference of the Cultural Studies Association of Australia, in Brisbane, December 2000. I would like to thank Albie Thoms for his support of this paper. A variant of chapter 6 was presented at the XIII biennial conference of the Film and History Association of Australia and New Zealand, Melbourne, November 2006. I appreciate the productive and supportive audience comments made on my papers at these events. Deakin University provided Research Publication Leave during semester two of 2005 which enabled me to make significant progress on the manuscript of this book. The Film and Television Studies Section at Monash University, Melbourne, provided me with a congenial environment during the final stages of the work. I'd especially like to thank Dr Deane Williams, Head of Section, in this relation.

For their unceasing support of my academic activities I would like to thank my mother, Beryl Beattie, my sister, Louise Thake, and my brother-in-law, Michael Thake. This book is dedicated to my father, Reg Beattie (1922–98), Collector of Customs, airman and sage, whose memory is a guiding light in everything I do. Any errors in this book remain, of course, my own.

introduction

Why can't we have a true theatre of documentary (non-fiction) filmmaking that entertains and excites?
  – D.A. Pennebaker and Chris Hegedus (in Macdonald & Cousins 1996: 390)

'Documentary is a clumsy description,' claimed John Grierson, 'but let it stand' (1998: 81). As awkward as it may be, the word was nevertheless useable to the extent that as early in its history as 1932, when Grierson made this comment, the features of the form he referred to as documentary were identifiable and rapidly hardening into a prescriptive formula. In this way, the theories, canons, expository forms, institutional arrangements and productive practices constructed, emphasised and applied by Grierson and his followers have historically functioned in English-language contexts to ignore, sideline and exclude alternate documentary representational approaches and forms.[1] Exclusion and marginalisation, and the restricted range of formal processes endorsed within the existing documentary canon, demand reconsideration. *Documentary Display* addresses this situation by re-viewing and retheorising documentary film and video as part of a process of recognising and understanding the complete range of formal and stylistic practices which can be denoted by the maladroit word 'documentary'.

The focus for the reassessment of the documentary tradition undertaken within this book – with its potential to inform, enlarge and enrich that tradition – is the processes, practices and protocols referred to here as *documentary display*. Such a display functions across, and invests, a broad range of works, and is analysed within this study through reference to practices operative within the popular and prominent forms of found-footage film, 'rockumentary', the city film, nonfiction surf film and video, and certain depictions of natural science topics. Display is not unique to any one form or film – it is a representational regime and process that features in and across the type of work analysed in this book and is recognisable in other works, including, for example, those in which 'documentary' footage is reframed within the context of avant-gardist nonfictional film and video. Though deployed in varying contexts, the practices and processes of documentary display are identifiable to the extent that display is a category that productively lends itself to analysis.

In these terms, display is not reducible to a mode in the sense of those summarised by film theorist Bill Nichols as expository (direct address to the viewer, typically via voice-over, in which images are frequently subservient to the words of the narration), observational (an abandonment of commentary within an intimate, sometimes voyeuristic, close depiction of subjects), interactive (based on witness testimony within interviews), reflexive (a self-conscious questioning of the documentary form), and performative ('an "excessive" use of style') (see 1991: 95). The formulation of 'modes' was Nichols' attempt to specify prominent features of the form referred to as documentary. Nichols' object was not to reify formal components of a documentary tradition, but to analyse characteristics which have historically been circulated in the service of documentary representation. 'Modes' constitute basic building blocks for theoretical interpretations of documentary's formal structures and generic identity. As such, modes constitute the basis of a broader assessment of what have been called documentary 'functions', a notion which offers a productive way to define and describe documentary display.

According to John Corner's useful analysis, both form and function, interacting across national media histories, have coalesced to the point that it is possible to speak of a documentary tradition. Beyond form and function, a third element, that of production practices, informs the constituents that make up a documentary text. As Corner notes, 'specific production practices, forms and functions all work to "hold together" (or not) the documentary identity at different times and places. Briefly put, they concern how a film or [television] programme was made (according to what recipes, methods and ethics), how it looks and sounds, and what job it was designed to do, what kind of impact and use-value it was to have for audiences' (2002a). In these ways the identity of a work of documentary is composed of the variable interaction of form, function and productive practices. Drawing on this approach to the generic components of documentary, Corner outlines four functions within which modes (notably exposition, testimony and observation) have variously been applied.

The first function is 'the project of democratic civics. Documentary is regarded here as providing publicity for citizenship. This is documentary in its classic, modernist-realist phase, funded ... by official bodies. In Britain, it is certainly this function that Grierson saw the documentary primarily fulfilling in the 1920s and 1930s.' The second function Corner identifies is 'documentary as journalistic inquiry and exposition. This is essentially the documentary as reporting, possibly the most extensive use of documentary methods on television.' A third function is that of 'documentary as radical interrogation and alternative perspective. This is documentary as developed within the independent cinema movements which have maintained a presence in the audio-visual culture of some countries. There is often a level of formal experimentation here not usually found in broadcast forms ... including techniques of disruption and distancing ... and kinds of personal testimony.' A fourth function is the recently emergent 'documentary as diversion. This is documentary as "popular factual entertainment" ... Performing this function, documentary is a vehicle variously for the high-intensity incident (the reconstructed accident, the police raid), for anecdotal knowledge (gossipy first-person accounts) and snoopy sociality (as an amused bystander to the mixture of mess and routine in other people's working lives)' (ibid.).

Each of these functions encodes practices which have been variously circulated across the history of documentary representation, and point within such an application to the existence of a canon of 'classical' or exemplary documentary practices and works which, through audience reception and critical attention (though not necessarily endorsement), have been centrally situated within the documentary tradition. Exemplifying this process the new kid on the documentary block – popular factual entertainment – has already moved from its slightly disreputable status as an illegitimate meeting of multiple forms (observation, exposition, 'entertainment'), to be included within the documentary tradition, with central works in the field (the multinational success of Big Brother, for example) verging on canonical status. As works of popular factual entertainment increasingly move away from their bases in observational practices to widely deploy voice-overs and interviews they are, perhaps inevitably, readily incorporated into a documentary tradition predicated on the dominance of such expositional practices.

In their move towards canonical status, 'reality TV' and popular factual entertainment deflect the critical anxiety which accompanied their first appearances.[2] For many critics, the rise of 'reality TV', followed by the emergence of popular factual entertainment, spelled the end or death of documentary, killing off various long-standing traditions, among them observational or socially-concerned documentary film and television programmes.[3] It was a case of après Big Brother, le deluge... However, debate over the emergence of popular factual entertainment and the 'end of documentary' argument has failed to register the vitality imparted to nonfictional depictions by another form of representation, that of documentary display, and the ways in which display attests to documentary's longevity, as in, for example, the presence of the practice within rockumentary, a form which has proven popular with audiences and will no doubt continue to be so into the future. The multiple forms which encode the capacities and acts of documentary display, while critically ignored or excluded from the documentary canon, constitute a significant documentary function which is additional to, and in many ways separate from, those set out by Corner.

Documentary as display is documentary in which the visual realm is maximised as the field of exhibitionistic, expressionistic and excessive attractions. Documentary display draws on the basic claim of documentary – 'Believe me, I'm of the world' (Renov 1993b: 30) – in its implication of a set of scopic practices which variously include, among other features, the performative body as the focus of spectatorial attraction; image enlargement through magnification, whether cinematic microscopy or IMAX frame and screen enlargement; the productive exploitation of the disjunctions and ambiguities within and between images which occurs in certain found-footage films; the sensational bodily affect exemplified in images that evoke tactility or a pleasurable sense of shock; kinetic movement within the frame and, alternatively, a meditative 'stillness' resulting from an emphasis on an observational fixed-frame long take.[4]

Documentary display operates across a range of audio-visual technology, including the 'new media' of electronic image and sound manipulation. However, the focus here is on expressions of display in film and video – whether screened in cinemas and other public exhibition spaces, or on television – as exemplars of wider nonfictional representational trends evident over the past three decades. Aspects of documentary practice such as processes of production, the political economy of documentary media, or audience attitudes are not the primary focus of this book, though the study does in places confront historiographic, political and cultural conditions and concerns and attends to the reception of certain forms. Principally, the operations of documentary display, and analysis of those practices, are approached here through the field of aesthetics, a category – following Grierson's emphasis on the public utility of documentary – that is often excluded from analysis of documentary representation.

The category of aesthetics, and the aesthetic functions of texts, implicates three important points: 'the organization of creative works, the experiences they produce (or, to signal a key crux, that audiences derive from them) and the modes of analysis and theory that can be used in investigation' (Corner 2003: 92). Such considerations are applicable to works of documentary in general, and to the expressive practices and capacities of documentary display in particular. In relation to the first point – attention to the organisation of creative works – documentary film producer and film theorist Jill Godmilow has argued that the documentary tradition reinforces a filmmaking practice that is 'ridiculously limited in terms of style' and is largely closed to influences from other art forms (quoted in Adams 1999: 5). The analysis of the forms, styles and capacities of documentary display undertaken in this book indicates that a range of practices beyond traditional and limited approaches are available to, and applied by, documentary filmmakers in the creation of expressive and innovative representations.

4

The experiences produced by and derived from documentary – the second point – have typically been defined in critical sources in terms of the genre's ability to relay information and knowledge. According to this position, documentary is instructional and educative and knowledge is expressed through argument, which is constructed in theoretical writings as the defining characteristic of documentary work.[5] In turn, argument, and its presentation of evidence, is commonly linked in critical and theoretical assessments of documentary to the explanatory strategies of exposition. The argumentative thrust of exposition – direct address to the viewer in the form of voice-over, onscreen presenter comments, and titles – can be summarised as 'telling', a mode that primarily seeks to explain, impart information and convey 'knowledge'. The presence of exposition within the documentary tradition, aligned with patterns of telling, beg questions that frequently go unasked, and hence unaddressed, in estimations and assumptions of documentary form. Certain questions demand to be answered, for example, 'why ... assume that all documentaries present evidence in making an argument? Might not some documentaries have other functions?' (Plantiga 1997: 103). A cogent analysis – one which embodies these questions – argues that 'we need ... to recognize the fact that some nonfiction films are concerned not primarily with argument, or with the assertion of propositions about the world, but have an aesthetic function that serves as their primary organizational principle' (ibid.). Beyond 'telling' there is another way of seeing and knowing.

Indeed, the image, released from a strict denotative literalism whereby it must serve as the vehicle or subject of evidence, is variously deployable as evocation, sensory affect, or 'poetic' allusion. Such effects pertain to documentary as 'looking' (as opposed to 'telling'), the scopic realm of documentary display. In this way documentary display embodies 'a notion of visuality that separates documentary looking from the regime of ... power/knowledge relationships' (Green 2006: 69; emphasis in original). The documentary image as a purveyor of information and knowledge is an aspect of documentary display, though no longer a privileged and exclusionary feature of documentary representation. Separated, or freed, from the immediate demands of knowledge production, documentary display entertains, startles and excites in ways which produce pleasure – the great repressed in analyses predicated on documentary as a sober discourse. Within its multiple enhancements documentary display helps shift documentary theory – the third and final consideration within the category of aesthetics – into new terrain, away from a focus on sobriety, rectitude, literalism, and a public service educative function, towards an emphasis on the arresting, playful, ambiguous, entertaining and pleasurable capacities of nonfiction imagery. The focus of this study on the expressive dispositions of documentary display offers new ways of seeing and understanding documentary – re-viewing it – as a contribution to the process of expanding the field of documentary analysis and theory.

Chapter one extends and informs the outline here of the core organisational features of documentary display. Works of display, and the scopic satisfactions derivable from an exhibitionistic 'showing' as opposed to an expositional 'telling', are grounded in a variable mix of formal practices in which sensation is frequently the vehicle of cognition and knowledge. The emphasis in documentary display on affective ways of knowing is the result of practices and protocols as diverse as, among others, various camera movements and associated markings of time and place; long takes which alternately frame action or a meditative stillness; and expressive pictorial stylings which mix 'poetic' and rhetorical functions. The revised ways of seeing, and an associated revision of knowing attendant on display, constitute a lineage distinct from that inaugurated by Grierson. Indeed, the origin of display is aligned with the series of visual excitements and shocks characteristic of an early 'cinema of attractions'. Beyond the cinema of attractions the lineage of display includes borrowings from the filmic avant-garde and its influence on a range of works, including modernist films such as the so-called city symphonies of the 1920s and 1930s to contemporary avant-gardist documentations marked by a high degree of visual and sonic innovation. The lineage of display also implicates capacities commonly associated with fiction film, including the arresting features of spectacle, a condition which frequently serves within display as a vehicle of knowledge. In a linked way the body – as a presence in urban environments and in performance – often becomes a focus of spectacular display. The body in documentary display functions in a way similar to its presence in certain fiction genres in which the body is a central depictive focus capable of evoking strong affective bonds and responses in spectators. The outcome of the practices and capacities of display is the displacement of seriousness and sobriety in works characterised by multiple pleasures, the latter a term not commonly applied to documentary representation. The presence of pleasure is part of the reason that works of display are also popular (to use another word not necessarily commonly applied to documentary). In its lineage derived from 'attractions' and the avant-garde, and in its variable mixture of spectacle, pleasure and popularity, documentary display revises the documentary canon and the traditional assessments it encodes concerning the nature of documentary representation.

Each of the forms examined here constitute cases or instances which broaden and augment the various features and capacities of the process of documentary display. In this way chapter two, 'The Corporeal and the Urban', examines the case of display as it operates within representations of the city, tracing such works from the city symphonies of the 1920s dealing with urban centres in Europe, to New York City films of the 1940s and 1950s, to contemporary films which explore non-Western cities. Within a focus on the corporeal – through which 'the city' is actualised as such – the city film innovatively combines elements of the avant-garde with the capacities of documentary to produce an expressive documentary display of place and people. Traversing a period from the 1920s to the present, the display of the city film implicates varying historical and political conditions, each of which provides a further context and informing perspective for the examination of the visual capacities of the documentary display which is the productive basis of the city film.

Chapter three examines the case of direct cinema and performance, specifically the ways in which the observational method of direct cinema is reworked within the popular form of 'rockumentary' and its grounding in the attraction of performative action. The chapter traces rockumentary from its foundation in the 1960s in D.A. Pennebaker's *Dont Look Back* (1967) to recent variants of the form. While works in this category vary in the ways in which they deploy and manipulate the practices and approaches of direct cinema, a common focus of such works is an emphasis on the performing body, whether onstage or off. The complexity of performance in both environments – and the interaction of onstage and offstage performative action – serves as the engaging appeal of the visually alluring and pleasurable display of rockumentary.

As the outlines of chapters two and three suggest, display is implicated with a range of considerations that contribute to the realm of the aesthetic. Following this line of analysis, chapter four further informs the formal and stylistic capacities of documentary display within the case of found-footage film. The chapter analyses the ways in which found-footage film constructs arguments about history – as a particular form of representation of experience – within the process of display. The basis of found-footage film's representation of history is an expanded notion of the concept of the visual archive, from which the found-footage filmmaker extracts images which are deployed to construct narratives and impressions of socio-historical experience. The core of such representations, and the foundation of the found-footage display, is located in collagist methods which release unrealised meanings and productive ambiguities inherent in source footage. Ambiguity – and its attendant 'double seeing' – results in a critical historiography operative through documentary display. This process is examined within various works, including *Tribulation 99* (1991), Craig Baldwin's witty history of US-Latin American relations, Bruce Conner's *A Movie* (1958), a review of media-saturated US culture, and Kenneth Anger's *Scorpio Rising* (1964), a film not commonly associated with found-footage practices though one which grounds its analysis of a particular subculture within the methods of collagist found-footage filmmaking.

Chapter five, the case of nonfiction surf film and video, attends to the intersection of avant-gardist and documentary proclivities within the popular and prolific forms of surf film and surf video produced over the past forty years. The stylistic differences between surf film of the early 1970s and recent surf video are mediated within a shared discourse which mixes poetic, expressive and rhetorical components into an avant-gardist documentary display. The sensorial impact of such a display is registered in the unruly and unrestrained audience reactions which frequently accompany public screenings of surf film and the fact that surf videos are often watched repeatedly in the home. Exemplifying the formal practices and patterns of audience reception associated with the form, the video works of Jack McCoy – analysed in the chapter – point to specific features and effects of the documentary display of surf texts.

The final chapter is concerned with the case of natural science film and display as a characteristic of the magnified image. Visual enhancement of documentary images in the form of microcinema, and its abilities to dramatically enlarge microscopic organisms, and the spectacularly increased size of images within large-screen projection systems, result in unique forms of scopic attentiveness to subjects. Typically, such technology and approaches have been directed towards the representation of nature, particularly marine organisms. The chapter examines this process within the microcinema of Jean Painlevé and the enlarged documentary representations of IMAX cinema. Painlevé's Surrealist-inflected enlarged images of aquatic nature, and the costly illusion of the real produced within IMAX representations of natural science subjects, construct documentary display as a technologically-enhanced expansion of the realm of the visible.

The coalescence within documentary display of an expansive field of the visible and impressions of reality in the forms and styles studied in this book point in one way to new, as yet unrealised, approaches to the depiction of experience and, in another way, return us to the origins of cinema. When in the late nineteenth century Louis Lumière demonstrated the invention that was the cinématographe, audiences were amazed by the sights on the screen. Film historian Erik Barnouw summarised the impact of those first screenings as 'the familiar, seen anew in this way, brought astonishment' (1983: 7). The astonishment attending new representations of the real: documentary display rewinds to this moment, and projects it into the future.

chapter one

Show and Tell:
Revealing Documentary Display

I find myself involved with ... the experience of seeing, looking and watching.
– Kevin Robins (1996: 5)

The film theorist and documentary filmmaker Jean-Louis Comolli noted in 1999 that as 'vague and variable as it may seem, the category called "documentary" is central to the cinema's experience and history ... The cinema began as documentary and the documentary as cinema' (1996: 36). No doubt; but the form of documentary film was foreshadowed early in its history in the English-language world by John Grierson's insistence that the awkward word 'documentary' denote a type of film which he famously called the 'creative treatment of actuality' (quoted in Rotha 1952: 70).[1] For Grierson, 'the creative shapings ... of natural material', applied in the service of public education, constituted the basis of documentary film (1998a: 83). While the forms and styles of a so-called creative treatment or interpretation of 'actuality' have been widely debated and critiqued in various sources, relatively little attention has been paid to the effects on the Griersonian documentary of the demands of its commitment to social pedagogy. The need to inform or instruct the public was associated with specific arrangements and practices implicated in the Griersonian documentary, chiefly that of sponsorship. Constructed by Grierson as a project separate from the funding regimes of the fiction film industry, documentary was deployed in the service of various government and corporate sponsors which relied on the new mode as a way of informing and forming citizens and consumers.

Following Grierson, sponsorship was institutionalised as the foundation of the documentary mode of production, and the continued prominence of sponsorship within the documentary tradition is exemplified in the fact that 'sponsored documentary' is a category that includes the majority of documentary output.[2]

Stuart Legg, one of Grierson's early collaborators, reflected late in his career on the role of government sponsorship in the British documentary film movement by noting that the relationship between the filmmaker and the governmental sponsor 'is at the root of everything we've done for the last forty years' (quoted in Winston 1995: 58). Legg conceded that the relationship was a problematic one, thereby pointing to the fact that civil servants did not necessarily understand or accept a filmmaker's ideas, aesthetics or politics. As documentary filmmaking continued to align itself through sponsorship with the demands of the civil service and commercial interests, sponsored filmmakers found it increasingly difficult to make films which expressed a point of view that contradicted or opposed the political stance of the sponsor. Harry Watt, who produced a number of films for the General Post Office Film Unit (GPO Film Unit) after Grierson had moved there in 1933 from the Empire Marketing Board (EMB), admitted that the 'truth is that if we had indulged in real social criticism to any extent, we would have immediately been without sponsorship and a whole experiment [in documentary film production] would have been finished' (quoted in Armes 1978: 133). Watt did not consider the fact that without the restrictions of sponsorship the 'experiment' may have taken very different forms, devoid of the self-censorship which he admits functioned to set limits on what documentary filmmakers could and could not say – and how they could say it.

One effect of the rise of the Griersonian documentary form in English-speaking countries throughout the 1930s and 1940s was that it tended in those countries to marginalise the modernist experimentations of filmmakers such as Dziga Vertov, Walter Ruttmann, Jean Vigo and Luis Buñuel. Indeed, works of political and formal radicalism, and agitational forms generally, are frequently overlooked or downplayed in the majority of critical assessments of the documentary tradition, with their emphases on the Griersonian form of sponsored documentary. Later in his career Grierson insisted that documentary 'was from the beginning ... an "anti-aesthetic" movement' (1998b: 105) and elsewhere he admitted, with less revisionist fervour, that the requirements of various government sponsors meant that British documentary films of the 1930s largely 'ceased exploring into the poetic use of the documentary approach' (quoted in Sussex 1972: 24). Those filmmakers who persisted with formal experimentation, such as Humphrey Jennings, occupied an unstable position within the documentary film movement. Jennings' 'poetic' style – which is frequently summarised in terms of 'beautiful' images and striking montages – challenged Grierson's emphasis on documentary as a project concerned with social pedagogy. In these terms Jennings' *Listen to Britain* (1942) was dismissed by Edgar Anstey, one of Jennings' colleagues at the Crown Film Unit, the successor of the GPO Film Unit, as a work of great beauty which 'will not encourage anyone to do anything at all' (1942: 8).[3] Grierson set the direction of such a critique when in the early 1930s he criticised the formal experimentalism of Ruttmann's *Berlin: Die Symphonie der Großstadt* (*Berlin: Symphony of a Great City*, 1927), and the rest of the so-called city symphony genre, for an 'aesthetic decadence' that, according to Grierson, failed to apply a 'sense of social responsibility' to fulfilling the 'best ends of citizenship' (1998a: 87).

The terms of this approach, within which documentary is constructed as a form of governmental or official information masquerading as a morally (and politically) correct practice undertaken in the worthy name of popular pedagogy, infused the documentary project with a serious, some would say dull, tone. Documentary theorist Bill Nichols captures this tone in his widely quoted reference to documentary as a 'discourse of sobriety' (1991: 3–4). The timbre or tone is expressed in, to maintain the sonic metaphor, what Nichols calls the 'voice' of documentary. For Nichols, 'voice' refers to 'something narrower than style: that which conveys to us a sense of a text's social point of view, of how it is organising the materials it is presenting to us ... Voice is perhaps akin to that intangible, moiré like pattern formed by the unique interaction of all a film's codes, and it applies to all modes of documentary' (1998: 50). In this sense 'voice' is a central organisational principle around which a documentary text is constructed.

A central component of such a principle is the arrangement of codes known as exposition, the dominant mode of documentary in its 'classic' or Griersonian form, which has continued since the 1920s to be the primary means within documentary of relaying information and persuasively making a case (see Nichols 1991: 34). In turn, the chief means by which information, knowledge and evidence is presented in the expository documentary (and, according to certain critical interpretations, documentary generally) is through argument. Nichols insists that 'at the heart of documentary is less a *story* and its imaginary world than an *argument* about the historical world' (1991: 111; emphasis in original). Nichols' distinction between narrative (storytelling) and argument suggests that the two functions are not complementary. In so doing he 'reintroduces the traditional criteria for documentary – as real and as non-narrative' (Cowie 1997: 55). In contrast, as various commentators have noted, narrative is the basis of documentary; though a narrative can be attenuated within works which feature a heightened degree of visual or auditory style.[4] Narrative – storytelling – informs exposition, to the point that within the construction of an argument in narrative the 'telling' function supersedes (though does not erase or displace, as Nichols' description suggests) the story function. In this way exposition, as narrative and argument, is a powerful and prevalent organisational 'voice' available within documentary.

Nichols accedes the place of narrative in documentary when he argues that the rhetorical devices of exposition (typically in the form of direct address to the viewer) ally themselves with the cause and effect structure of narrative. He states that the 'viewer of documentaries in the expository mode generally holds that a commonsensical world will unfold in terms of the establishment of a logical, cause/effect linkage between sequences and events.' In this way 'recurrent images or phrases function as classic refrains, underscoring thematic points or their emotional undercurrents, such as the frequent montages of artillery fire and explosions in combat documentaries that steer the progression of a battle, its physical means of implementation, and its human cost' (1991: 37). Nichols elaborates the cause and effect structure of the expository mode in his reference to the 'problem-solution' strategy adopted in certain expositional works which, he notes, 'plays a role similar to the role of the classic unity of time in narrative where imaginary events occur within a fixed period of time and often move toward a conclusion under some form of temporal urgency or deadline ... [However], rather than the suspense of solving a mystery or rescuing a captive, the expository documentary frequently builds a sense of dramatic involvement around the need for a solution' (1991: 38).

Direct address to the viewer, in the form of titles, voice-over commentary, or on-camera delivery by a studio presenter or reporter 'in the field', is a chief strategic presentational form of the arguments which are narrativised in exposition. Added to these processes the voices of interview subjects 'are woven into a textual logic that subsumes and orchestrates them ... From *Housing Problems* (1935) to the latest edition of the evening news, witnesses give their testimony within a frame they cannot control and may not understand ... their task is to contribute evidence to someone else's argument, and when well done ... our attention is not on how the filmmaker *uses* witnesses to make a point but on the effectiveness of the argument itself' (Nichols 1991: 37). The testimony of witnesses is frequently incorporated into the argumentative narrative via a voice-over commentary which interprets and directs the information provided by witnesses. The authority of this form of narration, as expressed in the term often used to refer to the strategy, that of a 'voice of God', is derived from, and seated in, the disembodied voice. The so-called voice of God issues from an omniscient position that is the (verbal) incarnation of critical judgement and knowledge removed from the fallibility of the human sphere. Mary Ann Doane stresses that 'it is precisely because the voice is not localisable, because it cannot be yoked to a body, that it is capable of interpreting the image, producing the truth' (1980: 43).

Certain practices have subjectified the anonymity of the disembodied voice of God. The use of various recognisable voices and speech patterns, as typified by the voice-overs provided by known Hollywood stars in *Dear America: Letters Home from Vietnam* (1987), 'personalise' narration. In another way an ironic narration, in which a voice-over playfully or mockingly contrasts with accompanying images, as in the subversive clash of word and image in Georges Franju's *Hôtel des invalides*

(1952), effectively reconfigures an overly-authoritarian voice-over. Beyond such examples narration is typically provided by a stentorian voice of God which legitimates points of view as authoritative in a practice which has contributed to the 'miserable reputation' of voice-over (Bruzzi 2000: 40). The practice has been criticised for its suppression of the voices of witnesses, closing off the experiences of subjects who otherwise could provide differing class or gender perspectives on the topic nominally under examination.[5] In this way Nichols comments on the 'overwhelmingly didactic' nature of an expository mode which dominates the communicative capacity of accompanying visuals (1988: 48). The point is forcefully carried in the estimation by compilation documentary filmmaker Emile de Antonio that voice-over is 'fascist', a technique that limits and controls the possibilities for spectatorial interpretation (quoted in Kellner & Streible 2000: 21). The various references to control, domination and authoritarianism prominent in criticisms of the mode expose the negative consequences of expository telling. More specifically, the imposition of textual meaning via *telling* – being told – displaces the possibility and potential of gaining information and knowledge through an open-ended process of interpretation which productively exploits the knowledge and pleasure (knowledge as pleasure) located in *showing* – the visual capacities of what is here referred to as the act of documentary display.

Display is based on the documentary claim to represent *the* world (as opposed to the fictional representation of *a* world), and in this case truth claims operate within and through a stylised scopic textual system.[6] Display is grounded in narrative, though the narrative function is often attenuated and placed in the service of the expressive visual effects of the work. The visual also supersedes, but does not displace, a work's auditory components, and the auditory register is frequently deployed to reinforce visual effects.[7] The textual emphasis on scopic capacities pointed to here does not reduce documentary display to observationalism, though display is often established through, for example, long takes, the privileged style of the observational mode of direct cinema. More particularly, display is operative within scopic forms and spectatorial effects reminiscent of those of early cinema. As David MacDougall notes, 'documentary was born in the pleasures of watching such ordinary events as leaves shimmering on a tree or a train arriving at a station' (1992–93: 36).

However, long takes of such arresting and pleasurable incidents fell into disfavour within the history of documentary filmmaking, primarily as a result of erroneous conceptions of audience expectations. MacDougall outlines this process through reference to the 'great enemy of documentary (and oddly, rather a taboo topic of discussion among filmmakers themselves)' which he describes as the '"dead spot" in which nothing seems to be happening. Film producers are terrified of such moments, for they are terrified of audience impatience' (1992–93: 38).

Andy Warhol tested the limits of such a theory in *Sleep* (1963) and *Empire* (1964), static long takes of many hours duration of, respectively, a person sleeping and Manhattan's Empire State Building. In these works 'our expectations [of narrative progression and 'action'] are deliberately confounded and we are provoked into supplying the images with meaning. Audiences, however, are generally asked to stretch the rules only so far. And when they are asked to do so they are usually offered compensation' (MacDougall 1992–93: 40). Such pay-offs may include multiple visually captivating segments, as in the series of two-and-a-half minute long takes of man-made environments that is James Benning's *El Valley Centro* (1999), or five whimsical long-takes of the sea and beach in Abbas Kiarostami's *Five: Dedicated to Yaujiro Ozu* (2003). The so-called rockumentary, which has been aligned in critical interpretations of documentary with direct cinema, applies the long take of direct cinema's observational mode in ways which offer multiple sonic and scopic compensations for the audience. Rockumentary typifies the revision of observation within an enhanced showing or display, an active process of representation, which contrasts with a (direct cinema) observationalism that is capable of verging on the passivity of surveillance footage.

The various stylings result in works which produce a viewing experience which is captivating, exciting and pleasurable. The pleasures derivable from display are grounded in the pictorial quality of a documentary image 'with its organisation of screen space into a plane both of reference and of formal design [in] combination with its kinetic properties ... [Such an emphasis derives] from the movement of things within the shot, the movement of the camera during the shot or, more broadly, the temporal organisation of continuity and change introduced by editing' (Corner 2003: 96–7). All three arrangements 'produce different kinds of scopic satisfaction' while the second feature – shifting perception brought about by camera movement (its glide, its drifts, its swoops, its trackings, its movements across documented space, its shiftings of the relationships of distance and proximity) – is one of the most familiar of aesthetic tropes in documentary practice' (Corner 2003: 97). The technique involves a

fusing of the reality of [the] world with the motivation of imaginative design [which] is often stimulating in its bringing together of recognition with kinds of 'making strange' or, less radically, what we must call 're-seeing'. Here, the connections made between our apprehension of the physical realities shown and the subjective (affective, conceptual or propositional) world that also forms the documentary topic are significant. Feeling and ideas condense upon objects, bodies and places, modified by the physical at the same time as the physical itself is perceived within the developing thematics. Such a dialectics, at once sensual and intellectual, referentially committed yet often possessed of a dreamlike potential for the indirectly suggestive and associative, is central to *documentary as an aesthetic project*. (Ibid.; emphasis in original)

Further, it can be added, such a 're-seeing' is a basis of a documentary display in which the expressive, aesthetic, formal attractiveness of a documentary work is amplified to the point of threatening to displace the 'referential such as to make the subject itself secondary to its formal appropriation' (Corner 1996: 123).

The range of formal practices and features identified here in relation to the act of documentary display are deployed to a marked degree in works which Nichols describes as performative, among them, for example, Trinh T. Minh-ha's *Naked Spaces: Living is Round* (1985) and Jonathan Robinson's *Sight Unseen* (1990). These works are less concerned with the real-world referent traditionally defined as the object of documentary than with the effective and affective capacities of a work's combination of expressive and highly stylised representational methods. Ever since *Turksib* (1929) and *Night Mail* (1936), notes Nichols, 'documentary has exhibited these qualities; what is distinctive here is their function as an organizing *dominant* for the text' (1994: 94; emphasis in original).

Reference to an avowedly 'political' work such as *Turksib* within an analysis of aesthetics alludes to what is elsewhere constructed as a divide between aesthetics and politics, a division that is typically framed in terms of mutual exclusions within in which the aesthetic denies politics, and vice versa. The separation of aesthetics and politics is recast within documentary display's circulation of a politics of aesthetically-organised vision. Such a politics is deployed, for example, in works which apply the city symphony form to analyses of social conditions within cities beyond the urban centres of the Europe-North America axis which have traditionally served as the focus of the form. The connections between aesthetics and politics are extended in the relationship between documentary display and the essay film. Paul Arthur points to the political stance of the essay film when he argues that 'the majority of [film] essays cast themselves as oppositional, interrogating received wisdom or status quo ideologies from left perspectives' (2003: 60). The practices of documentary display variously share a number of features with the essay film, among them a strong authorial presence, the possibility of movement between separate styles, tones, or modes of address, and the disruption of unities of time and place associated with traditional documentary practices (see Arthur 2003: 59). Essayists – among them Chris Marker, Harun Farocki, Patrick Keiller, Jean-Luc Godard, Raúl Ruiz and Johan Grimonprez – produce works which, in common with acts of documentary display, occupy an ambivalent position between documentary and the avant-garde. As with 'performative' documentaries, the analysis in essay films of historical events and experience may be subsumed within an emphasis on the expressive representation of such experiences, as in the case of Grimonprez's *Dial H-I-S-T-O-R-Y* (1997), a work which examines the processes of media representation of historical events within a self-reflexive commentary on the filmmaker's own strategies.

A similar subsumption of the historical referent within documentary display does not cancel out the construction of knowledge within display. Rather, the multiple formal innovations and the maximisation of expressive scopic capacities characteristic of works of display construct knowledge in particular ways. Display motivates knowledge differently to nonfiction works such as the long-form news documentary and its series of fact-based statements. The form of knowledge produced within documentary display is subjective, affective, visceral and sensuous and as such is a part of a broader visual culture that 'acknowledges appeals to the senses as a form of knowledge production. This form of knowledge production is distinct from appeals to the intellect or cognitive faculty. For the intellect, logic prevails over affect; for the senses the converse holds, bringing with it a distinct form of knowledge' (Nichols 2000: 41–2). In these terms, as Nichols notes, the 'visual is no longer a means of verifying the certainty of facts pertaining to an objective, external world and truths about this world conveyed linguistically. The visual now constitutes the terrain of subjective experience as the locus of knowledge' (2000: 42). Part of this form of reception is what Barbara Stafford has termed the 'sensationalized knowledge' available from and through visual spectacle as a means of 'demonstrating truth' and learning from 'the seductive coercion of perception' (1994: 51, 58). A sensuous and affective knowledge – a knowledge which is produced via the senses, primarily that of sight – and which operates through subjective, as opposed to cognitive, impressions and processes, draws on relations between sight and imagination. Sight, and appearances, says John Berger, impact on an imagination that constructs and animates our understanding of the world. 'Without imagination the world becomes unreflective and opaque' (quoted in Robins 1996: 159). Appearances inform imagination through which the world is apprehended within a form of visual knowing, a central feature associated with documentary display.

The shift from a cognitive to an affective path to knowledge characteristic of documentary display is produced within and through a variety of scopic regimes and protocols. Display variously configures forms, modes, styles and practices including long takes and other features of observation, kinetic editing, vibrant collage, dynamic movement within the frame, close-ups and expanded screen views within expressive representations of the socio-historical world. The description of display offered here leaves room for inclusions, and is not intended to be either exclusive or exhaustive. The description, and the following additions and supplements, outline characteristics of display in broad terms, while at the same time further specifying features and capacities that are recognisable within the category.

A fuller description of documentary display is achieved within attention to its foundations in what film historian Tom Gunning has evocatively called the 'cinema of attractions', its allegiance to forms and practices associated with the avant-garde, and through reference to certain other core features, principally bodily exhibition, and pleasure. Each of these features and components is discussed below.

Display and attractions

Gunning's notion of 'attractions' alludes to Eisenstein's analysis of the theatre in terms of a process through which a spectator is subjected to a 'sensual or psychological impact'. Eisenstein proposed that the theatre should be composed of a montage of such attractions which would create in the spectator responses notably different from those provided by 'illusory depictions' (1988: 35). Gunning applies Eisenstein's term 'attractions' to the aesthetic features of so-called primitive cinema (which in critical assessments is typically placed circa pre-1907, before the dominance of narrative forms of cinema). Gunning's description of an early cinema of attractions theorises cinema as a series of visual shocks derived from short scenes of action.[8] The capacity of such moments to captivate an audience was ignored by Grierson who condemned these works to the 'lower categories' separate from 'documentary proper' (1998a: 82). In his distinction between narrative forms of documentary and non-narrative forms of 'actualities', Grierson was here, as elsewhere in his theoretical writings, tending towards oversimplification.

The 'weak ontological frontier' between documentary and the so-called lower forms, and a dialectical intermingling of features across the frontier, was not banished by the sort of fiat Grierson sought to impose (see Levy 1982: 249). Miriam Hansen stresses this point when she argues that the majority of actualities were non-acted, 'ostensibly staged scenes that could be categorized as documentaries', including news films, views of everyday work and leisure, and a large number of travelogues. Hansen widens her argument by insisting that the imposition of 'the later distinction between documentary and fictional genres upon primitive diversity ... is problematic in several respects.' The distinction is complicated when, for example, it is considered that certain actualities involved fictionalised reconstructions, yet were not necessarily intended to deceive. Hansen notes that while 'the boundaries between documentary reality and mise-en-scène may have been relative, they seem to have mattered less than the kind of [visual] fascination ... [with the] sensationalist appeal of such films' (1994: 31).

Gunning emphasises this appeal in his description of the core of the cinema of attractions as an 'aesthetic of astonishment' whereby spectators were confronted with short works of often startling and shocking imagery which offered up a 'brief dose of scopic pleasure' (1994: 121). The aesthetic identified by Gunning was to be variously deployed in subsequent years in the service of longer works of documentary display. According to Hansen the goal of the 'aesthetic of showmanship' within the early cinema of attractions was to assault viewers with 'sensational, supernatural, scientific, sentimental, or otherwise stimulating sights', in contrast to the incorporation of such features into the illusion of a fictional narrative. 'The style of early films was presentational rather than representational; that is, they tended to address the viewer directly – as in frequent asides to the camera and the predominantly frontal organization of space – rather than indirectly – as classical [fiction] films do through perceptual absorption into a closed diegetic space' (1994: 137).

The aesthetic is exemplified through reference to the first film screened publicly for a sizeable audience, the Lumière brothers' *L'Arrivée d'un train à la Ciotat* (*Arrival of a Train at La Ciotat*, 1895). A foundational myth of cinema holds that at the sight of the approaching train on the screen 'spectators reared back in their seats, or screamed, or got up and ran from the auditorium (or all in succession) ... Credibility overwhelms all else, the physical reflex signalling trauma' (Gunning 1994: 114–15). Whether or not screenings of the film produced such a demonstrable reaction (and serious doubts exist whether panic occurred during the film's screening in the Salon Indien of the Grand Café on the Boulevard des Capucins in Paris), 'there is no question that reactions of astonishment and even a type of terror accompanied many early projections' (Gunning 1994: 116). Responses of this kind point to an intense spectatorial involvement in short scenes marked by startling imagery. Such images, and the exhibitionist attractions which bind them, is further exemplified in Thomas Edison's short film *Electrocuting an Elephant* (1903). In the film an elephant is secured to a large electrified plate, which is switched on. Smoke rises from the elephant's feet and shortly thereafter the animal falls on its side. 'The moment of technologically advanced death is neither further explained nor dramatised' (Gunning 1994: 122). As with *L'Arrivée d'un train à la Ciotat*, viewer curiosity is aroused and fulfilled in 'a brief moment of revelation typical of the cinema of attractions. This is a cinema of instants, rather than developing situations' (Gunning 1994: 123). The cinema of attractions eschews narrative action or empathy with characters; it is, instead, one which directly addresses the audience with spectacular sights. In this way the spectator 'does not get lost in a fictional world and its drama, but remains aware of the act of looking, the excitement of curiosity and its fulfilment ... This cinema addresses and holds the spectator, emphasising and foregrounding the act of display' (Gunning 1994: 121). Display in the cinema of attractions is organised so that showing or the presentation of a series of revelatory views or central sights takes precedence over an expository form of telling.

The relevance of the aesthetic of attractions to the concept of documentary display is highlighted through reference to Gunnings' elaboration of features of the aesthetic, which in its emphasis on exhibitionism, 'attractiveness', visual fascination and the 'very pleasure of looking', precedes, though comes to parallel and inform, documentary display:

> The attraction invokes an exhibitionist rather than a voyeuristic regime. The attraction directly addresses the spectator, acknowledging the viewer's response ... This encounter can ... take on an aggressive aspect, as the attraction confronts audiences and even tries to shock them (the onrushing locomotive that seems to threaten the audience is early cinema's most enduring example).

> The metapsychology of attractions is undoubtedly extremely complex, but its roots could be traced to what St. Augustine called curiositas and early Christianity condemned as 'the lust of the eye'. We could list a number of inherently 'attractive' themes in early cinema: a fascination with visual experiences that seem to fold back on the very pleasure of looking (colours, forms of motion – the very phenomenon of motion itself in cinema's earliest projections); an interest in novelty (ranging from actual current events to physical freaks and oddities); an often sexualised fascination with the body (female nudity or revealing clothing, decay, and death); a peculiarly modern obsession with violent and aggressive sensations (such as speed or the threat of injury). All of these are topoi of an aesthetic of attractions. (2004: 44)

Gunning informs this description within a contrast of the cinema of attractions and fictional narrative: 'Rather than a desire for an (almost) endlessly delayed fulfilment and a cognitive involvement in pursuing an enigma, early cinema ... attracts in a different manner ... Attraction's fundamental hold on spectators depends on arousing and satisfying curiosity through a direct and acknowledged act' of visual surprise and 'a cinematic gesture of presenting for view' which further approximates the documentary act of display (ibid.; emphasis in original). The aesthetic invokes a 'spectator whose delight comes from the unpredictability of the instant' (2004: 49).

Documentary display shares with the cinema of attractions an emphasis on spectatorial engagement, visual stimuli, and showing or presenting exhibitionistic views capable of visually arousing pleasure in the spectator, and, through such approaches, forms of sensational knowledge. Gunning emphasises that the effects of a cinema of attractions do not disappear with the dominance of narrative cinema, but instead form components of narrative films (as in the song and dance spectacle of the musical) and, significantly, inform certain avant-garde practices (1990: 57). It is this tradition – the cinema of attractions merged with avant-garde practices, as opposed to the Griersonian documentary film – that constitutes the central lineage of documentary display.

Documentary display and the avant-garde

The inscription in documentary film history of the Griersonian mode of social persuasion as the basis of the documentary form has functioned to deny 'not simply an overly aesthetic lineage but the radically transformative potential of film pursued by a large segment of the international avant-garde' (Nichols 2001: 582). As Nichols notes, from 'the vantage point of the avant-garde, the state and issues of citizenship [which concerned Grierson] were obscured by questions of perception ... [and] aesthetics ... These questions were more challenging imperatives than those that preoccupied the custodians of state power' (2001: 583). Nichols also points out that the 'historical linkage of modernist technique and documentary oratory, evident since the early 1920s in much Soviet and some European work, failed to enter into Grierson's own writings' (2001: 582). In fact the linkage is prominent in Grierson's influential essay 'First Principles of Documentary' of 1932 in which he relates his ideas on documentary to the formal experiments of Eisenstein's *Bronenosets Potyomkin* (*Battleship Potemkin*, 1925) and *Que Viva Mexico!* (1932), and modernist works within the city symphony cycle – notably Cavalcanti's *Rien que les heures* (*Nothing But Time*, 1926) and Ruttmann's *Berlin*. However, Grierson charges modernist innovation, notably as it is expressed in *Berlin*, with being a 'dangerous' model for documentary to follow (1998a: 88). Grierson's acknowledgement of the avant-garde, only to erase its presence from the documentary tradition, is a rhetorical move that is replicated in various theoretical quarters. Indeed, the separation of documentary and avant-gardist works is one reason for the continuing displacement of display from the history of documentary film, and within this separation works of documentary display are relegated to, and contained exclusively within, the category of the avant-garde.

A different approach, one which recognises many of what can be called avant-gardist documentaries, expands and informs the history of documentary film and video through the incorporation in that history of avant-gardist productions marked by features of documentary display. Examples here include works as varied as modernist city symphonies; the extended long take that is Michael Snow's *Wavelength* (1967); Werner Herzog's *Fata Morgana* (1971); Edin Vélez's video *Meta Mayan II* (1981) with its long takes, freeze frames and innovative observational strategies; Bill Viola's *Hatsu-Yume* (*First Dream*, 1981), which combines unusual views of rocks, wind and water in its report on Japan; Tacita Dean's video *The Green Ray* (2001) and its study of the effects of light associated with the setting sun; Michael Glawogger's series of global images in *Workingman's Death* (2005); and *Into the Great Silence* (2005), Philip Gröning's study of the silent lives of French Carthusian monks shot without commentary, interviews or musical score – a film which, in many respects, is a Western version of Robert Gardner's evocative study of Eastern religious practices, *Forest of Bliss* (1985). Stan Brakhage's *The Act of Seeing with One's Own Eyes* (1971) is a significant addition to this list. Brakhage's work is typically assigned within critical interpretations to the realm of avant-garde or experimental cinema. However, *The Act of Seeing with One's Own Eyes* differs from the majority of Brakhage's work in its deployment of a documentary approach to its subject. The film forms part of Brakhage's so-called Pittsburgh Trilogy, each film concerned with public institutions in the city. *Eyes* (1970) depicts the city's police force, *Deux Ex* (1971) a hospital, and *The Act of Seeing with One's Own Eyes* represents a number of autopsies performed in the city's morgue. The film is shot with a hand-held camera in an observational style reminiscent of direct cinema, though the lack of sound refuses the cues otherwise available in observational filmmaking. In the absence of any form of exposition, the film privileges a graphic showing over other forms of representation.

Showing in Brakhage's film is a function of access to what is otherwise forbidden from sight. Few films, whether classified as documentary or fiction, are as explicit in their dissection of their subject matter, although the cinema of Surrealism offers a number of points of reference for Brakhage's film. The slitting of an eyeball in *Un Chien andalou* (1928) enacts a metaphor of the curtailment of sight that is inverted within the open showing of dismembered body parts, including eyes, in Brakhage's film. Georges Franju's Surrealist-inspired *Le Sang des bêtes* (*Blood of the Beasts*, 1949) is another work that uses scenes of death – in this case animals being slaughtered – to assault the spectator. Like *Las Hurdes* (*Land Without Bread*, 1932), Buñuel's Surrealist critique of documentary as a form of knowledge, Franju's film wilfully disrupts the spaces or moral reassurance available within documentary through a series of shocks not dissimilar to those in *The Act of Seeing with One's Own Eyes*.

The shock associated with the visual presentation of otherwise proscribed sights can be traced to the cinema of attractions, which routinely transgressed the taboo concerning the representation of death and dying, albeit in a far less literal way than that of Brakhage's film. Like films of the cinema of attractions, *The Act of Seeing with One's Own Eyes* deploys a mode of representation that startles and shocks the viewer with graphic documentary images that point to the film's interrogative stance. Brakhage uses frank scenes of death and the dissected body as a way of reflecting on, as the film's title suggests, the very act of seeing. Brakhage posed a number of questions related to this act in the opening paragraph of his book *Metaphors on Vision* (1963):

> Imagine an eye unruled by man-made laws of perspective, an eye unprejudiced by compositional logic, an eye which ... must know each object encountered in life through an adventure of perception ... How many rainbows can light create

for the untutored eye? How aware of variations in heat waves can that eye be? Imagine a world alive with incomprehensible objects and shimmering with an endless variety of movement and innumerable gradations of color. (1976: 1)

Brakhage directs attention to the ways in which we see, as much as to the objects of sight. Here, as in the morgue film, Brakhage is concerned with analysing not the world itself, but the act of seeing the world. Brakhage offers a line of analysis and a direction for a form of representation which examines seeing through attention to the processes and contexts of showing or display whereby 'sight' is deployed. In this way Brakhage's film reflexively interrogates its form of representation, begging questions (as he did in *Metaphors on Vision*) of the ways in which documentary images are viewed and the types of responses demanded of such images.

The reflexive and implicatory method of Brakhage's film exposes the basis of its documentary display as a form which supplements documentary representation of the world with an awareness of the very process of representation evoked via the film's seemingly minimalist aesthetic strategies. Display in these terms involves the graphic ('unflinching') depiction of a subject and the provocation of questions concerning ways of seeing documentary depictions, questions which are commonly sublimated within the documentary drive to foreground content, as exemplified within journalistic or investigative modes of expositional representation. The emphasis on, and analysis of, 'seeing' and showing in the absence of expositional telling implicates the maximisation of the scopic regime which is spectacle. Spectacle extends documentary display, revising elements of the practice found in *The Act of Seeing with One's Own Eyes* wherein images provoke a conflicted spectatorial response of wanting/not wanting to see. The viewer of a spectacle, in contrast, is pleasurably captivated by 'explicit' imagery.

'A protracted stare': spectacle, knowledge, display

The conjunction of spectacle and documentary is an unusual one given that spectacle is typically described in relation to fiction film. Spectacle in fiction film is, as Laura Mulvey has pointed out, essentially atemporal, a moment of excess and stasis outside the temporal progression of the narrative (quoted in Doane 2002: 170). While fiction film is grounded in a narrative drive wherein all features of the work (from characterisation to *mise-en-scène*) are dedicated towards advancing the narrative, the 'excessive' nature of 'spectacle halts [a narrative] in a protracted stare' (Doane 2002: 170). In the paradigmatic example of fictional spectacle – the song and dance routine of the musical during Hollywood's classical era – what we find, according to Dana Polan, 'is an "entertainment" in its virtually etymological sense – a *holding-in-place*, a *containment*, in which awareness of any realities other than the spectacular gives way to a pervading image of sense as something that simply happens, shows forth, but that cannot be told' (1986: 56; emphasis in original).

In terms of a theory which predicates documentary on its expository ability to 'tell', a practice that endorses a reality which can be displayed though which 'cannot be told' is condemned to be cast negatively or denied. On the latter point, Brian Winston notes that the Griersonian strain of documentary theory, with its emphasis on sober expository modes of analysis 'meant, in effect, that a documentary of spectacle could not be pursued' (1998b: 168). Spectacle is thus an alternative to the features of Griersonianism. In one of the few studies to address this issue Elizabeth Cowie emphasises that 'for all its seriousness, the documentary film nevertheless also involves more disreputable features of cinema usually associated with the entertainment film, namely, the pleasures and fascination of film as spectacle' (1999: 19). This line of argument is extended in the recognition that such 'disreputable features' are productively inscribed within documentary representation through forms of display understood as the vehicle for a form of spectacle capable of producing knowledge.

Using documentary film as the basis of his analysis, Steve Neale defines spectacle as 'a specific form of the evocation and satiation of the scopic drive' in which images are exhibited 'to "catch" ... the eye' (1979: 66, 67). Such an approach situates spectacle within the scopic representational capacities that sustain it as a mode of 'fascinated gaze' (1979: 85). However, Neale, in contrast to Cowie and in common with numerous theorists of documentary, is suspect of this process, particularly the pleasure implicated in the alluring appeal of spectacle. For Neale, spectacle is not the 'visible as guarantee of veracity (of truth, of reality), but rather the visible as mask, as lure' which displaces 'knowledge, the essential ingredient in documentary, in favour of the construction of a mode of visual pleasure' (ibid.). Grierson lurks behind Neale's assessment that a pleasurable spectacle has no place within forms of documentary predicated on the serious (unspectacular and unpleasurable) business of purveying knowledge. Neale, like Grierson and other practitioners and theorists within the Griersonian tradition, refuses to acknowledge the spectacular as a vehicle of knowledge constructed within and through sensuous, entertaining and pleasurable documentary displays.

In contrast, Cowie's analysis of documentary draws a relationship between spectacle and a 'desire for reality', and notes that certain documentary films implicate 'desiring as well as knowing, spectators' (1999: 19, 20). Spectacle, as Cowie cogently points out, has long been associated with knowledge, as exemplified in the eighteenth-century institution of the European 'grand tour' 'whereby the viewing of the sights themselves and their visual appreciation' was deemed a necessary component of a 'young man's education' (1999: 25). In its capacity of constructing or communicating knowledge, documentary display draws on spectacle as 'an entertaining of the eye through form and light in a showing, and an entertaining of the mind in the showing of something known either as familiar or in a new or spectacular way, or something not yet known that thereby becomes known' (1999: 27). In such ways the viewer of spectacular documentary display is 'invited to look and, even without titles or voice-over, thereby to understand the seen' (ibid.).

A clear example of such a co-implication of spectacle and knowledge within documentary display is the scopic strategies deployed in *Lektionen in Finsternis* (*Lessons of Darkness*, 1992), Werner Herzog's reflection on the Gulf War and its aftermath. In *Lessons of Darkness*, as in certain other nonfiction works by Herzog, forms of visual spectacle are presented within the representation of landscape. Herzog's *La Soufrière – Warten auf eine unausweichliche Katastrophe* (*La Soufrière*, 1976), for example, depicts the island of Guadeloupe threatened by a massive volcanic eruption. His film *Fata Morgana*, filmed in and around the Sahara desert, focuses on the industrial detritus that litters the sandscape. The dramatic and bleak scenes of this film are that of the Earth polluted, and perhaps doomed, by Western technology as a form of environmental colonialism. In this sense Herzog asks, 'What have we done to our landscapes? We have *embarrassed* landscapes', and links such an 'embarrassment' with a loss of purity of image: 'How can we regain innocence of vision, our vision that has been so badly contaminated? We have to find adequate images again' (quoted in O'Toole 1979: 48; emphasis in original). The 'adequacy' or capacity of images to represent despoiled landscapes is a question begged by Herzog in *Lessons of Darkness*, a film which is divided into a prologue and thirteen sections. The condition of the landscape is immediately apparent in the prologue, which features a smoke-covered environment, and a man dwarfed by a huge fire. The following sections are introduced by titles which, in the English-language version of the film, are 'A Capital City' (long shots of prewar Kuwait); 'The War', featuring excerpts from television broadcast coverage of the aerial bombing of Baghdad; 'After the Battle', with its images of destroyed and damaged machinery and buildings; 'Finds from Torture Chambers', which includes instruments of torture laid out on a table in what was a torture chamber, and a woman's testimony in which she recounts the fate of her sons who were tortured to death in an act she was forced to witness. 'Satan's National Park' depicts fires from destroyed oil fields, and in the next section, 'Childhood', a woman recounts the murder of her husband and the brutalisation of her son, rendered mute by Iraqi soldiers. The following sections concentrate on the burning oil wells, torched by the retreating Iraqis, which littered the deserts of postwar Kuwait. 'And a Smoke Arose like a Smoke from Furnace' depicts the fires in the destroyed oil fields, and in

'A Pilgrimage' firefighters attempt to quell the flames with bulldozers, a scene extended in 'Dinosaurs on the Go'. 'Protuberances' examines the lakes of oil in the desert, and 'Drying up the Source' shows a number of burning wells being capped, while 'Life without Fire' depicts an inexplicable action: the relighting of two oil fires. Finally, 'I Am So Tired from Sighing; Lord Let it Be Night' is composed of shots of the oil fields aflame.

Critical references to the visual sublimity of Herzog's images often allude to Edmund Burke's interpretation of the sublime as a condition associated with fear, gloom and the majestic.[9] For Burke, landscape and its natural features and phenomena were frequently objects which inspired the sublime. Earthquakes, fires, storms, thunder and volcanoes were all capable in their excessive transcendence of the bounds of the natural world of inspiring the awe and dread that are aspects of the sublime.[10] However, for Burke the sublime object does not only cause terror; it can also result in sensations of excitement and feelings of exhilaration. Burke's oxymoron 'rapturous terror' captures the dual functions of the sublime, and something akin to this effect is achieved in the spectacle of Lessons of Darkness.[11] The panoramic aerial long takes, shot from a helicopter above the billowing smoke and massive fires of the oil-soaked desert, are capable of producing dialectically related responses of gloom and majesty, terror and rapture, horror and awe.

While evoking features of a Burkean sublime within its spectacle, the film also offers an essayist critique of the degraded 'spectacle' of events presented by the international corporate news media. In a commentary on his film, Herzog notes that oil-well fires had been widely screened on television and the 'whole world ... had repeatedly watched the same kind of images of the burning oil wells in Kuwait on CNN during and after the war. But these images saturated the public's consciousness only via news broadcasts and made very little impact because of their tabloid style.' According to Herzog, the 'stylisation of the horror in Lessons of Darkness means that the images penetrate deeper than the CNN footage ever could' (quoted in Cronin 2002: 244–5). Herzog reworks the images of commercial news media within a documentary mise-en-scène and an 'awe inspiring' framing of the scene. The 'majesty' of the sublime is reinforced in the use of music by Grieg, Mahler and Wagner on the soundtrack.

Herzog is alert to the fact that references to the 'stylisation' of horror can evoke critical misreadings of the film. Certain critics have condemned Herzog for not making an explicit antiwar statement, or for relegating the scenes of torture victims to minor or secondary roles against the lengthy scenes of oil fires.[12] Herzog admits that there is a 'slight imbalance' in the film and would have preferred to have included extra scenes of the human toll of the war, but was expelled by the Kuwaiti government before he could shoot such footage. The criticisms demand a different work entirely to that produced by Herzog (and if taken to their extreme would lead to the banning or censored exclusion of a work such as *Lessons of Darkness*). More particularly, such criticism misreads the fact that Herzog did not necessarily seek to engage the politics of warfare, but sought instead to represent the ecological consequences of war by focusing on landscape as a Goyaesque disaster of war.

The critical debate over the film highlights questions surrounding the place of spectacle in the presence of 'real world' concerns defined exclusively in terms of politics. John Corner's analysis of the dual operations of documentary serves to address such questions. Corner quotes Bill Nichols to the effect that 'a good documentary stimulates discussion of its subject, not itself' and adds that:

> Clearly, in one sense it is self-evidently true – a 'good' documentary must always, by definition, have the primary aim of directing its viewers down its *referential axis* towards 'real world' concerns. Yet ... there is an *aesthetic axis too* – a documentary 'poetics'. This does not merely comprise a set of presentational skills; it is centrally implicated in the production of the referential, and can be admitted to be so without distracting from the latter's primacy. (1995: 104; emphasis in original)

In this way the referential axis of *Lessons of Darkness* (the impact of war on landscape and a commentary on the representation of war) is achieved – foregrounded – through the aesthetic axis of a spectacle. Here, and in selected examples examined in the following chapters, display, and its implication with spectacle, is a vehicle for the referential within expressive forms of documentary representation. The works examined here inform conceptions of spectacular documentary display variously through, for example, the inclusion of kinetic and frenetic movement within the frame as in rockumentary and surf film, radically disjunctive moves between frames as in the case of certain compilation films, the awe-provoking magnification of the close-up, and the 'majestic' enlargement of IMAX. Such approaches, which construct and position an active spectator within the process of knowledge acquisition, are extended within views of the body, another focus of documentary display.

Bodily display

The relationship of documentary film, the body and display is informed through reference to Linda Williams' insightful analysis of the operations of bodily display in fictional film. Williams writes of pornography, horror and melodrama as 'body genres' which evoke 'ecstatic excesses – ... a quality of uncontrollable convulsion or spasm – of the body "beside itself" with sexual pleasure, fear and terror, or overpowering sadness' (1991: 5). Such genres not only 'sensationally display bodies on the screen', they share a spectatorial effect which is manifest as 'an apparent lack of proper aesthetic distance, a sense of over-involvement in sensation and emotion' (1991: 4). In this way, body genres both portray the body and 'affect the sensational body' such that 'it seems to be the case that the success of these genres is often measured by the degree to which the audience sensation mimics what is seen on the screen' (1991: 5).

Williams' analysis of fictional body genres can be aligned, to an extent, with Bill Nichols' comments on the role of the body in documentary film. Nichols argues that the body in documentary film can be considered from three non-exclusionary viewpoints: '(1) the body of the social actor who is agent and subject of historical actions and events, situations and experiences; (2) as the body of a narrative character who is the focus of actions and enigmas, helpers and donors all propelling the narrative toward closure; and (3) as a mythic, ahistorical persona, type, icon, or fetish which serves as the object of both desire and identification' (1993: 184). Each of these categories, notably the second and third, bears similarities to Williams' claims regarding the mimetic potential of the body on screen. More particularly, Jane Gaines (drawing on Williams' analysis) has informed the versions of the body in documentary outlined by Nichols. Gaines paraphrases the spectatorial effects of the body genres examined by Williams – pornography, horror and melodrama – in terms of 'making the body do things': 'horror makes you scream, melodrama makes you cry, and porn makes you "come"' (1999: 90). Gaines adds radical documentaries, such as In the Year of the Pig (1969), Word is Out (1979), The Battle of Chile (1979) and Berkeley in the Sixties (1990) to the forms that 'produce' an involuntary response in the spectator. Such documentaries feature images of bodies in struggle because the filmmakers 'want audiences to carry on that same struggle' (1999: 91; emphasis in original).

By adding radical documentaries to the category of body genre Gaines extends the analysis beyond fictional and semi-fictional genres (horror, melodrama, pornography) to include documentaries which provoke the spectator to mimic actions and sensations of the 'social actor' exhibited on the screen. Such responses implicate another body genre – that of nonfiction surf film. Whereas melodrama 'makes you cry' and horror 'makes you scream' and radical documentaries 'make you want to partake in political struggle', surf film 'makes you want to surf'. Like the genres analysed by Williams, surf film has had a 'low cultural status', even within the context of the most popular film genres (see Williams 1991: 4). Its 'low' status is further suggested in the fact that it evokes features of films which are 'disreputable' through effects which are visceral, kinetic and fast-paced. In an analysis of such features and effects in the 'new cinema of attractions' (the technologised special effects-based works of the so-called New Hollywood), Williams elsewhere argues that the appeal of such films, in their ability to produce a spectatorial absorption within and through sensational pleasures and visual and auditory 'attractions', can be compared to the pleasures of a roller-coaster ride – 'say the rickety wood and steel affair on Santa Cruz CA's boardwalk' (2000: 357). Surf film, with its kinetic imagery and its visceral and sensational effects, results in mimicry of the actions occurring below the Santa Cruz pier – in the surf. The spectator of surf film, drawn in the main from the surfing subculture, abandons traditional 'spectatorial discipline' within unrestrained or undisciplined reactions to the image (2000: 356). During the often raucous screenings of surf film, seated audience members frequently physically respond to images on the screen by 'throw[ing] their turn when the rider does ... [leaning] for a bottom turn and [pushing] back in their seat for a cutback', as Bob Condon, the producer of a number of surf films, has noted (quoted in Flynn 1987: 408).

The display of the body, as the source and focus of mimetic action, is also a feature of the performative body of direct cinema 'rockumentary'. While surf film 'makes you want to surf', the performative bodily display of so-called rockumentary 'makes you want to dance'. The specific sensational effects of the long take observational moments associated with rockumentary, in which onstage musicians are framed in intimate detail as they perform their music, have been noted in a description of spectatorial reactions to a screening of a first editorial cut of *Woodstock* (1970): 'As soon as [the audience was] seated ... we began to roll [the film]. And rock and roll we did! The screening would last four hours without intermission. The atmosphere [in the screening room] was so vibrant, so electric [that it] could never be ... duplicated ... Superlatives are inadequate to describe the synergy that bound everyone together for those four hours. It was a once-in-a-lifetime experience... After each [onscreen] act, [audience members] applauded and shouted' (Bell 1999: 229).

City film, in which the body is prominently featured in urban spaces, is another form aligned with the body genres of documentary display. While city film is not necessarily characterisable by the spectatorial mimetic function of other body genres, the body is a central organisational component of the form. In city films people are not only on display in urban environments; it is through the presence of people – a bodily presence – that the 'city' is activated as an urban and communal or social space. As with the other works included here, city films produce a range of visual, auditory and spectatorial effects and make available a variety of viewing pleasures. The display of the body, as an aspect of the broader form of documentary display, centrally implicates, as the references here emphasise, the role of sensation. The ability of documentary display to impact on the senses is extended in the pleasure derivable from the display.

The pleasure and popularity of documentary display

'Pleasure' is a problematic term in documentary film theory, and one which occupies an uneasy place in academic discourses of cinema generally. Within this
discourse, concepts of pleasure and distraction are commonly associated with
'mere entertainment' and aligned with the realm of fictional film. Film history
does admit the place of pleasure, as Gunning's analysis of the cinema of attractions demonstrates, though 'the more "difficult", more "enlightening" pleasures of non-narrative form and formal experimentation are affirmed over [the]
reassuring, conventional pleasures ... frequently associated with commercial or
mass culture' (see Rutsky & Wyatt 1990: 5). In this way Laura Mulvey's influential essay 'Visual Pleasure and Narrative Cinema' (1975) exemplifies film theory's
privileging of critical, 'difficult' pleasure. 'Only an oppositional or avant-garde
film practice, she argues, can "free the look of the camera" ... and the "look of
the audience" and therefore "destroy" the "satisfaction, pleasure and privilege"
of traditional narrative film' (ibid.). The sense of seriousness attached to oppositional and avant-garde (and documentary) works is, in turn, 'subordinated to,
in the service of, an external standard of judgement, a truth that, whether idealist
or materialist, is always rational' (Rutsky & Wyatt 1990: 6; emphasis in original).
One effect of the imposition of a representation of a rational truth as the core of
documentary is to reduce documentary to the realm of the serious, where pleasure
and associated conceptions of fun are weakened or attenuated – to the point that
documentary is characterised as a discourse of sobriety which, generally, is 'not a
lot of laughs' (Winston 1998a: 145).

An emphasis on seriousness in theorisations of documentary film can, however, be overstated. In this way, as Michael Renov has pointed out, a 'view of documentary which assumes too great a sobriety for nonfiction discourse will fail to
comprehend the sources of nonfiction's deep-seated appeal' (1993a: 3). However,
all too often attempts within documentary theory to account for the pleasure of
the documentary text inevitably limit the operations of pleasure. Nichols' (1991)
reference to 'epistephilia' (defined as the pleasure of knowing) is a case in point,
in which pleasure and enjoyment are restricted to a desire for knowledge and have
no broader operative function in the realm of documentary. While this form of
pleasure is available to the viewer of documentary, works of documentary may
also offer what are, in terms of a 'serious' academic theory of documentary, other
insalubrious pleasures. Such a recognition depends on an enlarged conception
of documentary – one which not only encompasses selected works canonised
within the documentary tradition but also includes the works analysed here, and
the pleasures they afford audiences beyond those linked exclusively to the sober
acquisition of knowledge. In this way Freud's account of scopophilia – the fulfil-

ment of the desire to see, and the satisfaction associated with this drive – more appropriately captures, than Nichols' neologism epistephilia, the multiple pleasures of the untheorised and excluded forms of documentary examined in this book.

Retrieving such pleasures reveals the productive bases of marginalised representational forms. The exclusion of pleasure from a theory of documentary film, or its exclusive restriction to the realm of cognition, is in many ways a legacy of a Griersonian emphasis on documentary as a didactic form of public education. The legacy is felt in Nichols' assessment of *Listen to Britain*, Jennings' innovative revision of Griersonian positions, which Nichols approaches exclusively in terms of knowledge production and a socially constructive 'epistephilia' (see 1991: 178–9). More astutely, Jim Leach, who examines the same film in terms of socially responsible war-time 'propaganda' and 'poetic' representation, concludes that 'the boundary lines in the debate over social utility and aesthetic pleasure are not as distinct as they might seem' (1998: 163). Brian Winston, in his book-length critique of Griersonian documentary, calls for the abandonment of 'the pretension to public education needs' as a way of increasing the acceptability and popularity of documentary. 'After all', he notes, one of the 'truly popular documentary forms, the rock performance film, has gratifyingly little public education sobriety about it' (1995: 255).

Winston's attention to another category commonly neglected in documentary theory – that of the popularity of the documentary text – focuses questions concerning the exclusionary functions of the documentary tradition as it is dominantly conceived. All too often theory and criticism construct a documentary tradition and canon from works which are unpopular with broad audiences. Reinforcing this point, Jane Gaines has observed that with 'the exception of some unusual films that enjoyed limited success as feature releases in the United States (*Harlan County, U.S.A,* 1976; *The Atomic Café,* 1982; *Roger and Me,* 1989 [to which can be added *The Fog of War,* 2004 and *Fahrenheit 9/11,* 2004], the films in the documentary canon have not been box-office blockbusters' (1995: 85). The key phrase here, of course, is 'in the documentary canon'. Beyond the relatively rigid boundaries and prescriptions of this canon, specific forms of nonfiction film – characterised in each case by documentary display – enjoy popularity with audiences. For example, rockumentary, as Winston notes, continues to attract audiences, as demonstrated in the success of *Metallica: Some Kind of Monster* (2004), among other recent variants of the form. The cultish identification with surf film within the surfing subculture is broadened through the fact that surf film is exhibited on television in a number of countries, and the form reached new markets and audiences with the opening-night screening of *Riding Giants* (2004) at the 2004 Sundance Film Festival. Natural science films, another form examined here in relation to documentary display, constitute a basic component of television schedules and a staple of the popular IMAX form of exhibition.

The pleasures derivable from documentary, and the popularity of certain documentary forms, inform new approaches to this mode of filmmaking. In this way the complex and various interaction of 'attractions', avant-gardist forms, spectacle, pleasure, entertainment and popularity construct and situate nonfictional representations which exceed the narrow confines of a documentary canon as it has traditionally been conceived and applied within and through critical and theoretical assessments. In the process, documentary display provides a unique way to re-view, and revise, common theoretical and critical assessments of the scopic and other formal capacities of documentary modes of representation.

chapter two

The Corporeal and the Urban:
From City Symphony to Global City Film

Films ... testify to bodies that were present before the camera.

– David MacDougall (2006: 13)

In the introduction to his history of the relationship between the body and the city in Western civilisation, Richard Sennett includes an anecdote about attending a cinema in New York. Sennett uses the story of watching film as a way of commenting on the place of the body and senses within urban settings and is concerned to document 'physical sensations in urban space' thereby addressing what he sees as the 'tactile sterility which afflicts the urban environment' (1994: 15). While Sennett's work performs an important task by drawing attention to various historical conditions implicated in urban and metropolitan experience, it is possible to rework the categories he deploys – bodies, the city and film – into a very different argument concerning representations of the city. Indeed the three categories coalesce in the so-called city film – works which include the 'city symphony' of the 1920s and subsequent documentary representations of urban spaces, among them the New York City films of the 1940s and 1950s, and films of non-Western cities produced in the decades from the 1960s to the present – within which the city is realised through a focus on people.

Common descriptions of the 'kaleidoscopic' and 'rhythmic' visual regime of the city film emphasise the city as a complex spatial arrangement of buildings, traffic, streets and boulevards.[1] While the kinaesthetic visual modes of the city symphony, for example, alluded to in references to 'rhythm', partially revive the visual intensity and pleasurable looking characteristic of the early 'cinema of attractions', all too frequently critical analyses of the extraordinary visual capacities of the city film ignore the fact that such a visual regime depicts cities which are traversed and occupied by people, 'as material presence ... as child and adult'

(MacDougall 2006: 2).[2] Specifically, representations of the corporeal in the form of individual and collective inhabitants of a city function in association with 'kaleidoscopic' and kinaesthetic depictions of the 'concrete' (buildings, streetscapes) to reinforce the documentary display of the city film.

In this relation, David MacDougall's term 'social aesthetics' draws attention to the role of the body in representation in a way that productively informs understandings of the city film and its capacity as documentary to construct knowledge about the world. As the term suggests, a social aesthetics foregrounds embodiment within what MacDougall identifies as the 'sensory and formal qualities of social life' (Barbash & Taylor 2001: 7). MacDougall applies the original meaning of 'aesthetics' – relating to perceptions by the senses – and in these terms the field of aesthetics is concerned with a wide range of culturally patterned sensory experience through which knowledge is produced (see MacDougall 2006). Michael Taussig explicates this process when he notes that everyday experience (the 'content' of documentary) includes 'much that is not sense so much as sensuousness, an embodied and somewhat automatic "knowledge" that functions like a peripheral vision, not studied contemplation, a knowledge that is imageric and sensate rather than ideational' (1992: 8).

This chapter takes up the reference to aesthetics as a form of representation that is located within and operates through a focus on the body and emphasises, following Sennett, the role of such an embodied aesthetic within the documentary display of the city film. In doing so this chapter reassesses and reviews the visual language and formal components of the documentary display of European city films of the 1920s – the so-called city symphonies – and New York City films of the 1940s and 1950s. The reassessment of the city film is informed by analysis of approaches to filming the city's inhabitants, as in the use of concealed cameras in the city symphony and the open acknowledgement of the camera in the New York City films. The traditional focus in city films and criticism on representations of European and North American cities has functioned to divert attention from the existence of representations of non-Western cities. Hanoi, Calcutta, Benares, Beirut and Tehran have all been represented in films which in their scrutiny of people and place deploy the camera in ways which extend the codes and styles of the city film. In these ways the city film has, from its inception, innovatively combined elements of avant-garde representation with documentary depiction. More particularly, the works examined here deploy a range of strategies to readdress and reframe the city. The resultant works reveal the city and its occupants – the city as its occupants – within the expressive capacities of the documentary display which is the productive basis of the city film.

Importantly, the study of the formal and aesthetic components of the documentary display of the city film implicates considerations of the historical and political contexts associated with the form. Michael Renov, one of the few critics to have drawn attention to the connections between the 'poeticism' of the city film and historical and political concerns, interprets the form in terms of a documentary mode of 'expression'. While the documentary tradition contains a number of examples of so-called poetic and expressive works, Renov identifies the city symphonies of the 1920s, among them Walter Ruttmann's *Berlin: Symphony of a Great City*, Dziga Vertov's *Chelovek s kino-apparatom (The Man with a Movie Camera*, 1929) and Jean Vigo's *À Propos de Nice* (1930) as works which combine an 'artfulness' derived from the 'function of purely photographic properties [with] the possibilities of editing to create explosive effects – cerebral as well as visceral' (1993b: 32). Renov informs the documentary bases of 'the powers of expressivity' of such works by recognising that the city symphony mode of representation is deployed 'in the service of historical representation' (ibid.). In this way the subtitle of Ruttmann's film was applied to numerous films within which practices of visual kinaesthesia constructed 'symphonies' based on the diurnal cycle of life in the modern metropolis, while simultaneously infusing avant-gardist perspectives with an historically and politically cognizant form of social criticism.

However, despite the presence of historical commentary and political critique evident within the form, charges of excessive formalism, with its inference of apoliticism and ahistoricism, were frequently levelled at the city symphony. A work as revolutionary – in terms of its Communist ideals and ground-breaking formal innovations – as *The Man with a Movie Camera* was not beyond such criticism. Eisenstein's infamous attack on what he interpreted as the 'formalist jack-straws and unmotivated camera mischief' of Vertov's film typifies a line of accusation which has been directed at the city film generally (1957: 43).[3] Within this critique the presence of formal experimentation within the city film – a poetics – is said to deny any sense of a politics defined as various expressions of power structuring or impacting on the production of city films. One aspect of this chapter is a revision of this dominant line of interpretation. Such a revision is undertaken within an analysis of the social aesthetics of the documentary display of the city film, which is historicised here through reference to varying political and historical contexts and filmmaking practices within and through which city films have been produced and circulated. The following delineation of these contexts and practices implicates works from the 1920s to the present thereby providing an overview of the texts analysed in the following sections and an outline of the structure of this chapter.

The city film and its contexts

Criticisms of the city symphony as a form which displaces politics within its aesthetics have congealed around Ruttmann's *Berlin*, a prominent example of the form. Contrary to widespread criticisms of the film, the aesthetic strategies of *Berlin* encode a specific political analysis, particularly a politics of gender and class. Indeed, it is through innovative narrative and visual techniques that gender and class are foregrounded within the film's depiction of cosmopolitan Weimar Berlin. One of the central strategies whereby class, gender and other aspects of content are realised in certain city films of the 1920s and 1930s is through the use of a hidden camera, a practice typically associated with social regulation and surveillance. Surveillance, as a 'top down' monitoring of people's lives, is recast in city symphonies as a way of displaying the demotic as a pressing reality, as in the use of a hidden camera in *The Man with a Movie Camera*. In *À Propos de Nice*, Vigo deployed a hidden camera and covert filming to construct a work within which the practices of intellectual montage critically document class differences within the city of Nice.

In contrast to the differing though decidedly leftist critiques in the city symphonies of Vertov and Vigo, the New York City films of the mid-twentieth century seemingly deny any sense of politics in their depictions of the inhabitants of the modern metropolis. However, the presence in certain New York City films of a subject's 'return look' to the camera brings issues of power and representation to the fore. The returned look demonstrates not only a familiarity with the camera but also an expression of a subject's refusal of its objectifying gaze. In these films the corporeal is not a disempowered presence before the camera. In such New York City films people openly (and literally) confront, return and playfully engage with the camera's powerful stare. Wheeler Winston Dixon has argued that this '"gaze of the screen", or "look back", has the power to transform our existences, to substantially change our view of our lives, and of the world we inhabit' (1995: 7). Such a hyperbolic claim does not necessarily do justice to the practice, though it does point to the fact that the 'return look' is, as Elizabeth Klaver argues, 'one of the most powerful looks operating in the media culture ... [and is one which bolsters] the opportunity for agency' (Klaver 2003: 286). In these terms the corporeal presence in certain New York City films is not the passive object of a gaze, but an active agent who openly confronts the camera. In this way the return look features as an important component of the city film which productively informs the vocabulary of the form beyond visual 'rhythm' or filmic inventories of architectural features. Within the return look in documentary – largely overlooked in accounts of the politicised gaze of 1970s and 1980s film theory – an object is exchanged for a subject in a way 'which might be termed Sartre's possibility of "being-seen-by-the-Other"' (quoted in ibid.).[4]

The irruptive presence of the Other was radically expressed throughout the 1960s in the processes of decolonisation and national liberation, and with them new ways of conceiving people within urban centres characterised by resistance and rebellion. One effect of such global political realignments and attendant filmic imagery was to shift the city film from its entrenched focus on the urban centres of Europe and North America to representations of the inhabitants of non-Western cities involved in struggles for national liberation. In this way, for example, while a central component of numerous city films – a day in the life of a city – was reinforced in the media's day in the life (September 11, 2001) of New York City in time of terror, another representation of a day in the life of citizens of a terrorised city in the throes of a war of national liberation, Hanoi in Santiago Alvarez's 1967 film *Hanoi, Martes Trece*, extended the formal capacities of the city film. Alvarez's film uses the 'day in the life' format to construct epistemological positions based on the individual within images of a city which had previously been beyond the conceptions and categorisations of the city film. Robert Kramer's film *Point de départ* (1993), similarly focused on Hanoi, also expands the language of the city film within its representation of the history and contemporary condition of the city's inhabitants.

As the works of Alvarez and Kramer attest, among the questions which became prominent as a result of the political disruptions of the 1960s were those pertaining to forms appropriate to the representation of people constructed politically as Other (and as politically Other). Not coincidentally such questions were addressed by filmmakers who recast the filmic practices of an ethnography which traditionally claimed to interpret the non-Western Other. Adopting such practices, Louis Malle's *Calcutta* (1969) and Robert Gardner's *Forest of Bliss* (1985) intervene within and revise the formal techniques of ethnographic film in their respective representations of Calcutta and Benares. Within this context both films provoked a marked amount of adverse criticism (and approbation) in their deployment and examination of an aesthetics of daily life which is the core of the works' documentary display.

The decolonisation struggles of the 1960s, and with them new modes of depicting the people of cities involved in such struggles, are echoed in the conditions of diaspora, exile and displacement experienced by the populations of various contemporary postcolonial cities, as represented in the practices of exilic filmmakers. Varieties of so-called Third Cinema and the closely aligned forms of exilic and intercultural cinemas, document postcolonial and emergent social conditions within and through a focus on the transformations wrought internally to a city and a nation by its citizens and externally by what is often an invasive military and political force. Hamid Naficy argues that the films of exilic and diasporic filmmakers, what he calls an 'accented cinema', are characterised by a 'tactile optic' (2001: 28). Such an optic informs the aesthetics of the documentary display of representations of cities of the Middle East analysed in the final section of this chapter. The emphasis in this section on a corporeal tactile or haptic optic as the basis of exilic representations of the city reprises Sennett's intention of writing a history which addresses and overcomes the 'dullness, the monotony, and the tactile sterility' of the urban environment. More specifically, the following analysis of the innovative representations of the city film is undertaken within the features of the varying political contexts and filmic practices outlined here. It is within these contexts and attention to the corporeal – the privileged site of the meeting of aesthetics and politics in the works examined in this chapter – that the documentary display of the city film is realised.

From the bowels of the earth to city streets: *Berlin: Symphony of a Great City* and its critics

The critical interpretations which have functioned to specify features of the city film were advanced through Grierson's contribution to the process of defining the notion of documentary. Grierson consolidated his thoughts on documentary film in a series of essays he published during 1932–34 in the journal *Cinema Quarterly* under the title 'First Principles of Documentary'. Notoriously contradictory and inconsistent in his writings, Grierson presented here a unified statement of his early position on the aesthetic, social and political approaches of documentary. Importantly, he referred to the essays as his 'manifesto', a word which evokes modernist declarations of creative (and political) intent and one which reinforces the systematic and purposive elaboration of ideas found in 'First Principles of Documentary' (1998a: 83). Though Grierson was later to revise a number of statements he made in the essays, the work nevertheless stands as an effective and significant summation of his early ideas on forms of documentary, including Robert Flaherty's *Nanook of the North* (1922), Ruttmann's *Berlin*, and his own film *Drifters* (1929). Grierson insisted that a documentary is organised via the narrativisation of incidents and events and praised Flaherty in this regard for his rigorous story form, structured from and around the actions of individuals. Grierson, however, was not entirely supportive of Flaherty's romanticised depiction of the individual. In a 1935 essay Grierson criticised what he called Flaherty's positioning of his subjects in natural environments in the form of a 'man against the sky' approach, preferring forms 'of industrial and social function, where man is more likely to be [working in a mine] in the bowels of the earth' (1979: 64).[5] In 'First Principles of Documentary' Grierson praises 'man', not in the bowels of the earth, but on the deck of a deep-sea fishing boat, as featured in his film *Drifters*, which he presents in the essays as a film which usefully depicts individuals as exemplary of labour in the modern industrial economy. Ignoring his developing criticisms of Flaherty, Grierson's film includes poetic images of the 'high bravery of upright labour' in scenes of fishermen at work at sea. Grierson acknowledged that the film's subject 'belonged in part to Flaherty's world, for it had something of the noble savage and certainly a great deal of the elements of nature to play with. It did, however, use steam and smoke and did, in a sense, marshal the effects of a modern industry' (1998a: 89). For Grierson, focusing on the individual was a method capable of 'cross-sectioning reality' to reveal 'complex and impersonal forces' (1998a: 86).

However, such an interpretation is not extended to Ruttmann's Berlin. Grierson found Ruttmann's associational montage – what Siegfried Kracauer, echoing Grierson, called Ruttmann's 'cross-section' of Weimar Berlin[6] – wanting in its capacity to produce documentary insights into daily life (see Grierson 1998a: 86). According to Grierson, in so far as 'the film was principally concerned with movements and the building of separate images into movements, Ruttmann was justified in calling it a symphony... In Berlin cinema swung along according to its own more natural powers: creating dramatic effect from the tempo'd accumulation of its single observation' (ibid.). Ignoring the film's representation of individuals, Grierson concludes that the innovative visual effects of Berlin were 'not enough' (1998a: 87). Grierson refuses to admit that it is via the embodiment of human subjects that the film performs the task of 'cross-sectioning' to expose the forces behind the 'daily doings' of the city (1998a: 85). It was through the representation of human subjects that, to paraphrase one commentator, the new language of rhythm and evocation through which the city symphony invigorated documentary was informed by a dose of reality and a capacity for social criticism.[7]

This capacity was achieved within an abandonment of the Griersonian representation of people as 'social types'. The form of social critique practised by Grierson in Drifters, as with his film criticism in 'First Principles of Documentary', stereotyped individuality or misrepresented identities (as in his reference to the fishermen in Drifters in terms of 'high bravery of upstanding labour', for example). A similar stereotyping or misrecognition of identities infuses criticisms of Berlin. Ruttmann's film conveys the accelerating pace of a day in the city through an aesthetic abstraction of shapes and a montage which juxtaposes images between scenes. The film's documentary display is fully realised in a combination of these elements within what James Donald has called 'an almost voyeuristic record of the little human dramas of public life. Children go to school, people chat in cafés, a policeman helps a little boy across the road, prostitutes ply their trade, street performers appear in silly costumes, a woman commits suicide' (1995: 86). Donald's recognition of the place of people in the film is, however, framed through a false identification of women as prostitutes. Such a recognition is widespread in criticism of the film and the scene, which is typically misinterpreted in these terms, involves a woman who turns a street corner and looks at a man, who returns her gaze, through the window of a department store.

As Anke Gleber notes, in 'criticism of the film by (male) critics, this woman has commonly been considered as a professional one, a woman who goes after her business as a "street-walker"' (1997a: 76). Gleber points out that Kracauer, writing in 1947, concludes his description of the film's street scenes with reference to the 'many prostitutes among the passers-by' (ibid.).[8] William Uricchio's analysis is similar: 'After several shots whose common element involves street-walkers as a subject, a specific mating instance is presented. A prostitute and potential customer pass one another on the street' (quoted in Gleber 1997b: 67). Sabine Hake reads the scene differently: 'The camera [follows] several young women on the streets by themselves: one as she is being picked up ... another as she waits impatiently at a corner, and yet another as she window shops on elegant Kurfurstenddamm' (quoted in Gleber 1997a: 76).[9] Gleber argues that the 'striking discrepancies in judging and naming these women might well provoke another look at the function and scenes of the female image in Berlin, Symphony of a [Great] City' (ibid.). Indeed, such a reappraisal could also note that far from lacking a narrative, as a number of critics have claimed to be the case, Ruttmann's film constructs a narrative line around the actions of women in the urban environment. The narrative is enhanced through the woman's unswerving gaze, a sign of the social and political status of women within the liberal Weimar republic. The story of women in the city is extended in a later (reconstructed) scene depicting the suicide of a woman, an incident that is structured into the narrative concerning the 'harsh modern city'.[10] Gleber informs understandings of the film's narrative development by noting that the scene involving a woman's suicide follows a scene depicting a fashion show in which women parade the latest styles. 'A narrative of women's lives is suggested that seems to connect their existence and demise in the city to the ways in which their images are exhibited and exploited in this society' (1997b: 77). In Ruttmann's Berlin display operates largely through a complex representation of gender which is structured into a narrative which features the so-called rhythm of the city.

The space left within the critical literature devoted to Berlin by the marginalisation of gender was filled to an extent by debate over another category of personal and political identity, that of class. Kracauer lamented the absence of references to class within the 'radius' of city spaces plotted in the film. In this way he asked where 'is the Berlin of the worker, the white collar worker, the shopkeeper, the upper bourgeoisie...?' (quoted in Natter 1994: 220). Nathan Friendlander echoed Kracauer when he argued that Ruttmann 'should have shown a day in the life of a proletarian or bourgeois from beginning to end' (quoted in ibid.). The argument is extended by Jay Chapman who, in an analysis of Berlin and Cavalcanti's city symphony Rien que les heures, contrasts the depiction of city inhabitants in both films. 'The city is its people; the people (different kinds and classes) are what make up the fabric of the city. In fact, one could almost go so far as to say that Rien que les heures is concerned only with people ... Cavalcanti is immediately concerned with people as individuals, while Ruttmann is more concerned with people as a mass. The people in *Berlin* are anonymous beings ... In *Rien que les heures* the people are specific individuals who also serve as symbols for specific types of people' (1979: 37). According to Chapman, Cavalcanti 'through his concentration on the poorer classes of people in the city ... turns *Rien que les heures* into a rather blunt personal statement which compares the mode of life of the wealthy and poorer classes' while in *Berlin* 'there is relatively little overt social comment about the various classes' (1979: 39–40).

Replicating Grierson's arguments, Chapman insists that for Ruttmann 'the essence of the city is its rhythm, and nothing else' (1979: 40). For Chapman the editing of *Berlin* produces a 'coldness' in the work which 'exhibits no real feeling for anything' especially 'not the people' (ibid.). Chapman here reformulates Kracauer's criticism of what he sees as Ruttmann's antihumanist position. According to Kracauer, human beings 'are forced into the sphere of the inanimate. They seem molecules in a stream of matter ... People in *Berlin* assume the character of material not even polished. Used up material is thrown away ... The life of society is a harsh, mechanical process' (quoted in Natter 1994: 220). Kracauer agrees with Carl Mayer (Ruttman's one-time collaborator, who disassociated himself from the film during production, arguing that Ruttmann had abandoned the original idea of 'a film about ordinary people in their normal surroundings' (quoted in Rotha 1952: 86)) that *Berlin* offers only a 'surface approach' (Kracauer 1947: 187). The reference to 'surface' alludes to the *Neue Sachhichkent* (New Objectivity), a term used in the 1920s to designate a modern economic order and related stylistic emphases in the cultural sphere, notably in the form of depictions of machinery, which gave close attention to the shiny – or 'modern' – surfaces of such objects (see Gaughan 2003: 41). Critics on the left charged that the New Objectivity reified aestheticised objects and celebrated the mechanical and mass-produced processes of modernity devoid of human agency. Kracauer espoused similar objections in relation to *Berlin*, arguing that the film's aesthetic formalism was at the expense of political critique (in Donald 1995: 87). Kracauer's critical line – one which has been replicated to the point of plagiarism within numerous successive interpretations of *Berlin* – is that Ruttmann's montage mechanises humanity by equating the body with machines. However, beyond a sequence in which images of mechanical toys are cross-cut to images of people on the city's streets, and a brief sequence of a stamping press, the film includes only a few shots of industrial machinery. In contrast, Vertov's revolutionary *The Man with a Movie Camera* (a film frequently contrasted to Ruttmann's *Berlin*) includes shots which tend to aestheticise machines.[11] It is therefore difficult to deduce from shots of machinery alone a depersonalised mass and the incipient fascism that many critics identify in Ruttmann's film.[12]

According to Kracauer, Vertov stresses formal rhythms but without seeming indifferent to content. His 'cross sections' are 'permeated with communist ideas' even when they picture only the beauty of abstract movements (1947: 187). For Kracauer, had Ruttmann 'been prompted by Vertov's revolutionary convictions, he would have had to indict the inherent anarchy of Berlin life. He would have been forced to emphasise content rather than rhythm' (ibid.). Kracauer here accepts Vertov's 'formal rhythms' though denies similar effects in Berlin. It would seem, as Wolfgang Natter comments, 'that formalism can be excused in a revolutionary society, while the treatment of Weimar Republic's society demands content (story) and interpretation' (1994: 220). Kracauer does not recognise that it is possible to interpret Ruttmann's film as a form of display which includes 'visual rhythm' and the prominent inclusion of representations of gendered and class-based subjects. Such an approach opens a productive line of comparison between the ways in which films in the city symphony cycle deploy the camera to represent human subjects, thereby implicating political and aesthetic issues not considered by Kracauer.

Displaying 'life as it is': the concealed camera of the city symphony

As it follows the peripatetic paths of the urban *flâneur* and *flâneuse* Ruttmann's film seems 'omnipresent', as Sabine Hake observes (quoted in Gleber 1997a: 76). A camera capable of capturing the errant and unmotivated gazes of its subjects is an unobtrusive presence in the profilmic scene. Indeed, much of the footage edited into the film was shot in the streets of Berlin over a period of a year by concealed cinematographers (see Barber 2002: 32).[13] Earlier in the century taking photographs secretly in the urban spaces of New York City and London was a relatively widespread practice conducted 'to provide documentation for certain forms of social discourse, as well as journalistic investigation' (Gunning 1999: 51). The camera's role at the turn of the century in gathering evidence used in the service of a reformist documentary impulse spurred the relatively well-known photographic work of Jacob Riis. An attenuated version of Riis's motives informed the actions of certain journalists of the day who used so-called detective cameras to surreptitiously take photographs of court-room proceedings and a similar attitude permeated the activities of street photographers who used hidden cameras to stalk unsuspecting subjects. The prevalence of such practices was reflected in incipient contemporary concerns with the intrusiveness of the camera and considerations of the new legal right to privacy.[14]

Ruttmann's use in Berlin of a concealed camera draws on certain elements of the documentary impulse which insists on unobstructed access to profilmic reality, and also partakes of the prurient drives behind unscrupulous journalistic conduct. Certainly the ethical questions circulating around the practices of filming secretly have yet to be addressed in relation to Ruttmann's film or other works in the city symphony cycle which employ the practice, such as Vigo's À Propos de Nice, a film which rigorously foregrounds its human subjects within its swirling montage. Vigo's outline for the opening of his film emphasises the ways in which the inhabitants of Nice feature within a 'kaleidoscopic' burst of images in which panoramic views of the city would be superimposed over images of a roulette wheel and its ball:

> The ball skips around. A hand throws in a chip. The ball slows down. A hand slides a chip along the table. The ball slows down. The croupier makes a sign with his finger. The rake pushes the chip back. A hand plays with some chips. The ball slowly skips around. Close-up of ball. Distorted view of the gamblers' faces. Impassive faces of the croupiers. A stack of chips seen in close-up. The rake. The stack of chips seen from a distance. The ball is spun again. The numbers on the green cloth. Travellers leaving the station. Travellers sitting on their suitcases. Commissionaires. Hotel employees. Taxis. Cars. The interpreter. A hotel door opening. Bellboys. A porter hurrying along. A terrace being swept. A restaurant. A headwaiter adjusts his tie. The hotels seen upside-down right themselves. A waiter checking the parting in his hair. A gnarled tree becomes a palm tree. A palm frond. A street cleaner's broom. A wave depositing garbage on the beach. The street cleaner sweeping. The casino on the promenade. A small pile of garbage near the street cleaner. The sea. The broom. The street cleaner leaves, pushing his cart. A view of the promenade desolate and tree-less. The beach chairs being set up. The sea. The gulls. The lines of trees. The clear sky. (Quoted in Salles Gomes 1972: 57)

During the filming Vigo realised that he should focus on the beachfront Promenade des Anglais and its many bourgeois patrons. Boris Kaufman, Vigo's cameraman, filmed such scenes using a camera concealed in a cardboard box or camouflaged on his lap as he sat in a wheelchair pushed by Vigo along the boardwalk (see Salles Gomes 1972: 58; see also Barnouw 1983: 77). For Vigo such a filming method was integral to his conception of what he called '*point de vue documenté*', an approach predicated on propinquity, concealment and direct access to subjects (quoted in B. Kaufman 1979: 77). If people became aware of being filmed Kaufman immediately stopped the camera. Vigo insisted that 'social documentary' is achievable only through close attention to individuals in order to reveal, in his own words, 'the hidden reason for a gesture ... [To] extract from an ordinary person his interior beauty – or a caricature of him – quite by chance ... conscious behaviour cannot be tolerated, character must be surprised by the camera if the whole "documentary" value of this kind of cinema is to be achieved' (quoted in ibid.).

Vigo's *point de vue documenté* was, he maintained, a unique way of filming which would reveal social and political conditions within the city of Nice. Vigo emphasised in his comments on a 'documentary point of view' that such an approach was the basis of 'social cinema', a form of analysis which implicates commentary on classes depicted in terms of distinctions between wealth and poverty. Vigo's 'social consciousness' is applied to the specific historical context of Nice to produce a strident statement which contrasts the lives of the idle rich with the experiences of the working poor. The montage featuring a roulette wheel is suggestive of the theme in its reference to Nice as 'a city which thrives on gambling' (Vigo quoted in Salles Gomes 1972: 55). Vigo's Surrealist-inflected politics and the montage of his intellectual cinema are evident in sequences in which wealthy female patrons of Nice's promenade are intercut with shots of an ostrich, and images of sun-bathers are accompanied by shots of crocodiles lazing in the sun. The critique of bourgeois conditions is extended in the contrast between scenes featuring wealthy seaside *flâneurs* and those depicting Nice's working-class quarter. While not as trenchant as the shots of poverty in Cavalcanti's *Rien que les heures*, Vigo's film effectively emphasises social distinctions within the juxtaposition of scenes of the leisurely and free-wheeling life of the Promenade des Anglais and shots of the narrow confines of the working district.[15]

Vertov, seeking in a similar way to capture 'life unawares' in his composite Soviet city constructed in *The Man with a Movie Camera*, employed the practice of concealed filming through which he produced a revolutionary image. In places the film abandons concealed filming within self-referential moments constructed in part through the responses of people within the film to the presence of the camera. The film includes, for example, a number of scenes in which workers reveal their awareness of being filmed in the form of indirect looks to the camera. The complicity between filmmaker and social actor results in a form of 'unconcealed empathy' with the camera and filmmaker (see Petrić 1993: 81). In other scenes, however, Vertov's commitment to *kino-pravda* (film-truth) is applied through means of filming with a hidden camera. In a valuable interview published in 1979 Mikhail Kaufman, the cameraman on the film, explained the filming method he and Vertov adopted in the film. 'The special problem', argues Kaufman, 'was filming people' (quoted in *October* 1979: 64). He added:

After an argument between us, Vertov decided to publish a sort of ban ruling out the 'kinokina' and temporarily ruling out the subject as an object of filming because of his inability to behave in front of a camera. As if a subject absolutely has to know how to behave! At that time I put it as follows: In the narrative feature one has to know how to act; in the documentary cinema one has to know how not to act. To be able not to act – one will have to wait a long time until the subject is educated in such a way that he won't pay any attention to the fact that he is being filmed. There's no school like that yet, is there? (Kaufman quoted in *October* 1974: 64)

Vertov supplanted his ban on filming people with a revised approach in which he conceived of the method of secretly filming subjects, a process he interpreted as an ethical component of a class-based mode of filmmaking. The method of hidden filming followed a principle of film-truth that maintained that a camera operator must film people in a way that does not impede on a subject's work – and, by extension, the realities of proletarian daily life. (see Petrić 1993: 82). Kaufman and Vertov therefore addressed the 'problem of people' in part within scenes in which social actors became such through the method of film-truth which documents what can be called a subject's 'performance of the real' through the use of concealed cameras.[16] 'Following that line of thought', notes Kaufman,

> I constructed a sort of tent, something like a telephone booth, for *The Man with a Movie Camera*. There has to be an observation point somewhere. So I made myself up as a telephone repairman. There weren't any special lenses, so I went out and bought a regular camera and removed the deep-focus lens. Standing off to the side I could still get things very close up, and that's why you saw those wonderful faces of the children and of the Chinese magician in *The Man with a Movie Camera*. This method supplied us with material which was more expressive. (Quoted in *October* 1979: 64)

In other examples Kaufman refers to practices of distracting people's attention so that he could shoot 'life as it is'. Kaufman emphasises that in these terms the revelation of film-truth produces 'totally new and fresh material' which informs the film's documentary 'display of emotions' (ibid.).

However, the documentary display of *The Man with a Movie Camera* was not merely based on observation. Kinaesthesia as a form of display results from a style of editing conducted to a set of principles which were almost mathematical in their precision. In his 1929 essay 'The Alphabet of the "Kinoks"', Vertov explains the method whereby shots and scenes function kinaesthetically (quoted in Petrić 1995: 16). According to Vertov the juxtapostional editing of shots must be considered in relation to '(a) the frame's scale, (b) the pictorial/graphic composition of the image, (c) the shooting angle, (d) the play of light and darkness, (e) the multidirectional motions within the shot, the physical movement of the camera, and (f) the differing speeds of the camera/projector (in order to create an illusion of fast or slow motion on the screen)' (quoted in ibid.). In Vertov's approach this 'film-eye', the montage of associated shots, interacted dialectically with film-truth (the ontological veracity of the shot) to reveal a new, progressive reality hidden below the surface details of experience. The combination of film-eye and film-truth vigorously inscribes a form of documentary display which relies on showing, not telling, to achieve aesthetic resolution and a perception of a revolutionary reality.

New York city films and the look to the camera

The indirect acknowledgements of the camera found in *The Man with a Movie Camera* were attended by a 'look back' at the camera by subjects in a range of works produced after Vertov's ground-breaking film, among them a number of city films made in New York City during the 1940s and 1950s.[17] New York City films of the mid-twentieth century were preceded by various nonfictional works from the 1920s and 1930s in which the city was depicted in a modernist focus on technology and architecture. One such work, *Manhatta* (1921) by Paul Strand and Charles Sheeler, is a six-minute paean to urban technology constructed from shots of ferries, skyscrapers and streets in a form derived from the pre-nickelodeon genre of urban panoramas. Panoramas, typically one-take short static vignettes depicting city views of traffic or buildings, also included shots taken with a camera mounted on a moving object, such as a tram, train, subway or ferry. Utilising a variety of such shots in its focus on the city as technology, *Manhatta* eschews the corporeal. Flaherty summed up the thematic perspective of the film when he pointed out that *Manhatta* is 'not a film of human beings, but of skyscrapers which they had erected, completely dwarfing humanity itself' (quoted in Horak 1995: 32). Flaherty's own city film, *Twenty-Four Dollar Island* (1925), similarly ignored the inhabitants of New York City, thereby contradicting the focus on individual protagonists in his films *Nanook of the North, Moana* (1926), *Man of Aran* (1934) and *Louisiana Story* (1948). Jay Leyda's *A Bronx Morning* (1931) is, following *Manhatta* and *Twenty-Four Dollar Island*, indebted to the European city symphony in its diurnal passage of time in an urban environment defined as a corporeal space. However, in comparing *Manhatta* and *A Bronx Morning*, Jean-Christopher Horak notes that Leyda's film is 'more celebratory of the city and also more humanistic in its view of city dwellers' (ibid.). Other works from the period, including Irving Brown's *City of Contrasts* (1931) and Herman Weinberg's *Autumn Fire* (1933), foreground the inhabitants of New York City as a way of criticising urban conditions (see MacDonald 2001: 153).

While the films of Brown and Weinberg suggest the possibility that the New York City films of the following decades would build on a legacy of socially-aware critique, such a possibility is denied within critical reactions to New York City films of the mid-twentieth century which were typically, as with the reception of Francis Thompson's N.Y., N.Y. (subtitled 'A Day in New York', 1957), characterised solely or exclusively in terms of 'visual interest' and a 'sense of the city as a sub-

lime, romantic environment, full of color, upbeat energy, and intellectual beauty'
(MacDonald 2001: 163). However, the emphasis on the urban dweller established
in works such as those by Leyda, Brown and Weinberg (and continued in Thompson's N.Y., N.Y., contrary to a critical focus that ignores the presence of the corporeal in the film[18]) points to the multiple ways in which subjects within certain New
York City films perform as 'social actors' before the camera, and in certain cases
openly acknowledge the presence of the camera. Such a practice and an associated politics are not necessarily concerned with social critique in the ways that,
for example, certain city symphonies of the 1920s were intent on revealing urban
class or gender divisions. Rather, the 'look back' at the camera foregrounds the
corporeal as a presence within the city film capable of confronting and resisting
the camera's objectifying gaze. It is within such a practice that people in a number
of New York City films from the 1940s and 1950s express mastery over technology
(specifically in this case, visual technology) which otherwise (in the form of au-
tomobiles, trains, and feats of engineering) is typically interpreted in films of the
city as swamping, engulfing or controlling subjects.

In this way Rudy Burkhardt's films – Up and Down the Waterfront (1946), The
Climate of New York (1948) and Under the Brooklyn Bridge (1953) – meld an intensive
focus on architectural features of the city with close observation of the city's inhabitants to reveal instances of the 'look back' at the camera. Under the Brooklyn
Bridge, for example, the most ambitious of the films within the trilogy, documents
the river and waterside near the bridge and begins with a sequence featuring door-
ways and windows of houses around the approach to the bridge. The following
sequences depict the demolition of a building near the bridge, and workers on
a lunch break. The next sequence documents young boys swimming in the East
River, followed by a sequence in which people leave work and walk home. The
film concludes with shots of deserted streets in early evening and views of the
Brooklyn Bridge framed against the lower Manhattan skyline in the background.
In his analysis of the film, Scott MacDonald pays particular attention to the sequence involving boys swimming in the East River. According to MacDonald the
sequence reveals what he suspects is 'a change in the way American boys relate
to the movie camera. Most of the boys in the swimming sequence are nude, and
they betray no particular consciousness of their naked bodies before the camera'
(2001: 158). MacDonald reflects on the representation of the boys by comparing
the process of their filming in Burkhardt's film with potential contemporary reactions to such a representation: 'It is difficult to imagine a group of 1990s boys so at
ease with themselves or with the fact of being filmed under these circumstances.
In the intervening half-century, Americans have become well aware of the power
and potential personal danger of the motion picture camera and automatically
suspicious of the motivations of those using it' (ibid.).

The open and unaffected acknowledgement of the camera in *Under the Brooklyn Bridge* is in contrast to the depiction of subjects in earlier city films. The hidden camera filming of the city symphonies was undertaken in order to avoid provoking a subject's response and in those shots in which subjects recognise the camera the look to the camera is in the main indirect or oblique. The direct look at the camera within *Under the Brooklyn Bridge* revises this approach and is extended in Burkhardt's *The Pursuit of Happiness* (1940) which assertively privileges the social actor through the inclusion of close-ups of faces. The 'fractured travelog' format of the city represented in his film *The Climate of New York* is reworked in *The Pursuit of Happiness* within a mode reminiscent of ethnographic film in which subjects in the process of being visually documented openly return the camera's gaze.[19] Here as elsewhere in his work, Burkhardt's camera captures individuals within the crowded city who unblinkingly look directly into the camera, 'eye to eye' (MacDonald 2001: 159).

The returned look to the camera was also a prominent feature of the city films produced in the early 1950s by New York street photographer Weegee (Arthur Felig). *Weegee's New York* (1950[20]), edited into two parts by Amos Vogel ('New York Fantasy' and 'Coney Island') is, according to MacDonald, 'one of the most under-recognized independent films of the 1950s' (2001: 161). The opening 'New York Fantasy' sequence begins in the early morning in Manhattan, and uses time-lapse photography to suggest an increasing pace in the 'awakening' city. Other expressionistic shots include scenes of New York harbour and Times Square at night, and time-lapse images of night-time streets. The Coney Island section captures the popular seaside boardwalk and beach on an extremely crowded summer Sunday afternoon. MacDonald observes that 'Weegee's Coney island reveals a population seemingly at ease with its bodies, even under the persistent gaze of the movie camera' (2001: 162). Weegee's film restages his well-known photograph 'Coney Island, 22nd of July 1940, 4 o'clock in the afternoon', a captivating image of the wide beach and neighbouring boardwalk next to the Coney Island amusement park crammed with sun worshippers. The photograph is echoed in the opening intertitle of the Coney Island section of Weegee's film ('A million people on the beach of a Sunday afternoon is normal') and the film's Coney Island sequence reproduces a similar unguarded and generous look to the camera by the numerous subjects captured in the beach photograph.[21]

Emile Benveniste called the 'return look' the 'great "repressed of narrative cinema"' (quoted in Vernet 1989: 48). Such a practice finds open expression in documentary film, and, as the examples of Burkhardt and Weegee demonstrate, constitutes a significant component of the visual display of certain New York City films of the 1940s and 1950s. Notably, this process is one component within and through which the visual language of the city film is informed and expanded beyond a focus on architectural features and 'kaleidoscopic' and 'rhythmic' visual styles typically ascribed to the form. Replicating the usual focus on such features and styles, Paul Arthur, in an essay entitled 'The Redemption of the City' (2005a), isolates various formal configurations and the presence of 'inventories' (of doors, windows, water towers, chimneys and other architectural features) within the city film. Arthur opens his essay with brief reference to the European city symphonies and German 'street films' before concentrating his analysis on American, specifically New York, city films thereby reinforcing an unstated aspect of criticism of the city film – that such representations pertain only to cities in Europe and the US. Eschewing Arthur's preoccupation with architectural features and his strict geographical focus, the category of city film can be expanded to include the visual language of a form deployed in the representation of urban populations in works which abandon a strict focus on cities within the Europe-North America geographical axis.

Beyond the European and North American city

Struggles for national liberation in various parts of the world in the late 1960s informed the content and form of representations of inhabitants of cities involved in such struggles. Liberation from colonial powers provoked a range of expressive works which sought to endorse and replicate political liberation in 'agit-prop' forms. In this way the 'descriptive poetics' of Santiago Alavarez's *Hanoi, Martes Trece*, for example, revise the visual grammar, prevailing apoliticism and excessive formalism of certain (New York) city films and constitute a profound engagement with the people of war-torn Hanoi. Unlike the directors of the portmanteau film *Far from Vietnam* (1967) Alvarez, as a citizen of a country allied with North Vietnam in its struggle against US imperialism (Alvarez's homeland, Cuba, named 1967 the 'Year of Heroic Vietnam'), was permitted to film in North Vietnam during the war. *Hanoi, Martes Trece* reworks the traditional diurnal schema of the city symphony to produce a poetic evocation of a city under siege. As with Humphrey Jennings' *London Can Take It!* (co-directed with Harry Watt, 1940), another film focused on a city at war – which, like Alvarez's work, is routinely ignored in analyses of the city film – *Hanoi, Martes Trece* depicts an urban population forging ahead in the face of intense aerial bombardment.

The title of Alavarez's film is the date, Tuesday the 13th (of December, 1966), of an attack by US warplanes on North Vietnam, an event which occurred soon after Alavarez and his cameraman, Ivan Napoles, arrived in Hanoi. Alavarez's scorching indictment of the US invasion of Vietnam is shot in black and white, though the film begins and ends with colour footage of paintings and engravings by Vietnamese artists which foreground the rich cultural traditions of a people whose history is presented in voice-over from a text dealing with nineteenth-century Vietnam (written by Cuban national hero, José Marti). The history is suddenly interrupted by a montage that constructs a rapidly-delivered savagely satirical biography of Lyndon Johnson. The biography begins with the title 'Nace un niño en Texas' – 'a boy is born in Texas' – accompanied by images of a baby's birth which are intercut with shots of a cow giving birth. The film returns to a different pace with images of Vietnamese fishermen and farmers, though the scenes of rural labour are transformed into the reality of war as workers in the fields abandon their tasks to operate antiaircraft guns against an air attack.

After the air raid a title fills the screen, 'We turn anger into energy', a statement of resistance which is enacted in the opening scenes of rural workers/fighters and in the second section of the film which concentrates on the activities of the inhabitants of Hanoi. Alvarez includes shots of street stalls, people going to work on bicycles and people moulding large concrete tubes which are embedded in the streets for use as air-raid shelters, another reminder of the continuous bombing and the originality of the Vietnamese people in the presence of the massive US aerial campaign. In the wake of a US bombing raid Alvarez depicts the effects on the civilian population of the city: people putting out fires with hand-held buckets of water, and shots of broken bodies and destroyed houses. Despite the destruction of its infrastructure and the killing and maiming, Vietnamese society is depicted as one which, in its fortitude, is capable of resisting the US onslaught. Alvarez's film revises the sociologically and journalistically inflected Griersonian approach in which subjects tend to be depicted as victims of historical conditions, a trace of which lingers in city films which implicitly allude to the city as a space which crushes or smothers individuals.[22] As Alavarez noted during the making of the film, the Vietnamese despised being framed as victims (quoted in Wilkinson 2001). Moving beyond the aesthetics and politics of victimhood Alvarez also avoided depictions of the Vietnamese as exoticised Other. Within a montage composed of a violent collision of images of war and daily life, Hanoi, Martes Trece foregrounds the Vietnamese people as, to revive an ignored term, agents of history.

The representation of the Vietnamese people not as victims, faceless enemy or exotic Other, was informed within Robert Kramer's film Point de départ, a film which in many ways can be considered a sequel to Alvarez's film – though in fact Point de départ was made as a follow-up to Kramer's 1969 film People's War. Twenty-five years after People's War Kramer returned to Hanoi to make a film on the effects of the war on the people of what was North Vietnam. Point de départ mixes archival footage from the 1960s, contemporary interviews and observation within a reflection on the passage of time and the reconstruction of post-war Vietnam. Well-known architectural landmarks in Hanoi provide a form of 'cognitive mapping' orienting the viewer within the city's urban space.[23] The mausoleum in central Hanoi containing Ho Chi Minh's body and the Long Bien Bridge, constructed by the French, are among the sites included in the film. Shots of the bridge, which was seriously damaged during the war by US bombing, and patched and rebuilt numerous times in response to each attack, are featured throughout the film and come to function as a metaphor for the city's reconstruction programme. The theme of rebuilding is extended in a direct and didactic way in a sequence depicting a brick factory and the laborious mode of producing bricks by hand. The analogous linking of the brick factory scenes to an interview with an urban planner reinforces the theme of reconstruction and the spatial refiguration of Hanoi exemplified in the building programme. In terms of the city film the interview with an urban planner is a wry comment on a work such as The City (1939), directed by Willard Van Dyke and Ralph Steiner and produced by the American Institute of Planners, which structures its city imagery around a thematic focus on urban planning. The Griersonian-influenced tradition of urban planning films (among them When We Build Again, 1943; Proud City, 1945; and Town and Country Planning, 1946) are also implicated in Kramer's reference to the planning of Hanoi's future in a way which is implicitly critical of the heavy-handed expository approach of a number of Griersonian documentaries.[24]

Point de départ removes subjects from Griersonian positions of authority and victimhood and confirms their individuality. Kramer ends the sequence in the brick factory with a long take of a factory worker framed against a (brick) wall who looks into the camera with a resolute gaze. In fiction film the extended shot of a character's face 'is not warranted by the simple communication of information about character emotion. Such scenes are also intended to elicit emphatic emotions in the spectator' (Plantinga 1999: 239). In Kramer's documentary portrait of a city, the long take of a subject mobilises empathy in the provision of knowledge. The long take, with its absence of voice-over or commentary, the site of authority and knowledge in the expository documentary, here articulates the knowledge and experience encoded in the worker's body which 'tells the story' of a city caught between the past and the future. The lack of finality or closure for the city – its continual planning and construction – is evoked in the ongoing static long take. The camera's scrutiny reveals the brick worker as a historical agent who will effect social and political change and whose body bears the memory of both the city and the nation. In this way the subject is positioned as a synecdochic representative of the fate of the nation within a Jamesonian national allegory of the conditions of Vietnamese history and society.[25] In these terms the story of the subject in Point de départ – implicit within the allegorical frame of Kramer's long take – encodes a different history of the urban environment to that evoked in the casual and insouciant look to camera of certain New York City films.

Revising the ethnographic in the city film

Kramer's *Point de départ* was conceived, as the title of the film suggests, as a starting place for a reflection on change, the passage of time and forgetting within the context of urban space (see Kramer quoted in Blum-Reid 2003: 98). These positions are enacted within the film in which Hanoi becomes a spatial metaphor for the lives of its inhabitants through whom the film functions as a reflection on the political past and future of the Vietnamese people. In a similar way Louis Malle's *Calcutta* constitutes what Malle called a 'departing point of a reflection' on the city and his direction as a filmmaker (quoted in Blum-Reid 2003: 91).

Paul Arthur's inventories of the formal components of the New York City film – in which he includes commonly used shots of windows, chimneys and doors – reveals the city filmmaker as archaeologist minutely documenting the hieroglyphics of physical objects for meaning (see 2005a). In contrast, Malle dispels a fetishistic fixation on objects within the language of 'uncontrolled' observation. His approach eschews the complex montage of the European city symphony or New York City film to attend to the actions of human subjects and the body as the focus of an understanding of the city *as* people. Within this equation Malle manages to avoid or revise certain assumptions implicit in an ethnographic approach which begins with the epistemological position that the filmic subject is Other, to be analysed and 'explained' to a (Western) audience. In contrast to such a form of ethnographic depiction Malle's reflections on Calcutta are mixed, and as Todd Gitlin notes of *Phantom India* (1968), Malle's companion piece to *Calcutta*, he 'seems aware of the risk he is taking, steering between total acceptance and his Cartesian skepticism' (1988: 537). Just as in *Phantom India*, Malle acknowledges the limits of documentary representation, admitting in voice-over that the camera is 'impossible' – that is, incapable of penetrating the Indian consciousness and culture – so too in *Calcutta* people unselfconsciously return and resist the camera's disciplinary gaze thereby mitigating the camera's predisposition to forms of ethnographic positioning and ways of knowing.[26]

Such ways of knowing are reworked in *Phantom India* in which Malle uses voice-over, typically the site of interpretation and analysis, to emphasise that he had failed to understand anything about India, and in *Calcutta* he eschews voice-over or titles. Malle's reliance in *Calcutta* on observation, as with Robert Gardner's abandonment of exposition in the 'ethnographic film' *Forest of Bliss*, forces the viewer to extract meaning from the visual domain. In these films observational techniques 'no longer give the impression of "capturing" the referential realm itself, the historical world as it is, so much as lend stress to qualities of duration, texture, and expression' within a focus on a city's inhabitants (Nichols 1994: 95). The representation of Benares and the city's cremation rites in *Forest of Bliss* is undertaken within the traditional diurnal cycle of the city symphony, though in other respects the film reworks established codes of the form. The locus for this revision is a mode of documentary display in which the capacities of 'showing' (operative within and through visual components, informed by aural features) take precedence over formal attention to 'telling' (expository claims concerning the experiential). This process is common to city films, including city symphonies, though in Forest of Bliss the 'showing' of display – which is marked to a degree not necessarily evident in other city films – results in a work of sensorial and affective intensity.

Forest of Bliss maps the holy city of Benares, concentrating on the area close to the Ganges – its streets, the Durga temple, a hospice, the steps leading down to the river and the Manikarnika ghat on the river's edge. The geography of the city is established within the lives of three individuals who traverse the river's bank: Mithai Lal, a healer, Ragul Pandit, a priest who daily worships at the river and at the Ganga Devi temple, and the Dom Raja, the 'King of the Burning Grounds' (the river-side cremation site). A spatial outline of the city is established principally through long sequences in which Mithai Lal is followed as he walks from his house to the river, and back to his house and to the Durga temple. The actions of these 'characters' is focused on the funerary rites conducted on the bank of the river adjacent to the city.[27] The depiction of death in Ruttmann's Berlin (a reconstructed scene of a woman's suicide) and in Cavalcanti's Rien que les heures (a staged murder) function as metaphors alluding to the essence of the city as a place which crushes or destroys individuals. In Forest of Bliss Gardner constructs a series of metaphors which support the interpretation that death is a transcendence of life and the holy city of Benares, the City of Light, far from a 'crushing' (or even 'kaleidoscopic') space, is the avenue to a transcendental realm.

The representation of individual lives, and death, is realised within a practice that Gardner refers to as 'telling the story by relying primarily on visual strategies' (1996: 176).[28] Gardner's emphasis on showing over telling, or telling via showing, and its move away from the expository construction of argumentation and knowledge, provoked a strong critical response within quarters of the ethnographic community concerned with maintaining ethnographic filmmaking practices based on certain formal strategies and distinctions.[29] Typical of the criticisms of Forest of Bliss were comments by Jay Ruby who admitted that 'I rarely can figure out what the people are doing [in Forest of Bliss] and when I can, the significance of the action is lost to me' (1990: 11). Ruby, as with another of the film's critics, Alexander Moore, insisted that the film requires a voice-over or titles to interpret the action (1988: 1).[30] Extending this line of criticism, the perpetually perplexed Ruby points to a distinction, and its effect on readings of the film, between (social) scientific interpretative approaches and artful positions (1990: 11).[31] Ruby's disquiet over the suggestion that ethnographic film is, or should be, 'art' was countered by defenders of Forest of Bliss who have argued that the film is not an ethnography and that it includes various devices to cue the viewer to this interpretation.[32] Such a position, however, inherently accepts Ruby's distinction between a 'scientific' visual ethnography capable of presenting and interpreting empirical evidence in the form of rational knowledge and a visual text dedicated to 'artistic expression' which therefore lacks any informational capacity.

Gardner's ethnographic city film obviates such distinctions through the application of a set of practices summarisable in terms of 'social aesthetics' (see Mac-Dougall 2006). The emphasis on embodiment within what MacDougall identifies as the 'sensory and formal qualities of social life' is, as Kevin Anderson notes, produced through immersion in the '"foreign" Benarese culture of death rituals ... Gardner's film invites us into this space of unfamiliar images and sounds in order for transformation to occur: a transformation in cognition, emotion, and the senses, a transformation that, ideally, stimulates and informs our ... cultural understanding'. The resultant encounter with 'the imagery and sounds of Gardner's film without [contra Ruby] the distraction of a literal translation of dialogue forces the viewer to prereflectively encounter the world Gardner is showing us' (Anderson 2003: 82).

Within the film's audio realm Gardner constructs a densely textured sonic tapestry composed of numerous recurring sounds, among them temple bells, dogs barking and growling, vultures and crows cawing, laughter, prayers, chanting, shouts, wailing, fires crackling, a conch shell blown like a trumpet, and creaking boat oars, the latter a sound which is repeated to the point of a 'symphonic' refrain. Gardner's visual montage is equally as complex, and includes an array of arresting images, among them, dogs fighting, children flying paper kites, cows and monkeys in the city's streets, the Ganges in morning mist, boats on the river, priests at prayer, and numerous shots of birds soaring, scavenging and darting across the Ganges. The effective force of such images is pushed to an intensity of emotion in the film's rampant imagery of death: the dead carried through city streets to funeral pyres built next to the river, the flames of the burning ghats, marigolds strewn over the body and the streets, the chants of priests and wails of mourners. Gardner's imagery does not merely replace or substitute the inventories and categories of the city symphony and New York City film, which contain the magnitude of urban experience within a 'kaleidoscopic' montage. In Forest of Bliss images powerfully and directly bespeak 'the city' in terms of the fate of the city's inhabitants. Gardner's death imagery evokes the shock Walter Benjamin accorded to the multiple sensory assaults of the city and informs it with an existential shock of death in the city.[33]

Counterpointing the images of death Gardner builds a web of imagery that serves as a buffer against the visual and sonic assault of the city and its shocks.

Gardner notes that as 'an *observer* who regards the city as having endless possibilities for confusion, I was no different from anyone else living in Benares. Here was a city of institutionalized chaos – and what can you do with chaos? ... Photographed, it just becomes visual noise, and the only way I could see to get away from the visual noise of Benares was to find refuge, almost literally, in [images of] marigolds or the wood [of the funeral pyres] or something extremely simple' (quoted in Gardner & Ostor 2001: 46; emphasis in original). The multiple images of the work associated with making funeral wreaths of marigolds, framing what becomes a 'marigold theme', is mobilised as a structural device through which Gardner balances the 'din and clatter' of populous Benares (2001: 47). The flower device gains its visual force through repetition and via seemingly unincorporated scenes such as those depicting people bringing marigolds into the city from the fields, and shots of hands picking marigolds, stringing marigolds as offerings, marigold wreaths on funeral pyres, and a holy cow devouring the flowers from rubbish in the street.

The chaos of the city is further balanced by attention to and sympathy for the people in the city, in particular the three central characters associated with the funerary rites – the healer, the priest and the Dom Raja. For Gardner these people 'are a great deal more to me than mere informants and characters in an anthropological field project. To me, they represent Benares in the best sense' (in Gardner & Ostor 2001: 33). The personality of each individual is revealed through certain details, as in the case of Mithai Lal descending steps to the Ganges, grunting as his arthritic limbs move him to the water's edge for his morning prayers. Gardner discusses the meaning of such details in an interview:

> The grunting on the [sound] track at this point was not as apparent in actuality as it is in the film. The sound was deliberately enhanced in post production ... [I changed] the balance and intensity of the sound so that it really stood out. Very often when you're doing sound and image at the same time you don't get good sound quality. The image concerns are usually greater and, as a rule, take precedence. So we had to really work on the sound to bring it up and make it clear that Mithai Lal was not wholly enjoying this stretching of his arthritic limbs right after having gotten out of a warm bed ... If everything is portrayed properly, the person is fleshed out as an individual. The camera can actually endow him with some personality or even some character. (In Gardner & Ostor 2001: 29)

Though Gardner admits that the 'very idea of finding a way to reproduce some reality that can be called another person is, on its face, a total absurdity' he does achieve character insights through sympathetic attention to each individual (quoted in MacDougall 2001: 79). Against the 'din' and 'chaos' of the city, such insights form a counter-narrative which is developed at a slower, more measured, pace than the funerary narrative with its inexorable movement of the dead being transported towards the Manikarnika funeral pyre. It is within the focus on individuals that Gardner captures moments of wonder and intimacy, as when he records the Dom Raja waking in the morning. At such times 'you're at the height of your power, at the height of your ecstasy as a filmmaker', says Gardner (quoted in MacDougall 2001: 83). The accretion and combination of such moments, which are informed by the visual shock of death, contribute to an aesthetic based in the sensory qualities of social life. Such an approach anchors showing and seeing – and the sensorial knowledge it produces – as the productive bases of the film's documentary display.

Sense and the city

The sensory aesthetic deployed in Gardner's Forest of Bliss is summarisable through reference to what David MacDougall calls the 'corporeal image', an intercultural focus on images of the body and the experiential presence of the filmmaker. As MacDougall states, 'corporeal images are not just the images of other bodies; they are also images of the body behind the camera and its relations with the world' (2006: 3). The subjective, intercultural cinema which MacDougall refers to is in certain respects similar to the practices of exilic filmmakers who, as a result of political disruption and forced exile or banishment are located between the homeland and their adoptive countries. Hamid Naficy has examined the ways in which the constraints of the experience of exile have resulted in a particular filmmaking style. According to Naficy, exilic filmmakers 'memorialize the homeland by fetishizing it in the form of cathected sounds, images, and chronotypes that are circulated intertextually in exilic popular culture, including in films and music videos. The exiles' primary relationship, in short, is with their countries and cultures of origin and with the sight, sound, taste, and feel of an ordinary experience' (2001: 26). Emphasising the sensory capacity of exilic films, Naficy insists that the 'dominance of vision ... is attenuated for the exiles by the prominence of the other senses, which continually and poignantly remind them of their seemingly irrevocable difference, loss, or lack of it' (2001: 28). Naficy adds:

> A particular fragrance on a hillside, a stolen glance in a restaurant, a body brush in a crowded street, a particular posture by a passenger in an elevator, a flash of memory during daily conversations, the sound of familiar words in one's native tongue heard from an adjoining car at a red traffic light – each of these [experiences] activates private memories and intensifies the feeling of displacement. (Ibid.; emphasis in original)

Significantly, as Naficy notes, memory occupies a privileged place as facilitator and mediator of sensory impressions which are central to the experience of exile and the evocations of exilic cinema. Naficy emphasises that exilic cinema 'is propelled by the memory, nostalgic longing, and multiple losses and wishes that are experienced by the diegetic characters, the exilic filmmakers and their audiences' (2001: 29).

Memory and its 'sensory reports' is, as Naficy and other theorists of exilic cinema note, a structural device prevalent within numerous city films produced by exilic filmmakers from the disrupted nations of the Middle East.[34] Within these terms filmmakers exiled from Lebanon, a nation wracked by warfare within and beyond its disputed borders, have structured filmic depictions of Beirut around the memories of the city's inhabitants. Zeini Sfeir's video *In Spite of the War* (2001), for example, focuses on those living in post-civil war Beirut and prominently includes interviews with members of a young generation who are nostalgic for the war. Their memories are ironically interspersed with a portrait of rebuilt downtown Beirut, a non-place in which all signs and memories of the conflict have been erased.

The themes of memory and remembrance are further examined in Lebanese American Walid Ra'ad's *In the Dead Weight of a Quarrel Hangs* (1996–99), a video composed of three works (*Missing Lebanese Wars*, *Secrets in the Open Sea*, and *Miraculous Beginnings*) which examines the history and memory of the religious, gender and class experiences of the wars. The theme of memory is extended in other city films dealing with the region produced by film and video makers who move between cultures and whose work is thereby not reducible to the experiences or discourse of a single culture. Such works include *A Place Called Home* (1998) by Iranian American Persheng Sadlegh-Vaziri, which traces the filmmaker's return to Tehran after years of living in the US. Sadlegh-Vaziri explores a new Tehran which is a very different place to her childhood memories. The revolution has altered lives and the physical terrain of the city, and within this scenario Sadlegh-Vaziri demonstrates the relationship of memory, people and place.

The documentation of memory, and the evocations of memories of the homeland, operates within exilic cinema in association with other identifiable filmic practices. Naficy argues that memory and nostalgic longing experienced by the diegetic subjects, exilic filmmakers and their audiences is a determining factor in the production of films which are marked by what he calls a tactile optics, 'that is, their nonlinear structure, which is driven by the juxtaposition of multiple spaces, times, voices, narratives, and foci – the montage effect' (2001: 29). Naficy's account of the formal features of 'tactile optics' is little different to descriptions of the practices of numerous avant-garde productions from the past twenty years; the essential difference is that Naficy emphasises that such practices are motivated by a sense of loss experienced by exilic filmmakers. Naficy's description of 'tactile optics' is informed by Laura Marks' references to what she calls a haptic visuality, a term she applies to the formal processes of intercultural cinema in a way which clarifies Naficy's less specific 'tactile optics'. Marks uses the term to refer to works which 'invite a look that moves on the surface plane of the screen for some time before the viewer realizes what she or he is beholding. Such images resolve into figuration only gradually, if at all. Conversely, a haptic work may create an image of such details, sometimes through miniaturism, that it evades distanced view, instead pulling the viewer in close' (2000: 163).

The term haptic (like tactile) emphasises the seemingly paradoxical role in visuality of a sense of touch which 'involves the body more than is the case with optical visuality. Touch is a sense located on the surface of the body: thinking of the cinema as haptic is only a step toward considering the ways cinema appeals to the body as a whole' (ibid.). The haptic features of the text are evident in Jayce Salloum's This is Not Beirut (1994) a video that, while composed of images of Beirut streets, visually reworks accepted notions of the city and the city film. Evoking the damage and destruction caused by the Lebanese wars, Salloum mixes scenes shot from a speeding car with static shots of buildings in rubble, with scenes of the city which are violently interrupted by jump cuts which also fracture and disrupt dialogue (see Marks 2000: 58). The emphasis in the work on the haptic qualities of the image – the surface texture and manipulation of the image – is matched by a nonlinear structure and a montage of radical juxtaposition of foci characteristic of a tactile optics. The effect of haptic or tactile visuality in Salloum's video is an implicit criticism of the ways in which the global news media have 'covered' Beirut and the political situation in Lebanon as a zone of chaos and unintelligibility. As Marks comments, more than 'an antiportrait of Beirut, the tape is a mediation on political representation' (2000: 59).

The freneticism of Salloum's anti-city film, and a resultant tactile or haptic effect, is also evident in Waël Noureddine's Ca sera beau. From Beyrouth with Love (2005), a tape which intersperses long tracking shots and short, rapidly edited shots of Beirut filmed over the course of days and nights (in an echo of the diurnal cycle of 1920s city symphonies). Images of a city scarred by war – pock-marked buildings and military patrols – recur within the video. Part of the human toll of war in Beirut is registered in drug-taking, exemplified in scenes in which Noureddine and his friends indulge in various narcotics. Ironically, and fittingly, Noureddine's 'city symphony' is scored to a soundtrack of punk music (as in the film's final scenes, which are accompanied by music by the Messageros Killer Boys).

The works of Salloum and Noureddine underscore the effects of national political disruption, displacement and exile, and the role of such experiences in the practices of exilic and intercultural filmmaking. Politically-informed contexts and effects have an influential role in the formal practices of the city film. With their primary emphasis on the corporeal, the representations produced by local and intercultural film and video makers construct the city film as it is defined here as a transnational form which is applied to differing locations in works which commonly deploy the corporeal image to 'physically' locate, describe and interpret varying cityscapes. The avant-gardist city film, for example, in its meld of documentary and 'experimental' forms constructs an insider and often subjective perspective on the corporeal presence of the people who inhabit a city. The variety of styles through which such a representation is constructed – from the 'kaleidoscopic' city symphonies of the 1920s to the revision of Western media modes in recent city films produced in the Middle East – operate through reference to varying political and historical contexts and effects to focus on the inhabitants of a city as the visual basis of the city film's documentary display. Such a display, with its emphasis on the body and spaces, is both a form of knowledge and a set of stylistic innovations which together produce a complex seeing in the form of an expressive documentary re-imagining of the city.

chapter three

Direct Cinema and Performance:
It's Not Only Rock and Roll

At times in life we meet people who we feel are acting.
— Michael Kirkby (1995: 47)

The documentary form popularly referred to as rockumentary has become, since its inception in the early 1960s, a staple of nonfiction film production.[1] The growth of the form has been enhanced by the fact that various Hollywood and independent directors not routinely associated with documentary film have produced works in this category, among them Martin Scorsese (*The Last Waltz*, 1978)[2], Jonathan Demme (*Stop Making Sense*, 1984; *Neil Young: Heart of Gold*, 2005), Gillian Armstrong (*Hard to Hold*, 1986) and Jim Jarmusch (*Year of the Horse*, 1998). However, despite (or because of) its enduring popular and commercial success, rockumentary has received scant critical attention within analyses of documentary film.[3] The relative absence of critical assessments of rockumentary is especially curious given the fact that many of the most notable works in the subgenre, including *Dont Look Back* (1966), *Monterey Pop* (1968) and *Gimme Shelter* (1970), were made by filmmakers associated with the early phase of an influential direct cinema – D.A. Pennebaker (*Dont Look Back* and *Monterey Pop*), Richard Leacock (*Monterey Pop*) and the Maysles brothers (*Monterey Pop* and *Gimme Shelter*).[4] Commentators have recently attended to the proliferation of observational reality television and 'popular factual entertainment' by noting the bases of these forms in the observational mode of direct cinema (see, for example, Brenton & Cohen 2003). Overlooked in the findings of such revisionism, however, is the fact that direct cinema has not completely dissipated into television 'reality' programmes, and continues to be deployed, in mutated forms, in the rockumentary.

The assessment that current forms of rockumentary rely on a variant of direct cinema suggests that a 'pure' direct cinema once existed, and indeed certain early practitioners of direct cinema based many of their claims for its efficacy on notions of an 'unperverted' form of unmediated observation, and, according to such practitioners of direct cinema, it was this characteristic which marked the difference between American direct cinema and French *cinéma vérité*.[5] Beyond the realm of nonfiction cinema, the rise of the rockumentary can be positioned in relation to the fate of the Hollywood studio system and the genres it maintained. Beginning in the early 1960s (with what was, arguably, the first example of the form, the Maysles brothers *What's Happening! The Beatles in the U.S.A.*, 1964[6]) direct cinema studies of rock musicians came at a time when established Hollywood genres were showing signs of exhaustion. This situation was exacerbated by the fact that Hollywood's traditional genres – notably the western and the musical – did not, in the short term at least, survive the demise of the studio system. Attempts during the 1960s to revive such genres often met with disaster (and the fate of the execrable *Paint Your Wagon* (1969) exemplifies the consequences resulting from a melding of the western and the musical into an ill-conceived cross-generic hybrid[7]). The combined circumstances – decline of the studio system and the impact of this situation on established filmic genres, in particular the musical – left a generic void which was filled by the rockumentary which, as David James notes, 'savagely reinvented the musical as genre' (1989 349).

The new form, in keeping with its associations with observational direct cinema, emphasised showing not telling; that is, rockumentary privileges a scopic regime over patterns of exposition such as voice-over or a reliance on interviews. Critics have argued that as a result of this orientation, direct cinema (and by implication rockumentary) fails to situate subjects within sociological or historical contexts, thereby contradicting the documentary project's emphasis on providing information and inspiring knowledge.[8] The position is overstated, as the case of rockumentary demonstrates. Rockumentary maintains a commitment to the traditional documentary project within a focus on youth subcultures and music subformations – and attendant perspectives on personal identity – which constitute the informational core of the form. However, rockumentary motivates knowledge in ways different to nonfiction works such as the long-form news documentary and its series of fact-based statements. In the rockumentary the provision of information ('telling') operates within and through a mode which emphasises and exploits the representational capacities of the visual register ('showing'). The form of knowledge produced within this mode is subjective, affective, visceral and sensuous.

The visual appeal of rockumentary is enhanced by its auditory features, though the soundtrack – while appealing in itself, especially to the fan/spectator attracted to rockumentary by the opportunity to hear particular music – is subservient to the image track. In most cases, the music performed live at concerts is available in recorded form and in this way people watch filmed versions of live concerts (and, perhaps, attend a live concert) to *see* the music being performed. The examples here highlight the relationship of image and sound as one in which image predominates and is foregrounded within the work of rockumentary. This chapter examines the visual regime of rockumentary as part of a project of identifying and examining formal practices which enlarge conceptions of the documentary canon. The analysis attends to the development of the rockumentary form from its foundation in the 1960s in *Dont Look Back* and *Gimme Shelter*, to *The Last Waltz*, to demonstrations of punk music performance, including Jem Cohen's *Instrument* (1999). Recent works in the rockumentary form – among them *I Am Trying to Break Your Heart* (2002) and *Metallica: Some Kind of Monster* (2004) – are also analysed with reference to the visual capacities of the focus of rockumentary on the performative body. The range of works examined here traverses the formal and stylistic features of rockumentary as derived from the form's core organisational principle, that of documentary display and its various manipulations of attendant 'attractions'. Notably, rockumentary's (direct) cinema of attractions is, as pointed out in the following section, centred on and conducted through the 'attraction' and display of onstage and offstage performance.

The body in performance and on display

Assumptions within established exegesis of the documentary of the form's unmediated and unreconstructed access to the real do not admit a place for notions of performance before or in reaction to the documentary camera. Rockumentary, with its relentless foregrounding of the performing body and the performance of music, revises this understanding. In 1965 the musician and composer Glenn Gould predicted that 'the public concert as we know it today [will] no longer exist a century hence [because] its functions [will] have been entirely taken over by electronic media' (quoted in Goehr 1995–96: 1). Gould's perception distantly echoes Walter Benjamin's 'Artwork' essay and its assessments of the potential of commercial mass production, notably in the form of the 'mechanical reproduction' of electronic media, to produce images and sounds which replace or stand in for the authentic work of art (see Benjamin 2005). Contrary to Gould, and functioning in a way that informs Benjamin's critique of the ability of modern media to reconfigure authenticity, the rockumentary insists on the place of live musical performance, to the point that, at times, the rockumentary performance is frequently staged to be recorded by the camera. Authenticity is, then, implicated with the rockumentary, though issues of authentic and staged performances are displaced by questions concerning the authenticity of the self – the authentic self – in relation to on-camera performance.

As with American avant-garde films of the 1960s, rockumentaries of the decade and those produced since that time, create a cinema in which the 'performing body [is] the central focus of the gaze' (Dixon 1998: 49). The performing body in the rockumentary is, however, not limited to onstage presentation and histrionics. A master trope of the rockumentary is the distinction between onstage performances and so-called 'backstage', an area which supposedly offers unmediated glimpses of the 'real' person behind the performance. The 'backstage' convention frequently exploits the hand-held camera of direct cinema and its capacity to film in confined and poorly-lit spaces such as dressing rooms, concert hall corridors, the back seats of limousines and in hotel rooms. Erving Goffman, in his sociological and psychological study of selfhood, *The Presentation of Self in Everyday Life*, examines various behaviours undertaken in particular social environments, among them 'backstage', the physical space behind or offstage in which a performer can relax and 'step out of character' (1969: 98). Such an understanding informs the convention of backstage as it operates in the rockumentary where, as Jonathan Romney argues, it is

> the most potent of all concepts designed to separate performer and fan. It is a space of privacy, a world behind the curtain in which the real being, the ineffable precious essence of the performer's self, supposedly lies shielded from sight ... The audience is not normally permitted behind the sacred veil, but it is a convention of the music documentary to include scenes which take us backstage and offer us tantalizing glimpses of the reality behind the show ... [Such scenes] offer us a fantasy 'Access All Areas' pass, one of those areas being the artist's very soul. Above all, they promise access to the truth, for backstage is imagined as a far more 'real' space than the stage in which the artists do their work. (1995: 83)

In Romney's account the convention creates a distinction between the public space of the stage, where a performer presents a persona constructed for the purposes of entertaining an audience, and the private spaces offstage in which the mask of the performer is dropped and the person behind the performer is revealed.

Bill Nichols' evocative phrase 'social actors', a term he uses to refer to the subjects of documentary, captures something of the performative presence in nonfiction representation.[9] Thomas Waugh's useful study of performance in documentary examines the ways in which performance (and the direction of action) is ingrained in the documentary tradition (see 1990). Waugh's essay is an acknowledgement that among other formal features documentary shares with fiction a performing subject. However, unlike the scripted performance of professional actors in fiction, documentary depicts social actors whose 'real' identity is expressed in performative action. Such recognition has been taken up within analyses of the 'reality television' phenomenon. Commentators have noted the difficulty in distinguishing on-camera authenticity and performance, and indeed much of the appeal for the spectator of popular factual entertainment is generated by an awareness of the on-camera subject's perpetual performance (see Roscoe 2001). In classic observationalism the subject does not appear to be performing; there is an attempt by both subject and director to treat speech and behaviour as 'naturally' as possible. In reality television and popular factual entertainment, in contrast, observation becomes the impetus for the non-professional to perform. One aspect of this process is exemplified in *Cops* (1989–present), among other variants of crime-based reality television in the US, in which producers were known to advise the police on performance techniques, and were willing to direct police in the delivery of dialogue and how to 'act' for the camera (see Andersen 1995: 181).

Similarly, docusoaps are populated by people willing, or seeking, to appear before the camera and who, in their modes of personal presentation, often adopt performative styles and attitudes.[10] However, this fact does not necessarily eliminate the possibility of depictions of 'real' or authentic behaviour. This understanding is implicated with the nature of self-revelation in performance, a condition related to the notion of everyday performance by people perceived to be acting. Such a situation

> does not mean that [people] are lying, dishonest, living in an unreal world, or necessarily giving a false impression of their character or personality. It means that they seem to be aware of an audience – to be 'on stage' – and that they relate to the situation by energetically projecting ideas, emotions, and elements of their personality, underlining and theatricalizing it for the sake of the audience. They are acting their own emotions and beliefs. (Kirkby 1995: 47)

This quality impacts in a specific way on viewers' experience of the docusoap, notably in the fact that they derive gratification from such programmes by locating the 'authentic' self within the performance. As Jane Roscoe has appropriately noted, audiences 'play the game of evaluating how well participants perform their role ... These moments of so-called authenticity – moments when we think we see the real person – take on key importance in these new factual hybrids. Such authenticity is both reassuring – linking us back to factual discourse and the "real" – and it is the prize in the audience game of performance, thus presenting us with a satisfying experience' (2001: 14).

The 'game' of 'performing the real' and locating the real within the performance is complicated within the gamedoc format of *Big Brother* (see Corner 2002). The viewer's search for moments of authenticity is increased in a programme that uses a non-natural setting – a house that is a studio – which reinforces self-conscious and self-aware performance, not naturalism, as the prime focus of the show. Finding authentic moments in *Big Brother* is further complicated by the process of eviction which serves as the programme's premise. In the presence of the threat of eviction participants must remain appealing to their fellow contestants, 'they have to perform the role of team player and good house guest – while also remembering that, ultimately, they have to win over the viewers to stay in the game' (Roscoe 2001: 17). The ways in which participants react to the various tests and contests posed to them, and interact with their fellow house guests, is a key element for the contestants and central to the viewing gratifications derivable from the programme. Annette Hill offers a useful way to understand the process of identifying the 'authentic' person within the performative role by replacing the notion of performance with the practice of 'self-display':

> Although many viewers are aware of press reports questioning the truthfulness of popular factual [programmes], and my research illustrates their cynicism about the reality in factual entertainment, this does not mean audiences have rejected the idea of authenticity in factual TV. In fact, audiences have developed viewing strategies that foreground authenticity in a highly constructed TV environment. For the average TV viewer, judging authenticity in popular factual programmes such as BB [*Big Brother*] is related to judging the integrity of the self. When contestants in BB are faced with emotionally difficult situations, they often reveal their 'true' nature. Audience attraction to judging levels of authenticity in BB is primarily based on whether contestants stay true to themselves, rather than whether the programme is truthful in its depiction of contestants. (2002: 336–7)

As Hill emphasises, *Big Brother* and other variants of popular factual entertainment rework the search for evidence of the real within a focus on the presentation of the self.

Interestingly, Hill echoes Goffman in her conclusions. In an analysis of 'belief in the part one is playing' in social situations, Goffman argues that 'the performer can be fully taken in by his own act; he can be sincerely convinced that the impression of reality which he stages is the real reality. When his audience is also convinced in this way about the show he puts on – and this seems to be the typical case – then, for the moment at least, only the sociologist or the socially disgruntled will have any doubts about the "realness" of what is presented' (1969: 15). Significantly, the conceptions by Hill and Goffman of the operation and function of self-display reinforce the practice of visual attraction in the rockumentary. As with popular factual entertainment, representational claims to the real or truth are attenuated, though still present, in the rockumentary. In ways which do not entirely conform to Romney's account of public and private space, the revelation of 'truth' in the rockumentary is not a simple function of a dialectical relationship between onstage and backstage spaces. Rather, conceptions of truth in the rockumentary are located within and emerge from the revelation of an authentic self within (onstage and backstage) performances, which are the core of rockumentary's documentary display. The process of performance – and the exposure or display of the performative self, the self as performer – is the structural basis of Pennebaker's groundbreaking work, *Dont Look Back*.

Dont Look Back: performing the documentary

As with other works of direct cinema, a rockumentary presumes to be an objective record of an event, in this case musical concert performances and offstage actions. However, as a species of direct cinema which focuses on performance, the rockumentary begs a number of questions concerning the effects of the camera on a subject's behaviour. Such questions are of particular relevance to *Dont Look Back*, which features multiple levels of performance. The film, a record of Bob Dylan's triumphant 1965 concert tour of the UK, includes a number of Dylan's onstage performances amidst scenes of life away from the spotlight. The intriguing aspect of *Dont Look Back* is the degree of attention the film gives to depicting the exploits of Dylan and his entourage in 'offstage' environments such as hotel rooms. Such scenes constitute another level of performance in which Dylan continues, in effect, to perform for the camera away from the stage.[11]

The film's prologue, which was suggested to Pennebaker by Dylan, exemplifies the filmmaker's willingness to abandon pure direct cinema by foregrounding offstage performance as one of the film's central concerns – not as something to be minimised or banished, but as an activity to be encouraged and highlighted. The segment features Dylan, standing in an alleyway behind the Savoy Hotel in London, holding large cue cards inscribed with hand-lettered words of his song 'Subterranean Homesick Blues', which plays on the soundtrack. During the sequence Dylan stands facing the camera flipping through the cards, the first inscribed with 'BASEMENT' (in the song Dylan sings 'Johnny's in the basement mixing up the medicine...'), continuing with others which bear various lyrics from the song: 'LOOK OUT!', 'WATCH IT!', 'HERE THEY COME!', 'LEADERS???' and so on. Dylan discards the cards one by one as the song continues to play. His act is replete with knowing looks to the camera which also depicts the alleyway in the background, empty except for the brief appearance of a bearded figure carrying a staff (the poet Allen Ginsberg). At the end of the segment, as the song is fading on the soundtrack, another man (Dylan's friend Bob Neuwirth) enters the frame, nods at Dylan, and the two walk away in opposite directions, with Dylan heading down the alley without looking back.

The prologue is a fully contained segment within the broader film, and it approximates what later became the 'rock clip', short interpretative works produced to accompany rock songs on television in formats such as those on MTV. (Indeed, Dylan's manager, Albert Grossman, had conceived of Pennebaker's film as an opportunity to produce promotional clips for Dylan's songs.) The segment positions Dylan 'centre stage' within a self-conscious performance. In these terms the prologue can either be considered out of place, even inappropriate, within the context of observationalism, or, alternatively, an indication that performance – an abandonment of the pretence of naturalism – will supersede the demands of a direct cinema committed to naturalism and observation. It is clear as the film progresses, and as Dylan continues to act for the camera, that his proposal to include the segment, and Pennebaker's agreement to do so, signals an emphasis on the performative which extends beyond the realms of the stage. William Rothman, in his lengthy and dense analysis of *Don't Book Back*, suggests that the purpose of the prologue is to announce that the film is not merely a 'documentary'; it is, instead, a 'collaboration in which filmmaker and subject are co-conspirators' (1997: 149). In this way the prologue functions as a marker that the body of the film will also be a 'performance by co-conspirators' (ibid.). This is not to suggest that Pennebaker consciously set out to 'defraud' or deceive the viewer. However, the 'collusion' between Dylan and Pennebaker does point to a manipulation, or transgression of the codes of direct cinema. The prologue, as with the rest of the film, constitutes Pennebaker's willingness to abandon 'pure' direct cinema, and to give rein, with Dylan's participation, to performance – both onstage and off.

Another indication of this willingness occurs during an interview between Dylan and a Jamaican correspondent for the BBC, one of the many interviews in the film. The interviewer asks, 'How did it all begin for you, Bob?' Dylan mumbles inaudibly and the film cuts to footage of a young Dylan singing 'He's Only a Pawn in Their Game' at a civil rights rally in Mississippi. As the scattered crowd at the rally applauds his performance, another cut introduces Dylan onstage during the 1965 tour singing 'The Times They Are A-Changin''. The cuts from contemporary action to the past depicted in archival footage, back to contemporary action, disrupts the temporal and spatial continuity that narratively orders observationalism, replacing it with the non-narrativised presence of performance. Elsewhere, Dylan's musical performances are structured into the narrative as he heads north to Manchester and back to London though, ironically, the narrative lacks the 'honesty' and 'integrity' of the Mississippi performance, a function of Dylan's constant performing offstage. Within these performances there is no way to get 'access' to 'the real' Dylan.

Such access is implicated with the convention of onstage/backstage. While *Dont Look Back* replicates the two domains of onstage and backstage, the film does not fully reproduce what are in other rock documentaries the attendant meanings of public and private space. We are permitted backstage, but not granted access to the 'real being'. Offstage, Dylan continues to perform, particularly in the presence of the many interviewers who appear in the backstage spaces. At certain times, Dylan seems to take delight in the interviews, and at other times he appears to be annoyed by interviewers, but both reactions seem to be calculated. He appears as a masterful role player, an obfuscationist, indulging in word games and gambits, willing to spin stories which are clearly fabricated at the interviewer's expense. In one particular interview, with Horace Judson, the London-based arts correspondent for *Time* magazine, Dylan launches a verbal attack on Judson and steps out of the role of interviewee by asking Judson unanswerable questions. The scene is unsettling – Dylan, the man of peace, indulging in verbal aggression – and it is difficult not to wonder whether it was another example of his performance. Judson felt that the scene was contrived as an entertaining sequence for the film to compensate for the fact that the recorded interview had gone flat (in Sounes 2001: 175).

In other, less overtly dramatic, moments the film captures, if not Dylan acting for the camera, then his awareness of the camera's presence revealed, however fleetingly, in glances at the camera. Having thrown a hotel assistant out of the room, telling him to go to his 'fop manager', Dylan looks to the camera. On another occasion, while playing music and talking with Alan Price of the Animals, Dylan starts a song and then looks directly at the camera, annoyed, it seems, that Pennebaker is at that moment still filming when, for once, Dylan would prefer he was not (see Bauldrie 1990: 48). In these moments, and particularly during his interactions with interviewers, the camera reveals or inspires performances which are, in effect, an acknowledgement of the camera's presence. The camera does not capture the man 'behind the shades' (as in the title of Clinton Heylin's book from 1991). As Pennebaker pointed out, Dylan 'knew that the camera was recording [him] in a way which [he] elected to be recorded. [He was] enacting [a] role ... very accurately' (1971: 192). By privileging and, in effect, licensing Dylan's offstage 'performances' for the camera *Dont Look Back* complicates direct cinema's foundational rhetoric of detached observationalism and the associated claim that the presence of a camera does not modify a subject's behaviour. More particularly, *Dont Look Back* effectively documents a consummate performer, and extends the opportunities (in the prologue and throughout the film) for Dylan to do so. Pennebaker is implicated in this process not as neutral observer but as co-conspirator colluding in Dylan's performances.

The performative self as attraction

The notion of onstage and backstage performance, and the complicity of the documentarian in such performances, is further problematised in Albert and David Maysles' film *Gimme Shelter*, a record of the Rolling Stones' 1969 tour of the US which ended in a disastrous concert at Altamont Speedway near San Francisco.[12] The Maysles brothers were originally hired by the Rolling Stones' management to film the band in concert at Madison Square Garden in New York, though subsequently the filmmakers followed the Stones' tour as it moved across the US from the east coast to the west coast. Prior to filming the New York concert Mick Jagger approached the Maysles and stated that, 'I'm not going to be an actor in this film. None of that Pennebaker shit' (quoted in Lewis 2000). Adopting Jagger's message, the Maysles brothers did not seek to replicate the performative aspects of *Dont Look Back* or Pennebaker's approach to Dylan's onscreen performance. Nevertheless, *Gimme Shelter* does complicate and expand the notion of performance in the direct cinema rockumentary.[13]

Gimme Shelter captures a band at the height of its career, delivering powerful versions of songs from its repertoire, and includes performances by other acts, among them a stunning version of 'I've Been Loving You Too Long' by Ike and Tina Turner. For the most part, the onstage performances are filmed in an unadorned direct cinema style though, in places, such as in the presentation of the Stones' song 'Love in Vain', the filmmakers employ slow-motion flashing optical effects. The failure of the techniques (ones which have been subsequently used and abused in numerous rockumentaries) to increase the song's affective potency points to the soundness of the decision to shoot the majority of the film in an observational mode. However, eschewing a sense of observational purity, *Gimme Shelter* subjects the mode to multiple revisions, notably in the film's climactic moments which involve a reworking of a strict observationalism.

The narrative climax of the film is the murder of a spectator at the Altamont concert by a member (or members) of the Californian branch of the Hell's Angels motorcycle club, allegedly hired to provide security for the event. Numerous commentators have suggested that the killing, which occurred in full view of the stage and the cameras, symbolises 'the death of the sixties' and the end of the countercultural innocence which, supposedly, informed gatherings such as Woodstock (see, for example, Miller 1999: 277).[14] In these terms 'Altamont' has gathered rhetorical force as a byword for a failure of the utopian hopes of the 1960s and a symbol of the destructive impulses dormant within sections of the counterculture which, according to this argument, were to find full expression in the murderous rampage of Charles Manson's 'family'.

In a scathing review of *Gimme Shelter*, the critic Pauline Kael accused the film-makers of exploiting the events at Altamont for their own profit: 'the violence and killing weren't scheduled, but the Maysles brothers hit the *cinéma vérité* jackpot' (1970: 113). Kael's qualms over what she perceived to be the bad faith and ethically suspect practices of the Maysles brothers led her to query the 'authenticity' of the premises of direct cinema (or *cinéma vérité* as she calls it): 'If events are created to be photographed, is the movie that records them a documentary, or does it function in a twilight zone? Is it the cinema of fact when the facts are manufactured for the cinema?' (ibid.).[15] The questions miss certain points. As Kael acknowledges, a film frequently included in histories of documentary (and often placed within the documentary canon), Leni Riefenstahl's *Triumph des Willens* (*Triumph of the Will*, 1935), was staged for the cameras. In another way, the direct cinema rockumentary *Monterey Pop* features an event that was staged to be filmed for sale to television (and was subsequently released theatrically). *Monterey Pop* demonstrates, among other aspects, that direct cinema practice did not necessarily eschew filming 'staged' events. Kael's comments imply that she accepts what was at one time a reasonably pervasive rhetoric concerning direct cinema practice as non-interventionist, a position which many practitioners of direct cinema had abandoned or were at the time of *Gimme Shelter* in the process of aborting (for example, Richard Leacock, a founder of direct cinema and a cameraman on *Monterey Pop*, subsequently disavowed much of the early rhetoric surrounding direct cinema as 'doctrinal bullshit' (quoted in Anon. 2001: 79).

Kael does not simply implicate the practices of filmmakers; her questions beg the suggestion that reality (or truth) is accessible if subjects refuse the presence of the camera and rather than presenting a persona 'manufactured for the camera' get on with 'being themselves'. That such a suggestion is available from Kael's comments underlines the fact that she misread the role of the subject in documentary generally, and in rockumentary in particular. Rockumentary foregrounds the performative self, a subject who is aware that he or she is on display. Admittedly, though, it took the emergence of 'popular factual entertainment' to bring to the critical fore many of the issues concerning the performative self in documentary. In a particularly astute reading of the popular factual television programme *Big Brother*, John Corner highlights relevant features of this process. Corner notes the 'degree of self-consciousness' and 'display' by the people in the 'predefined stage' of the *Big Brother* house (quoted in Hill 2005: 67). He comments, in what is in retrospect a critical commentary on Kael's process of reflection on Mick Jagger in *Gimme Shelter*, that the activities of *Big Brother* participants lead to 'thick judgemental and speculative discourse around participants' motives, actions and likely future behaviour' (quoted in ibid.). Corner argues that the activities of participants implicate a viewing process in which audiences attempt to locate moments in which participants are 'true to themselves'. Corner describes this viewing practice through reference to the term 'selving', which he uses to describe 'the central process whereby "true selves" are seen to emerge (and develop) from underneath and, indeed, through, the "performed selves" projected for us, as a consequence of the applied pressures of objective circumstances and group dynamics' (quoted in ibid.).

While not that far removed from Kael's idealist position that there is a 'real' subject behind documentary 'manipulation', Corner does, however, highlight the complex and often contradictory interaction of 'true selves' and 'performed self'. Given examples from rockumentary, the process that Corner describes is further complicated, to the point that 'true' and 'performed' selves coalesce – or, in a certain reformulation of the terms, the performed self is a 'true' self. This point was lost on one commentator writing soon after the release of *Gimme Shelter* who, though acknowledging the complexity of the interactions in rockumentary, reaches misleading conclusions:

> Let us take the live performance ... At such times, we as spectators must of necessity experience multiple vision, in that we are witness to a play within a play: we are watching the spectators who are watching the performer, who is performing for spectators of the concert, cameras at the concert and spectators who will see the film of the cameras at the concert ... Whenever a documentary is of the personality-profile variety, and whenever that performer being filmed is most aware of the camera filming him ... we can be reasonably sure that we are witnessing a lie and not a reality, an artifice as opposed to a truth, a performance as opposed to a true personality. (Van Wert 1974: 258)

As Corner's comments make clear, subsequent assessments of the performing self in documentary, especially those concerning popular factual entertainment, a format constructed around performance, undermine the position reached in the quotation. In another way, poststructuralist conceptions of identity, which anticipate recent arguments concerning the place of the performative self in popular factual entertainment, insist that identity is not a unitary construct, but is relational and as such is constantly reconstructed and in flux. In these terms there is no essential or fixed self, a position which admits the performative self – a mutable persona – as the expression of authentic selfhood.

The insight is particularly relevant to Jagger, the 'star' of *Gimme Shelter*, whose persona was constructed from his personal experiences, onstage performances and within a series of films. The frequent references in accounts of Jagger's career to the 'ambiguous sexuality' of his performances (see, for example, James 1996: 120), reinforced in Kael's reference to his 'polymorphous perversity' (1970: 113), in one way exemplify the reality of a persona that refuses to be fixed in unitary terms. That this persona connects with, or is an inherent expression of, selfhood is traceable through the development of the Jagger persona. The 'voice of the devil' in which Jagger sings 'Sympathy for the Devil', the song which the Stones attempt to perform as the fan, Meredith Hunter, is murdered by the Hell's Angels at Altamont, is an expression of Jagger as rock Lucifer. The themes implicated in the film's record of the song – bikers, the Devil incarnate, death, Jagger's effeminacy and the Hell's Angels' aggressive masculinity – were foreshadowed in Kenneth Anger's 1964 film *Scorpio Rising*, a work dealing with satanic homosexual motorcyclists given to the death drive, which uses a pastiche of popular songs as its soundtrack. As David James notes, 'large skeins of Jagger's persona are prefigured in the way the iconography of *Scorpio Rising* oscillates between effeminacy and hyper-masculinity' (1996: 120).[16]

The connections between effeminacy and masculinity, subcultural ritual and rock are extended in *Performance* (1969), the title itself an ironic reference to the persona Jagger expresses in the film. Co-directed by Nicolas Roeg and Donald Cammell, who had dabbled in the occult and Satanism, the film depicts a confrontation between the bohemian lifestyle of Turner (Jagger), an androgynous, reclusive former rock star living in a mansion in Notting Hill, and Chas Devlin (James Fox), a gangster on the run from his boss who seeks a hiding place in the mansion. 'In the course of their time together, Turner and Chas recognise bits of themselves in each other and, without quite realising it, would begin to merge and swap bits of their personalities – or, more exactly, the personae they had worn as personalities' (Levy 2002: 327). The inversions and transferences involved in the fictional scenario merged beyond the film into a mixing of Jagger's acted and authentic selves. Marianne Faithfull, Jagger's then partner who had helped him prepare for the film, 'saw the film ... as a remarkable window that opened their true selves to the world' (ibid.). According to Faithfull, most of the people in *Performance* 'weren't acting at all ... They were exhibiting themselves ... In the same way that some actors get to keep their wardrobe, Mick came way from *Performance* with his *character*' (quoted in Levy 2002: 333; emphasis in original).

Whereas certain spectators saw the persona as a pose, Faithfull astutely recognised it as the real thing, a persona as personification (see Levy 2002: 334). While many people involved with the film fell into drug addiction, nervous collapse, or lost their career path in the wake of the film, Jagger, as Faithfull notes, gained a new expression of his self as a result of acting in the film. 'Mick came out of it splendidly, with a new, shining and impenetrable suit of body armour. He didn't have a drug problem and he didn't have a nervous breakdown. Nothing really touched him ... Mick is so grounded as a person that he never loses his footing', she explained. 'He is able to observe the car crash at the moment of impact and escape unscathed – a quality that is extremely exasperating for the victims' (quoted in Levy 2002: 333–4).

The *sang froid* persona was for Jagger a reflection, as much as an expression, of self-hood. Reinforcing this point, Albert Maysles, in a commentary on direct cinema claims to veracity, adds that *Gimme Shelter* displays, rather than interprets, Jagger's (performative/authentic) self: 'we couldn't come out with a reading [of Jagger], except to present what we saw ... As I was filming him, I don't think that we'd missed anything that would have been more revealing. I wish it were more revealing, but it just didn't happen' (quoted in Economy 2000: 3).

The closure of *Gimme Shelter* includes Jagger watching replays of footage shot of the killing at Altamont, and the film ends with what one critic called an 'enigmatic freeze-frame of Jagger that still haunts, an impenetrably blank response to horror that is all the more troubling in its ambiguity' (ibid.). Roland Barthes in his analysis of the screened image of Greta Garbo's face argues that though an actress in fiction films, Garbo does not wear a mask: 'she is always herself, and carries without pretence, under her crown or her wide-brimmed hats, the same snowy solitary face' (2004: 589). According to Béla Belász facial expression 'is the most subjective ... of human manifestations [which] is rendered objective in the close-up' (2004: 316). Following Barthes and Belász, the final close-up of Jagger's face in *Gimme Shelter* displays Jagger's real (objective) character.

The technique, included throughout the film, of repeated scenes of Jagger and other members of the band viewing the Altamont footage, circumvents any prohibition concerning the incorporation of interviews within direct cinema. The Maysles adopted the replay technique as a form of 'interview' within which they elicit and document comments and reactions from the band members to the murder. Functioning in a way that is more effective than any of the situations constructed in popular factual entertainment, the technique pushes notions of the performative self to the limit. The sequences involving replays of the killing attract or demand attention for no other reason than the spectator wants to see how Jagger will respond to the images. The response is – like the final frozen image of his face – ambiguous, something that critics have found disturbing. Critical reactions have gathered around questions such as: is Jagger genuine, is he authentic, is this real, is he acting?[17] The premise of each question, with its distinction between 'real' and 'invented' or performed selves, overlooks the fact that for Jagger the two conditions coalesce. The central attraction of *Gimme Shelter*, achieved within a focus on Jagger, is the display of a performance of an authentic, enigmatic self.

The Last Waltz: image and sound

The relationship of performance, observationalism and levels of directorial intervention raised by *Gimme Shelter* is a critical component of Scorsese's *The Last Waltz*, a visual chronicle of the final concert given by The Band in San Francisco on Thanksgiving Day, 1976, which is interspersed with interviews with members of the band. If, as Stephen Severn has argued, the film 'represents a dramatic re-imagining of the possibilities inherent in the "rockumentary" genre' it does so by 'reimagining' (in the form of a revision) many of the formal aspects of rockumentary (2002–03: 25). Severn's comment that 'Scorsese's camerawork ... confounds the expectations of the genre by essentially eliminating the audience from the film' notes the way in which The Last Waltz revises one of the conventions of works such as Woodstock and Gimme Shelter (ibid.). In these films shots of the audience and, in the case of Woodstock, extended interview sequences with members of the audience, add another dimension to the rockumentary master tropes of backstage and onstage. Indeed Woodstock (following Monterey Pop) informs the stylistic language of onstage through widespread use of a shot from the back of the stage in which performers are framed against the audience in a way which depicts the size of the crowd and which establishes performers in symbiotic relationship with the audience. In contrast, The Last Waltz, as with Dont Look Back, rarely depicts the audience before the onstage performer.

The revision of established formal codes of the rockumentary in The Last Waltz is further evident in the film's abandonment of the direct cinema pretensions to observational purity which are alluded to in Dont Look Back. Whereas Pennebaker in Dont Look Back uses the questioning of Dylan by journalists as the basis of a form of exposition, and a similar effect is achieved in Gimme Shelter within Jagger's commentary on events as he watches a replay of scenes on the Maysles' editing machine, The Last Waltz openly employs the technique of interviewing the film's subjects. However, it is arguable whether such a development in Scorsese's hands productively expands the generic formal boundaries of the rockumentary. As Severn observes, Scorsese 'truly is a terrible interviewer – nervous [and] tentative' (2002–03: 28).[18]

Any sense of a so-called pure observationalism is further erased in the elaborate directorial planning of the concert footage segments. Scorsese prepared a two hundred page script of the shoot which incorporated specific details of the performance, to the level of 'scripting every [guitar] solo, every tambourine shake' (see Hernandez 2002). The approach not only abandons any sense of a direct cinema ethic of non-intervention in the profilmic scene, it also, in effect, denies 'backstage' shots of impromptu actions, music rehearsals and other unscripted moments.[19] In The Last Waltz the rehearsal is replaced by a closely scripted on-camera performance. Such revisions of the premises of observationalism do not, however, necessarily distinguish The Last Waltz from its antecedents. As with Dont Look Back, The Last Waltz privileges the image track above the soundtrack thereby foregrounding visuality – documentary display as visual spectacle – as the basis of the film's formal composition.[20]

The relationship of image and sound in the rockumentary was inverted within the representational format of music television and its paradigmatic expression, the cable television station MTV, which commenced broadcasts in 1981 soon after *The Last Waltz* was produced. Typically, analyses of MTV have pointed to the commercial basis of the format, and emphasised the role of music video as a promotional tool for the performers (in, for example, Frith, Goodwin & Grossberg 1993). On these grounds MTV is not necessarily distinguishable from the numerous rockumentaries which have been conceived or produced within the commercial framework of the popular music industry as promotional vehicles for the industry's 'products'. However, a notable difference between the dominant formal logic of the rockumentary and broadcast music video, one which inverts the image-sound relation pertaining in the rockumentary, is the fact that the ruling formal characteristic of the 'MTV aesthetic' is one in which editing is 'directed' by the tempo of contemporary popular music. As David James notes in his analysis of avant-garde imagery in music video, 'in almost all broadcast music video, the image track is controlled by the sound track; the visuals are assimilated to the song's rhythms' (1996: 236).[21] Despite the intervention of MTV within the visual and auditory representation of rock or popular music, the styles of music video on television did not set a standard for rockumentary's visual and sonic form and its relationship of image and sound. More relevant to the development of rockumentary than MTV was punk rock, which emerged at roughly the same time as MTV, and which provided new aesthetic forms for the representation of music performance.

Beyond observation

Punk music offered an alternative to the strands of utopianism, hedonism and consumption sustained by prevailing musical genres. The production of punk – a musical form which is 'militantly amateur, anti-music, deliberately rudimentary and abrasive' (James 1996: 241) – mobilised a 'do-it-yourself' mode of production that challenged the corporate production strategies of the mass-market music industry. The inevitable incorporation of punk by the music industry revised the 'DIY' aspect of the music, though punk's radical sonic alterity remained relatively intact and provided a basis for punk's musical successors, thrash and hardcore. Like punk music, punk cinema's *art brut* character was informed by a 'low-tech' approach to film production. Such an approach to filmmaking was rigorously expressed in the so-called cinema of transgression produced in New York during the 1980s and early 1990s. Filmmakers in this category – among them Richard Kern, Beth B, Nick Zedd and Vivienne Dick – exploited the availability of cheap cameras and projectors, notably synchronised sound super 8mm cameras, and later video technology, to produce fiction and nonfiction works which explored themes of drug taking, urban poverty, nihilism and sexual experimentation. The formal components of such works were marked by a wilful technical and aesthetic crudity.[22]

Punk music videos – documentations of punk music performance – partake of punk cinema's formal characteristics and production values. Produced, distributed and consumed by members of the subcultural formation addressed by punk music, punk music video functions in opposition to commercial television's broadcast practices and standards. As David James notes, 'though the category of "alternative" videos, playable only in specifically demarcated time-slots functions [within television schedules] as a holding-zone where the always shifting boundaries between assimilable and nonassimilable practices can be continually negotiated, certain videos are categorically inadmissible, even to the "alternative" reservation ... [Punk music videos] where the rudimentary quality of the music and the low production values of its televisualisation combine with unacceptable social practices, are a case in point' (1996: 243). Such works are distributed on videocassette or, in recent years, on DVD outside the channels of broadcast television. Through its mode of production and consumption, punk music video partakes of the stance identified by James as one in 'which the principles that produced the series of social and aesthetic projects mobilized as popular music were also manifest in film and in the practice of filmmaking' (1996: 245).

The connections between punk music and the formal and productive practices of punk music video (or DVD) are illustrated in the example of Jem Cohen's *Instrument*, a document filmed over ten years which deals with the Washington, D.C. hardcore punk band Fugazi.[23] Cohen's work reproduces the low production values of punk cinema and punk music video and utilises a mixture of film formats, including 8mm, super 8mm, 16mm and video. The inclusion in *Instrument* of various film stocks was not the result of a planned aesthetic. Rather, the incorporation of differing film gauges and stocks – and a collagist weaving of scenes shot in each format – was a response to financial restraints imposed on the filmmaking practice and a mode of production that included filmed segments of Fugazi performances donated by non-professional filmmakers. In this way the independent production practices and a DIY, assemblage method not only visually realises Fugazi's music, it sustains 'practices with the same social and aesthetic impulses as the music' (James 1996: 242). Fugazi's commitment to a truly independent form of music production extended to distancing itself from the major channels supporting commercial popular music. Band members declined to undertake interviews with the mainstream press and most music magazines, and the band's music was rarely played on commercial radio or MTV.[24]

In the spirit of Fugazi's anti-commercial position, *Instrument* was not devised as a promotional vehicle. Cohen had been shooting footage of the band for a number of years before Fugazi began to financially support what at the time was conceived as a documentary 'project', not a film.[25] The filmmaking process was undertaken as a collaboration between Cohen and members of the band and extended to editorial decisions and a soundtrack which, in contradiction of most music documentations, was produced specifically for the film. Cohen's commitment to the 'project' that became *Instrument* derives from a basic documentary impulse, which he referred to when he stated that his motivation for making films is 'to try to honestly capture something that goes on around me' (quoted in Savlov n.d.). However, Cohen was not concerned to replicate other documentaries about music, and to this end he understood that in order to 'create a filmic form that ... stepped over [visual] boundaries' he would not watch or study any rockumentaries (ibid.). Cohen wanted to 'capture music-making and [to] try to make something that felt, visually, like music, and something where the music was inextricably tied in with the moving pictures' (ibid.).

Instrument is composed of numerous segments comprising live performances, interviews with band members conducted over the years, and everyday scenes shot in motels, recording studios and on the road, during the band's tours of the US and Europe. The segments are separated by text from the lyrics of Fugazi songs, thereby visually representing one component of the band's music. More particularly, the attempt to visually represent Fugazi's performances and experiences results in visually arresting images which, combined, produce a trance or dreamlike quality. The effect is increased via the method of filming the band in concert which, like the live show itself, uses minimal white lighting, abjuring gimmicky staging. The near darkness of the stage depicts band members who, in Cohen's words, 'look like they're coal miners going to work' (ibid.). The dreamlike or hallucinatory effect is also partially the function of the film's compositional organisation and its constant and captivating movement between scenes of boisterous and uninhibited onstage performances and scenes which depict, in a manner verging on the surreal and the luminescent, lived experience on the road.

This approach, which functions as the basis of the film's visual appeal, stems from a revision of the documentary project in which everyday experience is represented in a realist mode as a rational world. *Instrument* depicts a reality out-of-kilter with common expectations and understandings. For Cohen, the world 'is insane. The world that we drive around in, [or see while touring] with the band ... is insane, and so the project should reflect that. It shouldn't just be about rock and roll, or indie rock, or four guys and what they're like ... It should be about other things which are central to lived experience' (ibid.). Cohen stresses that 'one of the reasons why I work with Fugazi and they work with me is that we enjoy travelling through this madness. It's what they write songs about and it's what I try to document in my films' (ibid.). The aim of this approach is, on the one hand, 'a simple evocation of what it's like to be a musician and on the other hand it's a not-so-simple evocation of what it's like to be a musician *in this very strange world*' (ibid.;

emphasis in original). Cohen's representations of Fugazi onstage, combined with an approach to a reality understood to be hallucinatory and 'insane', produces a film which exceeds the realist boundaries of documentary and becomes, like punk itself, a performance of an 'alternate' or oppositional array of experiences. In this way the performative display of *Instrument* constitutes the complete abandonment of the premises of direct cinema, thereby pushing the rockumentary beyond its traditional grounding in observational forms.

The crisis moment: blind faith and the act of seeing

The passing of punk, and the evisceration of its visual and sonic energies by the commercial practices of the popular film and music industries, was followed by the emergence of new popular musical genres, a resurgence of established musical styles and an increasing reliance on interviews in rockumentaries. Numerous rockumentaries, among them *Year of the Horse* and the films *I Am Trying to Break Your Heart*, *Dig!* (2003) and *Metallica: Some Kind of Monster*, include talking heads as a feature of the work. The emphasis in contemporary films on interviews, and a move away from the representation of onstage performance is, as with punk documentations, evidence of a certain abandonment of the observationalism that motivated the rise of the rockumentary. However, recent works do not as thoroughly abnegate the legacies of direct cinema as punk music film and video. In fact many recent rockumentaries renovate and recycle one of direct cinema's foundational principles, the so-called crisis moment.[26]

The crisis structure follows the logic that a person involved in a crisis is unlikely to be aware of the presence of the camera. The result, allegedly, is the revelation of the subject's true nature captured on film. This logic was translated into a number of direct cinema films which chose as their subject matter situations liable to result in crises. The dramatic potential created by impending or unravelling crisis was exploited within the structure of various works produced by a team of filmmakers working with Robert Drew for the ABC television network in the 1960s. The technique was pursued in *The Chair* (1962) and *Crisis: Behind a Presidential Commitment* (1963). Another Drew Associates work, *Primary* (1960), defers to the technique by choosing to follow presidential candidates involved in a hectic round of electioneering. Richard Leacock, one of the team responsible for shooting the film, argued early in his career for the efficacy of filming subjects involved in critical situations when he stated that as he filmed John Kennedy in a hotel room, 'I retired into a corner and got lost, sitting in a big comfortable arm-chair with the camera on my lap. I'm quite sure [Kennedy] hadn't the foggiest notion I was shooting' (quoted in Winston 1995: 150). The statement points to a problem inherent in the assumption that a subject will, in certain situations, be too preoccupied to register the presence of a camera. In this particular case Leacock denies the fact that it was highly unlikely that Kennedy, who at that time in his career was already a practiced and astute politician fully aware of the power of the media, would 'forget' or overlook the presence of the camera and its operator. Nevertheless, the crisis structure, and its assumption of an observational stance capable of revealing 'true' behaviours, continued in different ways to inform various direct cinema works of the late 1960s (such as the Maysles brothers' *Salesman*, 1969) and beyond (such as Craig Gilbert's television series *An American Family*, 1973).

Recent rockumentaries deploy crisis as a technique with the potential to provide unguarded insights into the actions of band members, though more particularly contemporary works recast crisis as a performative attraction. In this way, crises within a band's career – typically in the form of rivalry between band members (as in *Metallica: Some Kind of Monster*), or between one band and another, competing band (as in *Dig!*) – are structured not merely as a crucial 'moment' in a narrative, but inform extended sequences as the narrative core of the film and the basis of its spectatorial appeal. The process is exemplified in Sam Jones' *I am Trying to Break Your Heart*, a film which documents the Chicago-based group Wilco and the travails involved in the production of the band's fourth studio album, *Yankee Hotel Foxtrot*. In its intense focus on the recording of an album Jones' film evokes the studio recording sessions by the Rolling Stones captured in Godard's *One Plus One* (also known as, against Godard's wishes, *Sympathy for the Devil*, 1968). In another way, the subject of the film and the fact that it was shot with hand-held cameras using black and white 16 mm stock are reminiscent of Pennebaker's *Dont Look Back*, an influence which Jones readily acknowledges as important to his work (in DeRogatis 2002: NC4). Like Pennebaker, Jones grounds his film method within the practices and approaches of direct cinema. Echoing the direct cinema claim of 'access to all areas', Jones insists that he had complete and unfettered access to the band during the making of the film. According to Jones, Jeff Tweedy, the band's frontman, 'never complained or asked for space, allowing us to get incredibly close and intimate as this album was being recorded. Dave [Rudd, cameraman] has a lot of experience shooting music videos, and had no qualms about putting the camera three inches from the keyboard as Jay [Bennett] played a part, or laying on the ground [to shoot another scene]. The difference was these guys weren't rehearsing or lip-synching; they were making a record!' (2003). Jones reinforced the dual, though contradictory, direct cinema components of propinquity and anonymity when he stated that he attempted 'to get as close to the musicians as possible, and often found myself within a foot of Jeff as he sang into the microphone. To his and the rest of the band's credit, they didn't even seem to notice me ... I truly believe [that the band members] were having so much fun playing that they didn't even notice me or the crew walking amongst them' (ibid.).

The emphasis on unrestrained access to band members intersects in the film, in a tried direct cinema formula, with the notion of crisis. The crisis in the film includes the fact that during the production of the album the band went through major personnel changes with the replacement of long-standing member Jay Bennett and, more particularly, that the band's record company, Reprise, rejected the album, cancelled the band's contract, and left the band seeking another record company. For Jones, the combined conditions meant that 'things [then] started to get interesting from a dramatic point of view ... I watched anticipation turn to disappointment, relationships fall apart, and to a certain extent, eventual redemption. I tried to capture this as faithfully as possible in the editing room. These dramatic points helped the film fall very naturally into a three-act format that has a lot in common with dramatic feature films' (ibid.).

Starting out with a direct cinema insistence on unmediated access to his subjects during his 'fly on the wall' filming, Jones exposes the manipulated, 'dramatic', elements of (direct cinema) films structured around crises. The crisis structure partakes of features of melodrama (a drama set to music, a particularly fitting allusion in the case of rockumentary's musical performances), or soap opera, notably a reliance on narratives concerned with people in difficult or trying circumstances. Further, as with soap operas, the crisis structure is the basis of suspense and intrigue as the narrative moves (often in the way of a 'cliffhanger') towards a resolution of the crisis. As Jones' comments on the making of the film suggest, the narrative core of 'crisis' displaces, or, in terms of viewers' interest in the film, is at least comparable to, live performances of the band's songs. In this sense it is the 'crisis' (or crises) more than the band's resolutely 'indie' music which accounts for the film's appeal to a relatively wide audience.

In a similar way, Metallica: Some Kind of Monster exploits the crisis structure within its chronicle of the strains facing members of the phenomenally successful heavy metal band Metallica. During the recording of their album St. Anger the band members employ a so-called performance enhancement coach to negotiate the personal rivalries which threaten to destroy the group. The film follows the revelations of deep divisions between band members which are exacerbated by the departure of guitarist James Hetfield. After months in an alcohol rehabilitation clinic, during which time he had no contact with the band, Hetfield returns to the recording studio with a list of personal demands and strict limitations on the time he is willing to devote to the production of the new album. The situation rekindles and deepens tensions within the band, especially between Hetfield and drummer Lars Ulrich.

The film was co-produced by Joel Berlinger and Bruce Sinofsky, two directors trained in the techniques of direct cinema. Berlinger worked with the Maysles brothers and it was at the Maysles' production company, Maysles Films, that he met Sinofsky (see Stubbs 2002a). The legacy of their direct cinema training is evident in their recasting of the 'fly on the wall' approach of direct cinema. A variant of the technique is applied in *Metallica: Some Kind of Monster*, and is described by the filmmakers, referring to their constant filming presence, in terms of 'always buzzing around, like a fly' in the ears of all four members of the band (quoted in Brunner 2004). Further traces of the operational approach of direct cinema are evident in other comments made by the filmmakers. According to Berlinger and Sinofsky the 'presence of cameras tended to stimulate rather than stifle candour' (in Gundersen 2004), an assumption reinforced by Ulrich who commented that the camera 'can be a truth instigator' (in ibid.). More specifically, the film's lineage is marked within in the ways in which the filmmakers adopt and adapt the crisis structure of direct cinema as its core narrative function. Paul Arthur argues that the essence of the celebrated crisis structure of direct cinema is an intimate – in terms of a close physical proximity – rendering of a 'personality' who is 'struggling for self-definition in a web of institutional processes' (1993: 121). Such an assessment usefully draws attention to the personalisation of a subject that occurs within the formation, but ignores 'crisis' as a dominant structural account within direct cinema.

Attending to its role in this way, Brian Winston notes that the need to build a narrative without the assistance of commentary or interviews resulted in the care and attention given to structure within direct cinema (1995: 211). However, another view holds that the stress placed in direct cinema on being in the right place at the right time, and a resultant emphasis on the 'highly charged atmosphere', undercut narrative structure (quoted in ibid.). *Metallica: Some Kind of Monster* revises this claim, and points to the editorial attention to structure noted by Winston. The highly-charged atmosphere of the practice sessions in the recording studio, and the internal strife suffered by the band, constitute the crisis which provides a cogent narrative structure. This is not to suggest that the film merely deploys an unrevised form of 'crisis moment' derived from an earlier direct cinema. For the filmmakers the challenge was to show the tensions within the band, while simultaneously informing that view by explaining how and why the tensions had developed.[27] The framing method for such an explication is a series of journalists' questions of the band, which are interspersed throughout the film. These questions are 'answered' in the form of scenes which 'illustrate' or 'reply' to each point. The method resulted in a disruption of the temporality of filmed sequences, with scenes editorially ordered according to the logic of explaining or reflecting on the crisis. The shifts in the film in perception and time and the telegraphed narrative denouement that results from the structural emphasis on crisis echoes the Maysles brothers *Gimme Shelter*, which uses flashbacks to frame the crisis which is the film's emotional and scopic core. Like the Maysles' film, *Metallica: Some Kind of Monster* reworks the crisis in various ways, extending it from an isolated moment to function across the duration of the film. In this way the band's musical performances stand against the crisis in sessions in which band members interact as a unit, thereby alleviating (if only temporarily) the ever-present disunities that threaten to destroy the group. The context for both crisis and its release is performative action – in the sense of the band performing its music, and in the form of the 'backstage' emotional intensity which reveals the crisis besieging the group.

According to Sinofsky, observational, ever-present filming, and a commitment to accept the process without censorship, requires 'blind faith' on behalf of both subjects and filmmakers (quoted in Gundersen 2004). The result of such blind faith is an open willingness to examine the band's crisis, the 'truthful' visual and emotional focus of the film. The crisis climaxes in six minutes of screen time focused on an argument between Hetfield and Ulrich. Sinofsky notes that the 'purging went on for three hours. That was [Ulrich] projectile-vomiting 20 years of anger, anxiety and all the things he felt were wrong with [Hetfield], himself and the group. It was amazing. We were exhausted [by watching]. And we cut it down to just six minutes' (quoted in Gundersen 2004). The result is a remarkable performance – by the filmmakers and by the 'social actors', the subjects, within the scene. In this way, the truth which emerges from the scene (a 'demystification of the mythology of rock stars', according to Gundersen (2004)) interacts with and is grounded in a visual performance which is the basis of viewer captivation and attraction.

In *Metallica: Some Kind of Monster*, as with the other works examined here, performance – onstage in musical performances and offstage within enactments of the self – is the basis of a documentary display as it is constructed variously within, through and against either a recycling or a revision of the formal features of direct cinema. In this way documentary display, as the central formal principle of the works examined here, interacts with the category of the performative resulting in works which are visually alluring and pleasurable and which, as a result, constitute rockumentary as an immensely popular form of documentary practice which continues to exert a strong audience appeal. Giving close attention to the relationship between direct cinema and rockumentary, Brian Winston has claimed that direct cinema 'made the rock performance/tour movie into the most popular and commercially viable documentary form thus far' (1995: 205). However, in terms of the progression of the form plotted in this chapter, the inverse of this assessment may be closer to the mark: the rockumentary turned direct cinema into a commercially and widely available form, and rockumentary has at times returned to and superseded direct cinema in its scopic attention to performative documentary display.

chapter four

Found-Footage Film and History: Seeing Double

...the immanent ambiguity of reality...
— André Bażin (1971: 68)

Speaking of the abundance of images in the mass-mediated world of the late twentieth century, one observer has commented 'that the job of future document-ers may be more in the nature of editing than of creating' (Court 1995: 58). The observation points to the editorial manipulation of pre-existing footage, the basis of found-footage filmmaking, a procedure which film historian Paul Arthur, writ-ing in 1995, summarised as 'easily the most ubiquitous practice of the last twenty years' (2005a: 139). Typically, critical assessments of found-footage filmmaking cast the form in terms of the modes of avant-garde or experimental film, ignor-ing its place within the field of documentary film.[1] Constructed as a genre within the field of nonfiction representation, documentary has since its inception been composed of multiple representational strands, many of which frequently incor-porate pre-existing footage derived from a variety of sources. Working in such a vein, the found-footage filmmaker may combine nonfictional images selected from sources as varied as commercial stock footage, newsreels, home movies and fiction footage to construct an argument about the socio-historical world, thereby aligning the practice with the assertive and argumentative thrust of works com-monly canonised within the documentary tradition.

However, the found-footage filmmaker eschews dominant expository modes in favour of an assertive stance informed by the associational methods of filmic col-lage, as in the case of *Naqoyqatsi* (2002), the final film in Godfrey Reggio's 'Qatsi' trilogy (which also includes *Koyaanisqatsi* (1982) and *Powaqqatsi* (1988)). Approximately eighty per cent of the film's footage is composed of stock footage culled from sources which include newsreels, military and corporate films, television programmes and commercials, sports documentaries and animated cartoons. Lacking a voice-over or onscreen text or titles, Reggio's film reworks much of the footage in various ways (slow and quick motion, decolourisation, step printing, pixilation and digital enhancement) and recontextualises the images to construct an argument concerning the nature of contemporary warfare, the accelerated pace of life in the twenty-first century and the dehumanisation of social experience under the regime of technology. Criticisms of Reggio's films are divided between dismissive claims that they are kitsch recyclings of twentieth-century iconography that fail to penetrate their subjects, to approving references to their spellbinding visual effectiveness.[2] Dziga Vertov and Esfir Shub are often evoked in such criticisms, though works of both directors typically appear as a point of contrast to what Michael Dempsey argues is *Naqoyqatsi*'s abandonment of analysis 'in favour of a floodingly metaphysical, emotional "overwhelm"' (1988–89: 8).

While clearly Reggio's liberal humanist vision is not easily reconcilable with the historical materialist montage of Vertov or Shub, it is possible to draw comparisons between Reggio's work and, for example, aspects of Vertov's method, albeit with an emphasis on the formal as opposed to the political (if the two positions can be separated). Vertov's endorsement and elaboration of principles of found-footage montage in his manifesto on the camera as kino-eye resonate in certain ways in the associational argumentative structure and visual regime of Reggio's film: 'Kino-eye plunges into the seeming chaos of life to find itself the response to an assigned theme ... to organise the film pieces wrested from life into a meaningful rhythmic order, a meaningful visual phrase, an essence of "I see"' (Vertov quoted in Dempsey 1988–89: 12). Admittedly, Vertov's theoretical and practical emphasis on self-reflexivity is absent from Reggio's work, a point taken up by Catherine Russell when she argues that despite Reggio's 'use of experimental techniques such as slow motion, pixilation, and long takes, the films lack any extrinsic commentary on the filmmaking practice ... [and the] technical effects [applied in Reggio's films] may break the illusion of reality, but they merely enhance the illusion of mastery through vision in this new version of the "cinema of attractions"' (1999: 61). However, even Vertov could not fully dispel the illusion Russell refers to here. The ability to effectively delegitimate or subvert visual forms of mastery of a subject would, arguably, require a sustained challenge to, and reconfiguration of, post-Enlightenment modes of vision and the dominance of the modern regime of visuality. Encoding and contesting such a regime, the so-called cinema of attractions referred to by Russell frequently grounded its effects within nonfictional forms of showing and spectacle capable of disrupting dominant forms of vision, thereby providing new approaches to visual representations of experience.

It was such a potential that John Grierson banished from the realm of documentary by distinguishing between the 'actualities' of the cinema of attractions and a 'correct' documentary practice based on 'public purpose theories', which resulted in the conscious refusal of an aesthetically-informed documentary. 'We [in the documentary film movement] have all, I suppose, sacrificed some personal capacity in "art" and the pleasant vanity that goes with it' (1998b: 105). In this way, Grierson's conception of documentary as an historically and politically activated means of civic education and public service intended to promote the administrative and regulatory role of the state and 'responsible citizenship', developed in opposition to the formal innovations and aesthetic experiments which Grierson often associated with Robert Flaherty.

Grierson's legacy dies hard. The response to Ken Jacobs' Nervous System performance XCXHXEXRXRXIXEXSX at the thirty eighth annual Robert Flaherty seminar in 1992, for example, points to a distinctly Griersonian distaste for nonfictional aesthetics. The Nervous System apparatus works with a piece of found-footage film – a one and a half minute fragment of a 1920s stag film – which is screened via two 16mm projectors. Within the process a short strip of film is projected through the blades of a propeller which alternatively blocks the beam of each projector, producing a flicker and three-dimensional effect which slows the fragment of film to a screen time of two hours. Laura Marks, who was present at the screening, notes that 'we viewed a vintage porn film, which was both charming and explicit, for two hours, in a sort of cross between extreme slow motion and an intense flicker film ... At least a third of the audience walked out of the auditorium at various points during the screening. When the rest of us emerged, we found the walkouts divided roughly into those who objected to the film because it [was based on] pornography and those who were annoyed by what they felt was an extreme example of avant-garde viewing experience' (2002: 62).[3] Most particularly, Marks notes, the screening 'was criticized for ignoring [historical and political] issues beyond formal concerns' (ibid.). Against what is in the context of nonfiction theory and criticism a well-rehearsed argument which maintains that formalism denies politics and history, Marks notes that Jacobs' work embodies a sophisticated 'politics of vision' (ibid.). In a similar way, XCXHXEXRXRXIXEXSX confronts issues of gender and sexuality (as disgruntled members of the audience pointed out).

The analysis undertaken in this chapter contests the assertion that an (avant-gardist) formalism denies history and politics.[4] In doing so the chapter draws on a number of avant-gardist collage documentaries, notably Craig Baldwin's *Tribulation 99: Alien Anomalies under America*, Bruce Conner's *A Movie*, and Kenneth Anger's *Scorpio Rising*, a film that recasts found footage as it dispels any notion of a 'pure' formalism within its interrogation of sexuality and gender, the politics of popular culture representations, and the history of a subculture. These works are examined as examples of found-footage filmmaking which represent history within the process of documentary display. The bases of documentary display of found-footage film – the pleasurable 'attractions' of collage and shock, and a privileging of 'showing' over 'telling' – are attended to through reference to the status of the visual 'archive' of popular culture and questions concerning access to images in the 'archive', and within a contrast of compilation and collagist methods (the former illustrated through an analysis of Emile de Antonio's film from 1969, *In the Year of the Pig*). The representational process of documentary display is further informed by the filmic practice of ambiguity (what is here called 'double seeing'), which is understood in terms of a productive polysemy that operates as the foundation of a critical historiography. Found-footage film deploys such a historiography within the writing of history from popular culture sources while simultaneously critiquing such sources. In this way, metacommentary and historiography are implicated within a process in which source or 'found' footage is interrogated via filmic collage to release functional and valuable ambiguities inherent in the footage as the basis of the documentary display of found-footage film.

Source footage and filmic historiography

The historiographic potential of found-footage film – the ability of the form to represent history – is implicated with and dependent upon extant historical and exigent conditions which, as Fredric Jameson noted, 'set inexorable limits on ...praxis' (1981: 102). Such conditions include access to source footage, a problematic process which is frequently brushed over with facile statements which maintain that 'archival material is easy to obtain' by the filmmaker (Arthur 2005a: 163).[5] Access to images involves multiple factors, including the rules and restrictions imposed by archives maintained by various bodies and organisations (including government and scientific bodies, television stations, film studios and commercial stock footage collections), the cost of purchase from such archives and collections, alternate methods of obtaining relevant footage, and the risk of prosecution under restrictive national and international copyright laws associated with the re-use of footage. Producing found-footage films is an intricate, frequently expensive and legally fraught process which belies the suggestion of serendipity implied by the term 'found footage'.

The term found footage also implies the suggestion that the archive is infinite, a space which offers up endless possibilities and choices to the filmmaker who can readily locate whatever fragment of footage is desired. The impression of an infinite archive is contradicted by the cold, hard facts pertaining to the processes of image storage and retrieval. Examples here include the limitation that approximately only ten per cent of silent newsreels, a common source for found-footage filmmaking, has been archived in the US, and Hollywood's record of film preservation has run a similar course, a situation that is likely to continue in the future (see Sandusky 1992: 22). Preservation is the domain of the archive, though certain restrictions on the availability of and access to archival images are formally and informally imposed by such institutions. From his experience of researching in archives, film historian William Uricchio has noted the presence of 'structuring limitations'. Such limitations include overt and often stringent policies that deny or restrict access to the archive or to specific images, policies devised and adopted by an archive which define and implicitly restrict varieties of material which may be included in an archive, and a continual process of review of sources that functions to prioritise preservation practices thereby ignoring certain sources – or worse, the relegation of certain texts to destruction (1995: 256).

Such policies are not arbitrary; a certain logic rules archival practice. 'Archives', as Alan Sekula points out, 'constitute a *territory of images*; the unity of an archive is first and foremost that imposed by ownership. Whether or not the [film or photograph] in a particular archive [is] offered for sale, the general condition of archives involves the subordination of use to the logic of exchange' (1993: 116; emphasis in original). Such a commercial logic underwrites the consolidation or privatisation of source images and footage. Media theorist Herb Schiller has underlined the relationship between privatisation and its impact on access by noting that the 'private for-profit information industry in the United States is creating networks, establishing data bases, gaining access to government supplies of information originally gathered at public expense, and denying the library system the historic function of supplying the general public with information paid for by social subvention' (Schiller quoted in Katz 1991: 96). The base logic here is the cost of access to images. In the early 1990s commercial rates in the US for rights to reproduce privately-owned footage often exceeded $2,000 per minute (see Katz 1991: 97). The hegemony of advertising-oriented stock-footage collections, a central component of the so-called visual content industry, constitutes an extensive commodification of the image and installs the rule of fees and pricing as a crucial aspect of access to source material (see Frosh 2003: 46).

The dominance of the 'visual content industry' is supported by the expansion of copyright laws which restrict open access to information and reinforce the commercial logic of the industry. Copyright laws, and the creation of the category of 'intellectual property' which the laws are assumed to protect, sustains the privatisation of images within a market economy, thereby potentially affecting the cogency of representations of historical experience. In these terms the increasingly restricted category of 'fair use' of a copyrighted work is frequently insufficient for the purposes of constructing an adequate representation of a subject. Key US legal decisions on copyright exemplify the disturbing implications of the effects of copyright provisions for the writing of historical works. The cases of *Salinger v. Ran-*

dom House, Inc. and *New Era Publications International v. Henry Holt and Co.* concerned the use of quotations from unpublished letters or diaries in the manuscripts of biographies of, respectively, J.D. Salinger and L. Ron Hubbard. In both cases the court 'ruled that the expressive content of previously unpublished material could not be quoted. Though a recent [legal] decision concerning [another] biography ... has slightly relaxed the strictures against quoting unpublished sources, those decisions concerning fair use remain a serious problem for those who wish to make use of unpublished primary source material in the context of their historical research' (Buskirk 1992: 92). A similar effect pertains to found-footage filmmaking as historiography.

However, monopolistic global copyright laws are contested in sources beyond the courts. Various practices of appropriation of footage have emerged to confront and subvert implicit problems and overt restrictions associated with access to source footage. One such response was demonstrated by the compilation filmmaker Emile de Antonio during the production of his history of the Vietnam War, *In the Year of the Pig*. Much of the footage de Antonio required for his film was held in French military archives and the filmmaker admits to one of the more extreme measures he took to 'obtain' relevant footage from the strictly controlled military source:

> I ... got access to the French army's film library, the greatest collection of Vietnam footage that exists – it goes back to 1902 ... There's this beautiful shot in *Pig* of something you can't get in [the US]. It's Ho Chi Minh with Admiral d'Argenlieu, the French commissioner of Vietnam, aboard the battlecruiser *Richelieu*. It's ... a really symbolic scene, because [in the midst of Vietnam's anticolonial war with the French] ... Ho leaves the ship, with the French saluting, [and] takes a cigarette out of his mouth and, in that casual way of his, flips it over the side. I had to have that shot, so I said to [a French sergeant assigned to supervise de Antonio in the archive], 'Listen, I'm going to steal this. Would you mind going out, because I don't want you to be implicated in all this.' So I just cut that shot out of the roll of 35mm negative and stuck it in the pocket of my raincoat. I realised that since they knew who I was now, there was a good chance that the guys with the guns at the gate would stop me, and I could have gotten five years for that in France, but I thought it was worth it. Making films is risk taking. (Quoted in Crowdus & Georgakas 1988: 166–7)

The presence of increasing restrictions imposed by the provisions of global copyright laws placed on access to images has led to other, more sustained versions of image pilfering. 'Culture jamming' confronts the problem of access to and control of images through practices of image piracy designed to draw attention to the commercialisation of the image domain.

The proliferation of appropriative practices points to a politicisation of the issue of availability and access to source footage as reflected in forms of film-making that embody image piracy. However, not all material is obtained via such methods and source footage is variously deployed in filmmaking within practices referred to as compilation film, archival film or collage film. William Wees proposes three forms of filmmaking from found footage: compilation in which source footage is deployed in documentary realistic practice supporting and 'illustrating' an argument; collage as the redeployment of the image in a modernist avant-gardist method of juxtaposition; and appropriation as a post-modern recycling of archival images as simulacrum (1993: 33). Wees's labels are heuristic rather than constitutive, and in practice certain forms treat source footage in ways which are not reducible to a singular identifiable category. The varieties of found-footage filmmaking examined here are informed by each of the three forms set out by Wees though they are distinguishable from a strict realistic aesthetic which characterises certain compilation films. The complexities of the terminology and the variant practices subsumed within such terms is exempli-fied by the work of de Antonio, a filmmaker whose films rigorously interrogate official historical accounts as they simultaneously construct effective counter-histories. De Antonio's 'compilation' films provide a useful point of comparison and contrast with collagist methods.

In the Year of the Pig: 'radical scavenging' and radical history

Emile de Antonio produced a number of films concerned with events within US history. His compilation films include among others Point of Order (1964), which utilises television footage to examine the McCarthy hearings of the late 1950s; America is Hard to See (1971), his most conventional compilation work, which exam-ines Senator Eugene McCarthy's unsuccessful bid for the 1968 Democratic presi-dential nomination; Millhouse: A White Comedy (1971), a scathing satirical analysis of the political career of Richard Nixon; and In the Year of the Pig, an interpretation of the Vietnam War from French colonial rule, through US invasion of the coun-try, to the Tet offensive of 1968. In the latter work, de Antonio was not concerned with representing the war; his intention was to examine the causes and effects of US involvement in the war.

A number of television documentaries had dealt with the war in ways which failed to achieve the type of analysis de Antonio sought to undertake. The CBS television special Christmas in Vietnam (1965) and the films The Anderson Platoon (1966-67) and A Face of War (1968) focused on the actions of individual US sol-diers, an approach that has been endlessly replicated in the stream of US fiction films dealing with the Vietnam War. Within this representational focus, the GI is positioned as the principal, if not exclusive, agent of political interpretation and historical understanding. '[The US soldier's] experience of the war, always weightier and more authoritative than ours and circumscribing any experience we can have', notes film scholar David James, 'is proposed [in these representations] as the moment of authenticity and knowledge – as authenticity as knowledge – upon which the war can be evaluated and validated' (1989: 198). The focus limits analysis of the war to the level of personal knowledge, thus restricting broad analysis of topics such as the reasons why the US was involved in Vietnam and the political effects of the war on the Vietnamese. The documentary *Why Vietnam?* (1965), produced by the US State Department (the title an echo of Frank Capra's World War Two production for the Pentagon of the *Why We Fight* series) presented US involvement in Vietnam from a standpoint of official US policy towards the war. Upholding the debatable claim that the US was drawn into the war after its warships were attacked in the Gulf of Tonkin, the film repeats the arguments made by President Johnson that the US was involved in the war to assist 'a free people defend their sovereignty' against Ho Chi Minh's 'reign of terror' (see James 1989: 202). The absence of analysis of the issues and events asserted in the film denied an informed historical understanding of the war. De Antonio, however, held television news most accountable for its absence of interpretive critique of the conflict:

> There is nothing as bad that's happened concerning the war as the networks' coverage of it, because it seems as if they're covering the war whereas in fact they're not. The networks have made the American people comfortable with the war – because it appears between commercials. There's never the question asked, 'Why are we doing this? What is this war about?' It's never suggested by anything that occurs on television that we should even be interested in that type of question. Television is a way of avoiding coming to terms with the fact that we're in this war. (Quoted in Waugh 1985: 215)

In the Year of the Pig functions to readdress television's lack of analytical coverage of the war and, unlike *Why Vietnam?* and its unified and univocal history structured around the notion of US 'liberation' of Vietnam, de Antonio's film constructs a provocative history of the US invasion of Vietnam from multiple and competing discourses. The film's visual images were assembled from extensive searches of various sources in a process of what de Antonio referred to as 'radical scavenging' (quoted in Weiner 1971: 3). Images were obtained from archives in East Germany, Hanoi, the offices of the Vietnamese National Liberation Front in Prague, the archives of US and British television companies, notably the ABC and the BBC, and other sources, including the French army, the offices of UPI and newsreel footage shot by the film company Paramount. De Antonio weaves interviews he conducted with a number of contemporary figures with archival footage in which politicians and other observers comment on the war. The assembled selection of voices includes observations by, among others, Ho Chi Minh, Lyndon Johnson, Robert McNamara, Daniel Berrigan, Generals Paul Le May and William Westmoreland, US scholars Paul Mus and David Halberstam and French scholars Jean Lacouture (author of a biography of Ho Chi Minh) and Phillippe Devilliers (the editor of an academic journal devoted to the study of southeast Asia). The film adds to the auditory register of spoken comments through various musical and sonic overlays. In this way, for example, a US Department of Defense film, 'Communist Guerrilla Becomes U.S Ally' is accompanied by an excerpt from a Mahler symphony. The soundtrack also features several tunes played on traditional Vietnamese folk instruments, which are used in one scene, ironically, to perform a version of 'The Marseillaise' over images of French military defeat at Dien Bien Phu.

The complexity of the relationship of the film's visual and auditory discourses is exemplified in its opening sequence. Seemingly chaotic images and non-synchronous sounds become, in de Antonio's approach, powerful pieces of evidence of the methods employed by the US in the conduct of the war. Within the opening segment de Antonio links Vietnam to other American wars and in the process criticises attempts to justify and legitimate the war in Vietnam through such comparisons. References to the Civil War, located in the opening image of the soldier from that conflict and in a subsequent image of a Civil War memorial, are interspersed with words from the Revolutionary War: 'When I heard of the revolution, my heart was enlisted.' Such allusions to 'honourable' wars are accompanied by references, contained in a series of images, to the exorbitant amount of violence involved in pursuing the war in Vietnam: a still image of a GI's helmet inscribed 'make war not love', images of frightened Vietnamese civilians fleeing a destroyed village, footage of a monk who has set himself alight to protest the war, and a still image of an American soldier loading a helicopter gunship with shells, his body almost completely obscured by the ammunition. Accompanying the visual images is the sound of helicopters – a sound popularly associated with the Vietnam War and one that is used in the film as an aural motif – that suggests the auditory overload of the war itself and the 'noise' of verbal commentary associated with the war, examples of which are incorporated in the form of comments by US Vice President Hubert Humphrey and President Lyndon Johnson. Coming as they do after images of the violence suffered in the conflict by the Vietnamese, statements about the US as peacemaker (Humphrey) and the ethnocentric focus on an America which punishes itself with self-criticism (Johnson) are particularly offensive.

After the introductory montage the film turns to an analysis of the French occupation of Vietnam. Pre-World War Two footage shows French colonialists abusing rickshaw drivers. The history of the Vietnamese struggle continues in the following scenes in which de Antonio outlines the rise of Vietnamese nationalism under Ho Chi Minh, and the French re-occupation of Vietnam after Japanese control during World War Two. The end of French rule is signified in footage from a Soviet re-enactment of the Vietnamese victory at Dien Bien Phu. The following sequences examine US support for South Vietnamese president Ngo Dinh Diem amid evidence of the corruption of the Diem regime. American policy-makers discuss full-scale US military involvement in the Vietnamese war amid an analysis of events in the Gulf of Tonkin. The next section examines the US military conflict in Vietnam, focusing on the war in the countryside and the (racist) impressions of US soldiers and generals of their adversary. De Antonio contrasts these estimations of the enemy with images of the US ally, South Vietnamese premier Nguyen Cao Ky, and his authoritarian rule.

The final sequence contains a number of comments on the war by US observers, among them the journalist Harrison Salisbury of the *New York Times*, who describes the effects of US bombing on North Vietnam. The last words in the film are by the scholar Paul Mus, whose comments are directed at the American audience for the film: 'You are not the first people who destroyed villages in Vietnam, unfortunately. And so, they are used to that, and it's a great tradition that the village is not lost even when it disappears from the surface of the ground.' The observation intimates that Vietnamese fortitude and perseverance will outweigh America's military power, a suggestion extended in an image in the closing montage sequence of wounded American soldiers in Vietnam awaiting evacuation. The final sequence includes the same image of a Civil War statue of the young man who died at Gettysburg featured in the beginning of the film, here used in negative. Through a reversal of the image de Antonio subtly evokes the notion that the Vietnam War was the reversal of the Civil War, 'that our cause in Vietnam was not the one that boy had died for in 1863' (quoted in Crowdus & Georgakas 1988: 168).

De Antonio readily acknowledged that his work is opinionated: 'I happen to have strong feelings ... and my prejudice is under everything I do' (quoted in Rosenthal 1980: 211). His open abandonment of the presumption of objectivity was mirrored in his condemnation of the seemingly neutral and objective stance of direct cinema, a style which he called a 'joke' and a 'lie' for its refusal to make manifest its inherent 'prejudices' (ibid.). He argued that his approach, in contrast, was one of 'democratic didacticism', a method which presents aspects of an argument while constructing a conclusion which is ineluctable (quoted in Waugh 1985: 244). By acknowledging his didacticism de Antonio sought to diffuse the negative connotations of the term while reworking the position in ways which, he argued, do not condescend to his audience. De Antonio expanded on his method by stating that:

> I have been a teacher. My work is didactic ... I only want to think that [In the Year of the Pig] is more complicated, has more levels of meaning than there are in a slogan or in a purely didactic message. I don't believe that such a message has any more sense than to shout in the street 'Down with war!' ... The goal of a truly didactic work is to go beyond that and to suggest the 'why'. I like to describe my own feelings as democratic with a small d, which means that if you don't want to teach things to people but to reveal things to them, you will permit them then to arrive at the same conclusion as yourself. That's a democratic didacticism, without having to say 'firstly, secondly, thirdly'. And that's why I insist on the word 'reveal'. (Quoted in Waugh 1985: 244–5)

De Antonio's 'democratic didacticism' is, in this way, democratic in the sense that the viewer is asked to interpret information without reference to explanations imposed in a voice-over. De Antonio argued against what he interpreted as the manipulative technique of voice-over:

> I've always thought that it's wrong to explain things to audiences. The material is there, and interpretations can be made. I mean, I could have stopped the film and inserted outside explanations, but I'm really not terribly interested in that. I disagree with that approach from every point of view aesthetically and even politically. (Quoted in Waugh 1985: 245)

The film scholar Thomas Waugh has called the verbal the 'dominant logic of the de Antonio film' (1985: 249). The reference is to the role of interviews in de Antonio's films and the depth of content contained in such a method, which contrasts with the often facile and brief interviews of television journalism and which avoids the reign of personal reminiscence that stands in for historical analysis in many interview-based reports. Whereas, commonly, archival images are sequentially ordered by a voice-over narration, in de Antonio's film comments by an interviewee establish a contrapuntal and critical relationship with the images, judging and recoding them (see Waugh 1985: 245). De Antonio acknowledged that spoken comments available in interviews form the basis of the film around and against which he organised archival images: 'Words are very important in [In the Year of the Pig] and all of my work, that's how I do the editing: I start with the transcription of the soundtrack and put all those pages up on the walls of the big editing rooms where I work and begin to assemble the pages before the film: that's how the structure begins' (quoted in Waugh 1985: 249). This methodology differs from a strict adherence to a pre-planned script and a ready-made thesis to which the documents must conform.

However, attention to the word does not result in an uncritical acceptance of the opinions of interviewees. Comments by individuals are juxtaposed in ways which call into question the perceptions and claims of different commentators. It is a strategy which reveals that no one witness holds the definitive interpretation of events. Within this strategy the film 'cross-examines' interviewees via a process in which the verbal statements made by one commentator are juxtaposed with the observations of another. The process is exemplified in interviews relating to the Gulf of Tonkin incident. Statements by the United States Secretary of Defense, Robert McNamara, that the US warship Maddox returned fire only when attacked by North Vietnamese patrol boats are contested by testimony given by a sailor from the Maddox who denies that the North Vietnamese attacks took place. The process of 'questioning' is extended in those places within the film in which images are used as evidence to undercut the veracity of verbal statements. In one scene, for example, the claim by US Vice President Hubert Humphrey that Communist prisoners are not being ill-treated is juxtaposed with images of a captive Vietnamese man being kicked and beaten.

Elsewhere the film enters a complex process of exposing the evidential inadequacies of both film footage and verbal comments. The process is exemplified in the film's attitude to Ho Chi Minh, who in many ways occupies the ideological and emotive centre of the film. While the visual and the verbal domains coalesce in a hagiographic representation of Ho, at the same time such modes of representation are revealed as incapable of fully realising the North Vietnamese leader. Throughout the film Ho remains silent. In a sequence near the beginning of the film Ho's words emanate, in a form of ventriloquism, from Paul Mus. It is part of de Antonio's approach that Ho remains an enigma, a historical figure who cannot be contained by characterisations achievable via archival film and contemporary interviews.

Through various means, then, the film's interrogative process results in the destabilisation of the evidentiary status of both verbal comments and visual images. History, as a stable interpretation of past events, is not located in either the verbal or visual realms of de Antonio's film, but in the dialectical relationship of the verbal and visual operating in the film as a whole. De Antonio's method – one which forms the practical basis of a fully-realised and effective compilation film practice – exceeds both the juxtaposition of archival images and the counterpointing of testimony and images. Within the film the illustrative and evidentiary capacities of multiple images and sounds are questioned and reworked to produce a history which contests the official record of US involvement in the war encoded in many of the sources that de Antonio criticises, recontextualises and recodes.

'Speaking for itself': the assumed neutrality of found footage

De Antonio's method contests the stability of history within an interrogation of the semantic and referential 'stability' of sound and image. Rarely in de Antonio's sophisticated deployment of archival footage do statements by subjects or the ideological dispositions encoded in images go unchallenged. However, at times de Antonio seems to accept the commonsensical notion that archival newsreel footage can indeed 'speak for itself'. In this way, referring to footage of French officers in colonial Vietnam imperiously dispersing and ignoring a group of Vietnamese rickshaw drivers, de Antonio argued that the imagery was 'the equivalent of a couple of chapters of dense writing about the meaning of colonialism' (quoted in Crowdus & Georgakas 1988: 167). The suggestion that archival footage is, in its unrecontextualised state, a neutral bearer of meaning is itself an ideology within which found footage is reduced to the status of unassailable historical fact, the very condition that the collagist methods of found-footage filmmaking seek to contest.

The idea that archival or newsreel footage 'speaks for itself' continually seeps into critical commentary on compilation and collage film. Within its focus on newsreel footage, one of the few book-length studies of compilation film, Jay Leyda's *Films beget Films*, recognises formal components of newsreel footage such as 'composition', 'rhythm of movement' within the frame and the role of recorded sound (1964: 22). However, Leyda at times implicitly tends to treat newsreel footage as a 'window on the past' capable of unproblematically providing insights into historical events and personages. Closer attention to the contexts in which newsreels were shot and distributed points to factors which dispel the illusion of neutrality and expose positions ideologically encoded within newsreel footage. Separate studies of the newsreel by Nicholas Pronay (1971, 1972, 1976), Raymond Fielding (1972) and Tony Aldgate (1979) agree that the format of the early twentieth-century newsreels produced by leading production companies replicated discursive and political positions similar to those of newspapers and that the professional ideology of newsreel personnel and the organisational structures of newsreel companies equated to those of the Press. Rather than offering 'neutral' or 'innocent' (purely denotative, objective and non-ideological) images, newsreel footage was structured by and encoded with journalism's news values and a (tabloid) journalistic ideology that privileged modes of entertainment, 'fast-breaking' stories and a focus on human interest items. The outcome, as Fox Movietone newsreel commentator Lowell Thomas has noted, 'situated the newsreel between journalism and show business' (quoted in Cunningham 1984: 123). Early in the history of compilation film Vertov and Shub recognised that newsreel footage contained 'suppressed' ideas and ideologies that could be released within formally innovative montage practices.

Paul Arthur has argued that the notion of source images as neutral bearers of meaning is reproduced in the writings of a number of film theorists, among them Bill Nichols. As Arthur points out, 'Nichols advises us that the presence of a "perspective, and therefore a representation or argument, differentiates a text from mere film or raw footage", and implies that decontextualised fragments act as "value-free reproductions of the historical world". The recycled fragments thus seem to resemble Eisenstein's "montage cell": a shot that acquires coherent meaning only in juxtaposition with other shots' (1998). Traces of Nichols' attitude to source footage are also evident in his interpretation of the narrative bases of historiography, a position he derives from Hayden White's (1987) theory of history. According to White it is narrative, and its components of causality, plot and metaphor, that structure historical interpretation. Similarly, Nichols interprets 'classic realist [historical] representation' in terms of linear causality and teleological determination (1996: 57). Narrative in any *post facto* realist theory, Nichols maintains, 'is always a matter of storytelling: our reconstruction of events must impose meaning and order on them, assign motivations, assess causes, and propose moral judgements' (1994: 32). While critical of the realist historical text, Nichols suggests that the naïveté of such works is in part a function of the ways in which they deploy images as visual evidence within narrative frameworks.[6] Ignoring his own observations elsewhere that the source image is always already ideologically encoded, Nichols is here willing to propose that realist histories motivate the 'neutrality' of images as evidence in a narrative framework of 'telling' (1994: 32).

Montage and collage

The so-called neutrality of the image is forcefully exposed in a conception of history in which sources are circulated not as unmediated bearers of meaning but in the form of 'quotation' deployed as a commentary on the process of history writing. Such a method informs Walter Benjamin's materialist conception of historiography, a theory which in various ways offers a number of parallels and insights into the orientations informing found-footage film. In opposition to the proscriptions of 'telling', Benjamin's characterisation of his massive historical inventory of early twentieth-century commodity culture, *Passagenwerk*, the so-called Arcades Project, privileged the visual capacity of montage and collage. Benjamin said of the method, 'I have nothing to say, only show' (quoted in Wees 1993: 52). In his notebooks on the project, Benjamin set out the method of 'showing' as one in which he will let 'the rags, garbage' of the past 'come into their own' (quoted in Higonnet, Higonnet & Higonnet 1984: 393). The critical stage of his newly-devised method of 'heightened descriptiveness' was the application of a specific technique as the basis of history writing: 'The work must develop the art of quoting without quotation marks to the highest point. Its theory is most closely linked to that of montage ... For a piece of the past to be touched by the present, there must be no continuity between them ' (quoted in ibid.). The aesthetic and epistemological function of the work rested, then, on the 'shock-like' juxtaposition of source materials (quoted in Wees 1993: 52).

Elsewhere Benjamin reinforced the shock apparent in representations of history when he argued that to 'write history ... means to *quote* history. But the concept of quotation implies that any given historical object must be ripped out of its context' (quoted in Wees 1993: 42; emphasis in original). The epistemological insights derived from images violently removed from their original contexts – in a process Benjamin referred to as the 'blasting' free of images from their place in the homogeneity of a sterile historicism – are released within the recontextualisation of images within a new history (quoted in Higonnet, Higonnet & Higonnet 1984: 393). Within the image so recontextualised, said Benjamin, 'the Then and the Now come together in a constellation like a flash of lightning' (quoted in Wees 2000: 76). As William Wees notes, 'in this special sense, archival images not only represent or illustrate the past, they also illuminate it when they are subjected to analysis and critical re-readings, or as Benjamin put it, when they arrive at "the Now of recognisability"' (ibid.). Susan Buck-Morss summarises the method through which images are made recognisable as history as 'the dialectics of seeing', a process she describes as 'the interpretative power of images that make conceptual points concretely, with reference to the world outside the text' (quoted in Wees 1993: 53). Such a dialectic informs the methods of found-footage filmmaking and its principles of collage and montage, terms which signify similar though distinguishable practices.

In his analysis of found-footage film Wees slips uncomfortably between the terms collage and montage, resulting in some definitional legerdemain such as 'what I have been calling collage, Adorno or Burger prefer to call montage' (1993: 52). Perhaps recognising the lack of specification and precision in his use of the terms, Wees abandons the process and the specificity of the referent when he states that 'as far as I am concerned, either term [collage or montage] will do' (ibid.), a curious conclusion in a work dedicated to an analysis of visual and verbal signification. Yvonne Spielmann argues that collage 'means to cut, to remove by cutting, and to insert and layer elements that have not originally been related. The essential characteristic of collage lies within the combination of heterogenous elements into one single form. Because of its techniques of inserting and layering the collage has mainly been used in fine arts to break up the close surface structure of painting and to express the modernist idea of fragmentation and simultaneity in the arts' (1999: 138). Spielmann notes that in a different way 'montage developed mainly within the emergence of cinema to fulfil the need to structurally or

narratively connect fragmented elements in a linear structure to express parallel
action, and/or eventually conflicting information. As an aesthetic feature in the
art of the moving image montage has a dual function: it separates and connects
different elements in a spatial-temporal continuum. Montage has been widely articulated in the film medium to structure the ordering of images and the narrative
in a linear way' (1999: 139).

The revision of traditional montage practices within Eisenstein's dialectical
montage brings with it a collagist layering and juxtaposition of images. Spielmann uses the term 'cinematic collage' to describe a form of moving image
construction in which montage techniques 'that usually transport continuity are
crossed with matte and layering techniques' (ibid.). She focuses on the type of
image 'that transforms montage into collage, meaning that the complexity and
amount of matte and layering counters or even dissolves the montage function in
favour of "spatial effects"' (ibid.). Spielmann notes that this process occurs via the
use of digital tools in filmmaking. In a less technologically-mediated form, cinematic collage is the basis of found-footage filmmaking. In this way Spielmann's
summary of 'cinematic collage' can be paraphrased to provide a useful working
definition of the formal expressions of found-footage film: filmic collage refers to
a form of the moving image in which dialectical montage techniques are used to
construct an expressive visual documentary display.

The potential of such a form to produce effective historiographic and cultural commentary and critique has been queried by Paul Arthur. Surveying certain
found-footage film practices, Arthur finds fault with examples in which the 'simple retrieval and display/recombination of images is construed as sufficient for
the task of cultural critique ... Inchoate or even manifest themes are subject in this
work to continual qualification or obfuscation due to a refusal to provide enough
clues to a given film's abiding principles of organisation' (2005a: 144). The ability
to motivate a rigorous and effective historiographic practice of the type alluded to
in Arthur's criticism of simplistic associational forms is implicated with the ways
in which filmic collage produces what can be called a 'double seeing' of the filmic
image, a process which is closely linked to that of recontextualisation.

Among the numerous terms interchanged and circulated in critical interpretations of the formal characteristics of found-footage collage – including bricolage,
pastiche, assemblage and mosaic – the term recontextualisation most accurately
applies to the formal basis and historiographic potential of the found-footage
film. Recontextualisation is not simply a juxtapositional recombination of found
images, or a deferment to the authority supposedly inherent within the archival
image. Instead, as Arthur points out, 'the process of recontextualisation will inevitably, and should, vitiate the integrity of the original footage, [and expose the]
fidelity to technical standards (e.g., exposure, speed, cropping) of prior represen-

tations as neither a possible nor desirable goal. Similarly the prerogative of radically de-forming found footage is based on a recognition that the site of revision is less the semantic content of borrowed images than it is the material traces and dominant visual/aural codes which they embody' (1998).[7] Via such a recontextualisation newsreel footage, for example, is scratched, scraped and physically abused as a sign of mocking disrespect for its claims to referential authority in a manner aimed at exposing the codes and ideology – such as those of the 'showmanship' of journalism – embedded in the newsreel image. In this way found-footage film becomes a documentary practice, one which reveals the 'truth' of the image in the construction of a new historical representation. Recontextualisation openly foregrounds the differences between the production values of the source footage and those exhibited in the reworked film. This exhibitionism, a component of the documentary display of collage, results in a film in which each frame demonstrates conflicting authorial intentions. It is through this method that found-footage film critically comments on its sources, as it reworks and constructs narratives and new historical meanings from these sources. The dialectical method is extended in the self-reflexive metacommentary on, and critique of, the meanings so constructed. Recontextualisation and the associated 'double seeing', then, reflect and productively exploit the dual connotation of the word historiography, as the writing of history and a critique of the writing of history.

The dual operation of writing history from found sources and the simultaneous critique of and metacommentary on the textual construction of a history based on such sources – history and counter-history within the same work – results in a viable and constructive form of ambiguity. Maurice Mandelbaum captures the relevance of the concept of ambiguity to history when he states that 'any event is far too complex and ambiguous to sustain any single meaning' (1980: 42). Such a recognition of the ambiguity of history forces historical representation to adopt new strategies capable of delineating and analysing this core characteristic of experience. However, within documentary theory ambiguity and 'indeterminacy' have, typically, been cast as negative conditions to be banished from a form allegedly predicated on 'definitive' univocal interpretations. Importantly, found-footage filmmaking challenges and overcomes such proscriptions within its recasting of ambiguity as a productive polysemy within the documentary text.[8] Christophe Bode has pointed to the redeeming components of polysemy in an interpretation of ambiguity as 'the capacity of a work … to allow or even provoke different interpretations, all of them pertinent and comprehensive' and, it can be added, comprehensible (quoted in Gamboni 2002: 13). The production of different meanings within a single work through a process of a collagist documentary display is the central organisational feature of Craig Baldwin's *Tribulation 99*, an innovative and witty history of US intervention in Central and South America.

The trials and tribulations of Craig Baldwin: argument and ambiguity in found-footage film

In an essay on the 'trials and tribulations of Rodney King' Bill Nichols readdresses and expunges any trace of the suggestion that images 'speak for themselves' as neutral evidence. In his analysis of the court's use of the George Holliday amateur video of the beating of Rodney King by members of the Los Angeles Police Department, Nichols states bluntly that 'Mr Holliday's videotape is raw footage ... It does not speak for itself' (1994: 33). Nichols' analysis of the reception of the image within legal and semiotic contexts points to the ways in which the very concept of 'visible evidence' is problematised. The various uses of the video footage demonstrated that images can be reconfigured in various contexts, and that via such recontextualisation images reveal new, unintended or previously unrecognised meanings. As Nichols points out, the 'trial and tribulations of Rodney King place us squarely within a social arena where a struggle for interpretative hegemony unfolds' (1994: 18). This is the same arena occupied by found-footage film and within which the multiple meanings released by Baldwin's *Tribulation 99* contest accepted historical interpretations of the US role in Central and South America.

Using images culled from Hollywood science fiction, news and other television programming, and instructional films, among other sources, Baldwin's 48-minute filmic collage interrogates conspiratorial and paranoiac versions of history within the construction of a rigorous counter-history. In this way the polysemy of the film is produced within ascending levels of sources and critique. On one level, Baldwin exploits the ambiguities inherent in source footage – as symptom and reflection of the ideological predispositions encoded in the found imagery – and applies the multiple meanings released from their original source to criticise history as conspiracy. On another level, the film constructs multiple and competing, and in this way ambiguous, narratives which inform the film's critique of US intervention in Latin America.

The first narrative thread is that constructed in the opening sections of the film. Accompanying a montage of images from science fiction films and other sources a whispered voice-over describes an invasion of Earth by extraterrestrials named Quetzals, who, on their arrival on Earth, burrow underground from where, when threatened by US nuclear tests, they declare their intention to wage war on the US. The science fiction narrative is progressively displaced by another narrative which presents certain recognisable historical conditions in the tone of tabloid news and conspiracy theory. Voice-over and image argue that post-World War Two US foreign policy has been directed by the threat of alien invasion. As further information is provided the film exposes its own allegory in which Quetzals represent Communists, and as the film moves across various countries in Central and South

America US foreign policy is interpreted in terms of fear and panic in the presence of what is deemed to be the threat of certain governments in the region.

The multiple meanings produced within the dialectically related narratives of science fiction and spurious history are extended in Baldwin's critique of the conspiratorial tone he has applied in the construction of these narratives. An excessive, occasionally heavy-handed irony marks the conspiracies contained in the film and exposes the banality of conspiracy theories in general. The whispered voice-over (reminiscent of the mode of narration in Jean-Luc Godard's *2 ou 3 choses que je sais d'elle* (*Two or Three Things I Know about Her*, 1966)) evokes the arcane, secret elements of conspiracy. In place of the 'reasonable' and commonsensical tone associated in documentary with the 'voice of God' narration, the voice-over of Baldwin's film presents US foreign policy in the terms and tone of bizarre fantasies and racist and reactionary views. The irony is compounded in the contrast of voice-over and image, as in the 'explanation' of US funding for the Nicaraguan contras, which is presented over images of the Chiquita banana label: 'US President Ronald Reagan champions a compassionate campaign to resupply the freedom-fighters with the machine guns, C-4 plastic explosive, and other humanitarian weapons that they so desperately need in their struggle against literacy teachers, health clinics, and agricultural cooperatives.' As Michael Zryd notes, 'Baldwin's satire speaks the voice of racist, right-wing, apocalyptic ideology, inviting us to mock it – but not to dismiss its threat' (2003: 43). The black comedy of the science fiction and 'historical' narratives is reframed in the form of what Baldwin calls a 'pseudo pseudo-documentary' (quoted in Zryd 2003: 53). However, Baldwin's fake documentary is ordered by a rhetorical stance based in historical conditions – that of US involvement in Central and South America – which thereby moves the film towards the realm of the traditional documentary. Zryd points out that 'where fake documentaries typically use conventional documentary formats to fashion ironic fictions, Baldwin fakes a particular subgenre of marginal documentary film – the 'pseudo documentary'... – which range from 'science' documentaries like *Chariots of the Gods* (Germany, 1970, Harald Reinl) to *The Hellstrom Chronicle* (USA, 1971, Walon Green/Ed Spiegel) to far-right conspiracy narratives (post-1950s anticommunist films like *The Commies Are Coming, The Commies Are Coming* [aka *Red Nightmare*, USA, 1962, George Waggner]), to fundamentalist Christian apocalyptic warning films' (ibid.).

The critique – via 'faking' – of the 'pseudo documentary' implies the ambiguities inherent in *Tribulation 99*. Baldwin applies the multiple meanings released from their original source to criticise the representation of history as conspiracy. He emphasises the point when he comments that 'I wanted to make a statement that was critical of the CIA and [US] meddling in foreign countries, and [*Tribulation 99*] seemed to be a new use of... these paranoiac rants. I saw the CIA as being truly a conspiracy. I wanted to make a black comedy instead of a Noam Chomsky kind of thing ... I wanted to make [a film] that was satirical – one that would lacerate, tear apart, shred the CIA by burlesquing [it], by using these great [source] materials' (quoted in Cox 1998).[9] The film, then, contrasts conspiratorial interpretations of history purveyed by popular media and government to a history behind or implicated within conspiracy theories. To release this suppressed or 'hidden' history Baldwin parodies the very methods of those sources in which history is fabricated. 'Look at the records and history of the CIA', argues Baldwin. 'You've got a greater, more interesting conspiracy novel than any fiction writer could come up with, all you can do is just tell the real history, the real story' (quoted in Sargeant 2001). Exposing the 'real' story evokes the domain of documentary and Baldwin's documentary demonstrates the ways in which various sources can be motivated in the service of an historically accurate representation of experiences and events. In an apposite summation of this historiographic process Zryd notes that 'the film less *represents* history than *analyses* the historical discourse and political forces that motivate historical events. A committed leftist satire directed at American foreign policy and media culture, *Tribulation 99* shows how found-footage collage, through metaphor and irony, can offer highly condensed metahistorical analysis and complex political critique' (2003: 42; emphasis in original).

In an extensive assessment of the film, Catherine Russell misreads Baldwin's critique when she argues that *Tribulation 99* 'is an extremely ambivalent film, symptomatic of its own paranoid strategies that ultimately curtail the possibility of historical agency in the inaccessibility of a "real" outside the onslaught of images' (1999: 263). In contrast to such an assessment, Baldwin's ironic representation is openly critical of reactionary 'paranoid strategies'. Russell's criticism implies a call for a univocal narrative which would banish irony and parody, or at least limit polysemy and the number of narratives released or available in a single text through found sources. The possibility of such a suggestion is a function of a misreading of ambiguity as ambivalence. Baldwin dispels ambivalence in a rhetorical position that simultaneously criticises US intervention in Latin America and the governmental and media discourses which obfuscate the reality of this intervention. It is via the multiple, competing narratives which are constructed within this rhetorical position that *Tribulation 99* is informed as a productively ambiguous work.

The release, then, of multiple meanings within and through a collage of contesting narratives is activated through the mode of 'showing'. In this case 'showing' (as opposed to telling) is an exhibitionistic recasting of source footage in the production of (fake) 'historical' narratives and (a counter) analysis of historical discourses. The outcome has been called 'a new vernacular of film history' in which the scopic and analytical impact of the rapid-fire collage is combined within an effective political and historical critique in the form of documentary display (Katz 1991: 96).

The cinema of (coming) attractions: Bruce Conner's *A Movie*

Baldwin, as with numerous found-footage filmmakers, is heir to a tradition of collage film developed by Bruce Conner, whose *A Movie* is a paradigmatic example of the form.[10] Divided into three sections, Conner's 12-minute film combines a range of found footage, including stock footage of old Hollywood films, newsreels, brief excerpts from 'stag' films and sections extracted from instructional films, into a densely-layered comment on catastrophe and aggression in a media-saturated society. The first section, after a brief introduction comprising the film's title and the director's name, includes rapidly intercut shots of a runaway wagon train, horses galloping, a charging elephant and military tanks ploughing across fields. The pace of the sequence, and the accompanying music (Respighi's *The Pines of Rome*), intensifies around images of cars speeding on race tracks, multiple shots of cars crashing and those of an early model automobile tumbling over a cliff, followed by the title 'The End'. The practice of inserting titles within the film, perhaps borrowed from Joseph Cornell's collage film *The Children's Party* (c. 1938), mocks commercial media's insistence on illustrating or explaining self-evident action. The second section features shots of a dirigible, acrobats performing above a city street and a submarine in which an officer looks through a periscope. The image cuts in a punning fashion to a shot of a bikini-clad model posing on a bed, and the sexual innuendo is completed in a cut to a torpedo being fired from the submarine. The sequence continues with footage of an atomic bomb blast, followed by shots of surfers, water skiing accidents, a motorboat crash, motorbikes on a muddy track, people riding awkward bicycles, an aeroplane crash and a bridge collapsing. The final section of the film develops the theme of catastrophe as it builds to a climax within an avalanche of images of disaster and violence: a burning airship, a collapsing bridge, a firing-squad, bodies on a scaffold, a dead elephant, dead soldiers, a repeated image of a mushroom cloud from the detonation of a hydrogen bomb, and images of starving children. The film concludes with underwater shots of divers inspecting a sunken ship.

In organising the structure of the film Conner was influenced by the relatively new medium of television and the flicker of imagery that results from continually switching channels. More particularly, Conner was impressed by the previews of forthcoming film programmes screened in cinemas – the 'coming attractions' – which featured potted highlights of a number of films in quick succession. Conner has said in an interview that 'I remember scenes like Barbara Stanwyck throwing a glass of liquid in a man's face and saying "I hate you! I hate you!" And the next was of a railroad train going off the side of a cliff. I also saw weekly adventure serials where the sequence of events at the end would lead you to believe the consequence of those events was totally disastrous to the hero. But the hero would survive the next week since something had been left out of the sequence ... It became apparent to me that you can create an emotional response which is very different from what was socially agreed upon as a narrative structure' (quoted in Wees 1993: 78–9). The format of coming attractions – narrative intimations and revelations of sensational effects – is reminiscent of characterisations of early film as a cinema of attractions marked by visual spectacle, astonishment and revelation which confronted the spectator with a series of shocks.

In a related way, A Movie makes reference to the methods and effects of the cinema and other media, in particular their focus on violence and disaster. In these terms Conner's film broadens its critique within a commentary on the construction of history as violence. With reference to this effect, Catherine Russell argues that apocalypse 'is linked to the instability of representation, which Conner aestheticises as a kind of melancholy elegy for a lost depth of representation, betraying his modernist orientation' (1999: 248). Russell tends to misread and conflate positions held by the media and those contained in A Movie. Conner criticises the media's lack of depth and in place of melancholy or mourning for modernity the film evokes nostalgia for a history devoid of the media's excesses. By refusing the mass media's orientations Conner's work bears marks of the positions later promulgated by postmodern theories of utopia and the historical real. As Russell herself notes, modernist theories of utopia are grounded in the transcendence of reality: 'In postmodernity, "reality" is placed in question, and utopia becomes a search for the real, not a transcendence of it ... Huyssen summarises the Baudrillardian notion of postmodern simulation culture thus: "What is lost according to this account of a society saturated with images and discourses is not utopia but reality. At stake is the agony of the real..."' (1999: 254). Conner's collage criticises the loss of the real within a cinema and society which circulate an exploitative spectacle of sex and violence.

The complexities of A Movie also reveal another perspective. The film can be interpreted 'as presenting the devastating consequences of unbridled energy. The horrors of the modern world – warfare and the hydrogen bomb – are linked with more trivial pastimes, like sports and risky stunts' (Bordwell & Thompson 1997: 163). Within this form Conner's film comments on the media's representation of history as violence, while at the same time it analyses the consequences of aggression and violence. What Russell correctly identifies as the 'radical ambiguity of the collage form' (1999: 252), and what David Bordwell and Kristin Thompson recognise as the constructive ambiguity of A Movie (1997: 163) does not result in indeterminacy or the negation of meaning. In the case of Conner's film, a productive ambiguity is developed from and within a critique of the media's representation of history, and a simultaneous suggestion, implicit in the critique of the consequences of mediated violence and catastrophe, that other histories and knowledge reside beyond the representations of the popular media.

The implication is carried in the style of editing which is in distinct opposition to the continuity editing of dominant cinema. Stan Brakhage has commented on the reflexive qualities of Conner's editing and the ways in which the film draws attention to itself as a fabrication: 'He is ... very anxious that you see the splice and that you see whatever the mechanics are of putting two pieces [of film] together' (1989: 135). Conner exploits such practices and the potential of the associational editorial style to produce a disruption of the temporal and a disjunction of spatial understandings. The rapid accumulation of images and the frenetic manipulation of spatial and temporal relations between shots produce a palpable sensuous effect most commonly characterised as shock. P. Adams Sitney, for example, points out that Conner cuts 'at the point of maximal shock ... The montage follows an ideological structure; it amasses images, contrasts them, or synthesizes them in an unexpected way' (1979: 311).

The effect of shock, together with rhetorical ambiguity, inform the film's documentary display – a 'showing' in the form of access to meanings constructed in and through the scopic and visual domain, which contrasts to 'telling' and its curtailment of possible meanings in the proscriptions of exposition. The production of multiple meanings via showing and its associated capacity to provoke the senses and thereby extend meaning is exemplified in the final scene of the film which depicts, via one of the longest continuous pieces of found footage included in the film, a scuba diver exploring a sunken ship. The scene can suggest salvation, an escape from the freneticism and catastrophe of the world, creating 'some sense of hope and transcendence', according to one interpretation (Moritz & O'Neill 1978: 40), or, alternatively, the shot can be read as an end of action and events to suggest 'humankind's final death' (Bordwell & Thompson 1997: 163).

As the existence of diametrically varying critical interpretations suggests, the placement of the footage, and the scene it depicts, creates ambiguity. The equally valid and accessible meanings produced within the film's collage structure are informed by the affective impact of the footage and its ability to provide or provoke knowledge in ways not reducible to the cognitive effect of expository works. Bordwell and Thompson point to this effect in the observation that the final scene 'serves to relax the tension aroused by the mounting disasters ... It demonstrates the power of an associational formal system: its ability to guide our emotions and to arouse our thinking simply by juxtaposing different images and sounds' (ibid.). In this way the film's documentary display, operating within and through a constructive ambiguity, provides multiple rhetorical meanings concerning the history and impact of mediated society which gain resonance and are informed by the sensational and shocking effect of the film's collage. The ambiguity and attractions of A Movie – attractive because they are ambiguous – attest to the productive and meaningful effects of documentary display.

Scorpio Rising: collage, critique, shock

Within its ironic and 'ambiguous' analysis of popular culture and its media, *A Movie* is comparable to *Scorpio Rising*, a film that combines found footage and footage shot specifically for the film in a work which melds formal elements into an innovative representation of the lives and experiences of a group of 'rebel' motorcyclists. Writing in 1967, a year after the film's production, Sheldon Renan described the film's themes and formal concerns as a 'portrait of violence, an exercise in black humour, a document of motorcycle cultists, and one spectacular death wish' (1967: 111). Renan accurately identified the basis of *Scorpio Rising* as a document though Juan Suarez's description of the film as a 'documentary of sorts' (1996: 141) incisively captures the film's ambiguous status as avant-garde documentary.[11] In this sense *Scorpio Rising* shares characteristics of 'underground films' which, as Patrick Brennan notes, 'were neither purely documentary nor purely fictional; instead, they borrowed from both approaches. They were fictional in that their makers staged the situations they recode. Nevertheless, in accordance with their makers' claims, these films were documentaries as well: they recoded the spontaneous behaviours of performers who acknowledged both the artificiality of their dramatic situations and the presence of rolling cameras' (2002). Anger only partially scripted the actions of his real-life members of a Brooklyn motorcycle gang caught in their daily activities of languishing in bedrooms, cleaning and assembling their heavily chromed motorcycles, getting dressed, attending a party, and riding their motorbikes. The reality of the bikers' everyday activities opens the film to a greater degree of actuality than that emphasised by Brennan in his comments on the fictional staging of situations in underground film. Within and against the documentary footage he shot for the film, Anger intersperses a variety of found footage and other popular images, artefacts and music to create a layered collagist representation of a subculture in early 1960s America.

Among the found works structured into the 13 distinct segments of the film are footage of Marlon Brando in *The Wild One* (1953); extracts from *The Road to Jerusalem*, produced by Family Films, dealing with the life of Christ; images of Hitler; Gary Cooper in *High Noon* (1952); Bela Lugosi as Dracula; Mickey Rooney in *A Midsummer Night's Dream* (1935) directed by Max Reinhardt and William Dieterle; numerous photographs of James Dean; comic strips ('Li'l Abner', 'Dondi', 'Freckles and His Friends'); and a series of popular hit songs from the early 1960s.[12] Indeed, pop music forms a central organisational component of *Scorpio Rising* and the significance of this inclusion extends beyond the textual boundaries of the film, as David James has noted: 'Coming two years after Bruce Conner's scoring of Ray Charles's "What'd I Say?" in his film *Cosmic Ray* (1961), Anger's *Scorpio Rising* (1963) was the first major film in the American avant-garde to shift its musical point of reference from jazz to pop, and both films are commonly invoked as the most significant forerunners of contemporary music video' (1996: 231).[13]

In a related way *Scorpio Rising*'s soundtrack of excerpts from pop music songs (among them 'Leader of the Pack', 'Blue Velvet', 'Wind Up Doll', 'Devil in Disguise' and 'He's a Rebel') prefigured the recurrent use of rock songs in the motorcycle saga *Easy Rider* (1969), a film which combined short narrative segments, jump cuts and vibrant colours in what was another source of MTV music video. While *Easy Rider* utilised the lyrics of rock songs as a simple reflection of narrative action (Steppenwolf's 'Born to be Wild' played over the opening scenes in which the hippie bikers abandon the 'straight' world of Los Angeles for the open road is an obvious example of this process), *Scorpio Rising* deploys popular music and song in ironic counterpoint to its images. The song 'I Will Follow Him', for example, is rendered ironic via its insertion over images from *The Road to Jerusalem* of Christ and his followers, which in turn suggests the bikers' adoration of their leader, Scorpio, who is linked through death and demonic imagery to Hitler. This song, then, is embedded within, and opens onto, a skein of intertextual references which play on and with the song's pop nostalgia and recasts the associated imagery as deeply ambiguous. In other cases irony and ambiguity are developed through associations of image and sound in a way which tends towards a replication of an Eisensteinian vertical montage within which sound and image interact dialectically. A case in point is a cross-cut sequence depicting the bikers dressing in black leather and chains while the soundtrack is composed of the lyrics of the song 'Blue Velvet', which detail the gown worn by a female lover.

The homoerotic imagery of the ceremony of male dressing, one which has been replicated in commercial fictional cinema, and its interrelationship with the song's lyrics, turns the scene into a fantasy of cross-dressing.[14] Here, as James comments, by superimposing 'homosexual and female implications on the hyperbolic masculinity of the image of the motorcyclist, Anger destabilises it but also valorises it as the embodiment of a sexuality which cannot be unified ... Around this indeterminacy an entire lexicon of cultural icons is reinterpreted' (1989: 153). The ambiguity in the film surrounding sexuality and the capacity of such a representation to shock and startle situates *Scorpio Rising* within a tradition which Susan Sontag labelled 'the poetic cinema of shock' (1967: 207). Whereas certain works in this category, such as Georges Franju's *Le Sang des bêtes* and Luis Buñuel and Salvador Dalí's *Un Chien andalou* are capable of evoking shock through images of violence, shock in *Scorpio Rising* and Jack Smith's *Flaming Creatures* (1962–63) – another film in the tradition Sontag identifies – is the product of homoerotic exhibitionism, which in *Scorpio Rising* is combined with a different sort of violence to that found in the films of Franju and Buñuel. The homoerotic looks and gaze of *Scorpio Rising* merge in the second half of the film with found and other images of death and violence (including images of Hitler, swastikas, skulls, and references to motorcycle crashes) to represent the bikers as a sadomasochistic group bound by violence and rituals of death and demonism. Shock, then, in Sontag's sense, stems in *Scorpio Rising* from a 'subversive' form of homoeroticism which, in turn, is developed within and through the sensuous effects associated with a hyper-edited collage of popular archival sources.

Beyond shock, ambiguity also surrounds the film's representation of the lived experiences of members of a sub- or countercultural formation. The subculture of gay bikers and the popular culture sources which are the basis of the film's social critique are presented as both reactionary and utopian. 'Celebrating even as it satirises the counterculture', observes David James, '[*Scorpio Rising*] oscillates in self-perpetuating ironies that solemnise the banal even while pushing its own solemn affirmations to the edge of absurdity. *Scorpio Rising*'s critique of its hero is doubly articulated, the narrative accumulation of the popular cultural motifs that define him is reiterated in a similarly ambiguous formal assimilation of fragments from commercial films and music' (1989: 153). In this dense process the film refuses to curtail its social critique within a didactic imposition of meaning. The meanings – reaction and utopia – ascribed to the subculture, and more broadly to popular culture, the source of the film's meaning, are available within the film's documentary display grounded in collage. Far from alienating viewers, the film's display of sexuality, lifestyle and popular culture contributed to its notoriety and ensured its wide circulation.

In its various representational practices *Scorpio Rising*'s investigation of a particular subculture, as with Conner's incisive analysis in *A Movie* of a media-saturated culture, simultaneously comments on and critiques the sources upon which its analysis is based. In both Conner's film and Anger's work the resultant exploitation of the productive polysemy and ambiguities produced within and through a collagist documentary display is indicative of the form's capacity for the representation of the socio-historical world. Such works eschew expository or didactic modes of instruction or 'telling' in favour of a privileging of the visual domain of 'showing' as the vehicle of knowledge. The terms and features of the analysis undertaken here – with reference to the 'archive' of found images, distinctions between compilation and collage, and forms of collage and shock, ambiguity and 'double-seeing' evident within the work of Baldwin, Conner and Anger – provide a lexicon and critical approach to a broad understanding of documentary display as it operates in works which contest the boundaries of 'documentary' within the assimilation of so-called found footage.

chapter five

Nonfiction Surf Film and Video:
Sick, Filthy and Delirious

Since what Mr. Palomar means to do at this moment is simply see a wave ... his gaze will dwell on the movement of the wave that strikes the shore until it can record aspects not previously perceived...
    – Italo Calvino (1985: 4)

Specialised and specific documentary depictions of surfing styles and the surfing lifestyle constitute a popular and prolific form of nonfiction representational practice. The unrestrained and unruly response by audiences to public screenings of such works points to the ways in which surf film and video are integrally connected with, and integrated into, a broad surfing community. Such unruly public demonstrations suggest a communal viewing process wherein members of a subculture affirm common bonds and revel in an 'insider' perspective on surfing. The affective response also implies the strong emotive and cognitive investments audiences make in, and derive from, such works. This chapter examines such issues with reference to the formal expressive styles of surf film and surf video, focusing on examples from Australia, which, in tandem with California – the source of early influences on the development of surf film – is a prolific producer of surf film and video. More particularly, surf film and video comprise a significant contribution to nonfictional representational practice in Australia, and in this way, according to one enthusiastic commentator, such representations form 'the most significant ... development' in the history of Australian film production (Thoms 1978: 89). Various features of the surf film industry have been quoted in support of such a claim. Local producers of surf film were, it was argued, 'the only ones to have created an independent, vertically integrated film economy to control production, distribution, and exhibition' (Thoms 1978: 85). The predominant form of exhibition of early surf film – in local halls or under-utilised cinemas, often with the filmmaker present to provide an introduction or accompanying voice-over – 'helped to break down assumptions about exhibition and audiences that had dominated the trade for decades' (Pike & Cooper 1980: 307). In another way, features of the surf film industry have been linked to output, as in the claim that Bob Evans, a pioneer of Australian surf documentaries, 'was [Australia's] most prolific filmmaker in the 1960s' (Jarratt 1977: 44). Patterns of production, exhibition and reception inform the distinctive textual features of 'surf movies', the significance of which resides, primarily, in the fact that such texts meld documentary and experimental stylistics and practices in an expressive and innovative documentary display.

The meeting of avant-garde and documentary practices is, however, a proposition which threatens the resultant text with abandonment to the edges of film theory. Television theorist John Caldwell, for example, writes of the 'generic no-man's land' which is produced by the meeting (1995: 239). Indeed, while film history contains a number of examples of texts in which documentary and avant-garde modes intersect, frequently such examples illustrate the problematic and conflicted nature of the intersection. One example, from the early 1960s, demonstrates the difficulties for theoretical understandings and filmmaking practice posed by such a confluence. In 1963 Jonas Mekas, polemicist and practitioner of New York underground filmmaking, together with a number of his colleagues, visited, uninvited, the annual Flaherty documentary film seminar in Brattleboro, Vermont. Mekas brought with him Jack Smith's *Flaming Creatures* (1963) and Ken Jacob's *Blonde Cobra* (1963) to screen at the conference, which that year was dedicated to an analysis of works of direct cinema. The meeting of two traditions (on the one hand, the avant-garde, represented by Mekas and other members of the Film-Makers' Co-op, and the films they intended to screen, and, on the other hand, documentary film, represented by the seminar) was not a happy one, and Mekas and his associates were refused entry to the event. What has been called the 'two, nonexclusive tendencies (documentary and the avant-garde)' (see Nichols 1995), have, in practice – as the events at Brattleboro illustrate – been rigorously separated into two distinct strands. Such a division has been reinforced within and through documentary film theory which has determined that texts such as those Mekas sought to screen are outside the realms of documentary.

This position is rendered ironic when it is considered that *Flaming Creatures* is an effective documentary representation of a particular subculture. As film historian Marc Siegal has pointed out, assertions about 'the documentary nature of [certain] films irritated Mekas and other critics who valued underground film for its aesthetic innovation' (1997: 92). However, 'by legitimating underground films solely on aesthetic terms, these critics avoided a consideration of how aesthetic innovation can be integrally related [to documenting] particular (sexual) subcultures' (ibid.). In Siegal's analysis, Flaming Creatures is an avant-gardist documentary, one that has been denied the status of documentary – a 'documentary which dare not speak its name' (1997: 93).

Similarly, surf film and surf video – texts which blend documentary and experimental or avant-garde characteristics – have been excluded from the documentary canon and receive scant, if any, attention within (documentary) film theory. Challenging this exclusion is the recognition that the textual strategies and production and exhibition practices of independent surf texts pose a challenge to the assumptions that inform documentary theory and the canon of texts it supports and reinforces. The practices of documentary display – including the stylistic innovations of certain 'pure surf films' of the late 1960s, notably The Innermost Limits of Pure Fun (1970), Morning of the Earth (1972) and Crystal Voyager (1973), and various contemporary surf video productions – demand a revised understanding of documentary representation, and in so doing serve to enlarge the approaches and positions that function as the foundations of documentary film and video theory.

Discourse of delirium

The term avant-garde is used here to refer to experimental or innovative filmic styles and formal practices. As it is applied within this chapter the term is not necessarily linked to the traditions of the two avant-gardes identified by Peter Wollen (1982) – the formal and the theoretical-political – though it does derive aspects of its meaning from certain features examined by Wollen. The surf film Morning of the Earth, for example, borrows from, on the one hand, the formal innovations wrought by the New American Cinema and, on the other, from a lineage of poetic and imagistic avant-garde documentary film. Similarly, the primitivist stylistics of independently produced nonfiction surf videos are largely intelligible through reference to the textual practices of varieties of 'underground' film and video. Both surf film and surf video in their respective representations of lifestyles that transgress or offer alternatives to accepted social and political practices invoke the political component of the avant-garde noted by Wollen. Indeed, the documentation of 'alternatives' is a characteristic shared by surf film and surf video and avant-garde film and video works. Surf texts and avant-garde works, and their overlaps and intersections, can be contextualised within a common rhetoric of anti-traditionalism which derived much of its force from its connections to 1960s countercultural ideology.[1]

The countercultural context contributes a number of themes common to both surf texts and those texts produced explicitly as 'avant-garde' works, in particular an emphasis on personal freedom, hedonism and, in their shared distrust of industrial technology and its effects, various allusions to a lost pastoral ideal. The appeals in surf film to such culturally 'radical' characteristics finds a correlative in an emphasis within surf film and video on the documentation of surfing styles, particularly those styles which are innovative and aggressively expressive, that is, styles which were once defined by the surfing subculture as 'radical' and which, in the vernacular of the contemporary surfer, are described as 'sick' and 'filthy'.

Wollen's two avant-gardes intersect with the two 'radicalisms' outlined here – cultural radicalism and innovative surfing styles and manoeuvres – in surf texts which deploy a documentary mode that is not obsessed with truth or knowledge claims. Nevertheless, surf texts, like other documentaries assert – as with all documentary discourse – that the events and actions they present 'occur or occurred in the actual world' and achieve this task without recourse to textual strategies which reject aesthetic innovation (Plantinga 1996: 310). In doing so the previously marginalised and hence untheorised forms of surf film and surf video challenge and supplant the documentary discourse of sobriety with a structuring aesthetic that can be termed a discourse of delirium, a core component of the works' documentary display.

The phrase 'discourse of delirium', as it is applied here, is borrowed and reworked from Bill Nichols who uses it in a discussion of the evidentiary styles of the documentary *Who Killed Vincent Chin?* (1988). Nichols places this text, together with a number of other works, within the category of what he calls performative documentary. He interprets performative documentary as an emergent mode which deflects 'documentary from what has been its most commonsensical purpose – the development of strategies for persuasive argumentation about the historical world' (1994: 94). A structural 'emphasis on the poetic and an abundant use of style tempt relegation of such films to the avant-garde' (1994: 95). For Nichols, *Who Killed Vincent Chin?* pushes the features of performative documentary to their limits. Only in the last instance – through its claim on direct access to a real referent – does the text retrieve itself from being totally committed to the avant-garde.

According to Nichols, the film's excessive visual style 'poses the risk of sliding toward a discourse not of sobriety, but delirium' (1996: 59). *Who Killed Vincent Chin?* presents the spectator with:

> a fraying away of the historical event … the analytic impossibility of determining causality, internationality, or motivation from the visual record; the heightened intensity brought to bear on the isolated event itself … to yield up its secrets, its meaning. All of these factors burden the interpretation of the event with an excess that threatens to become pure delirium. (Ibid.)

The interpretative relevance to surf film and video of the evocative phrase 'discourse of delirium' is manifest through reference to certain features of the discourse, including a general lack of concern with an historical event and the eschewing of causality or motivation (see ibid.). The threat of an aesthetic 'pure delirium', a 'flailing, wild hysteria' is, in a positive and non-derogatory sense, achieved in the aesthetic tensions and accomplishments of the display within surf film and surf video (see Nichols 1994: 132).

The documentary representation of the world is extended and informed within an emphasis on spectacle evident in surf texts. Spectacle is at 'the very least ... a feast for the eyes' (Cowie 1999: 25). Surf film and video implicates a delirious display as formal excess, a 'promiscuous visual surplus', to the narrative economy of the text (James 1996: 216). The visually spectacular, excessive, features of surf film and video are enhanced through aural elements, particularly soundtracks which replace a voice-over, a staple of the expository documentary, with varieties of contemporary music. The visual elements, together with the aural aspects, contribute to a discourse which in its documentation of events and actions, is based on sensory experience. In these ways, the 'delirious' melding of avant-garde and documentary styles and practices of surf film and video is characterised by, to paraphrase Nichols' description of delirium, a heightened and frequently excessive visual and aural intensity brought to bear on the isolated action of surfing in order to reveal its secrets and meanings.

Hootin' and hollerin': delirium and audience reception

The audience for surf film, though primarily composed of surfers, has at times included a wider public. Common venues throughout the 1960s for the exhibition of surf films were community or church halls that comprised part of an informal chain of coastal exhibition sites during the summer months. Audiences at these venues often included holidaying families seeking an evening's entertainment. In other ways, Bruce Brown's *The Endless Summer* (1964) received general theatrical release worldwide, and *Crystal Voyager* had a limited theatrical release in Australia and London. Such patterns of exhibition opened surf film to an audience beyond its regular primary constituency of practising surfers. However, it is within this latter audience that the powerful effects of the discourse of delirium are evident. The viewing experience for this audience suggests a text that, in its banishment of sobriety, effectively documents essential aspects of surfing and associated lifestyles in ways which establish an intense form of identification with the text. The intensity of viewers' identification resulted at times in rowdy, occasionally violent, behaviour.

Typical of the unrestrained reactions to the public exhibition of surf films were those responses noted by world champion surfer Nat Young who attended the screening of a surf film in Sydney in 1963. According to Young it 'seemed it was almost surfer instinct to go wild over the screaming of surf guitars and [images of] the pounding of huge waves at Sunset [Beach]. As in California, the theatre proprietors and the public could not understand or tolerate this behaviour, especially when a glass mural depicting the Anzacs in battle was smashed and seats were ripped out of the auditorium; the surfers were ushered out by numerous police' (in Young & McGregor 1984: 91). As Young notes elsewhere, audience and community reactions in California were similar to those in Australia (see 1998: 178). The point is reinforced by surfer Sonny Varderman, who recalls the scene during a screening of *Search for Surf* (1960), a film produced by big wave surfer Greg Noll, which was exhibited in the Santa Monica Civic Auditorium: 'We had a pressure-packed, raucous crowd the first night. Greg had the music going before the film started ... Prior to the film, Greg would usually go up on stage, introduce himself and tell a little about where the film was taken. This evening, the crowd was just going crazy, and Greg was up on stage, getting pelted by beer and soft drink caps. He finally retreated and turned on the film and, again, everyone settled down at once' (quoted in Noll & Gabbard 1989: 87). Surfer and entrepreneur Randy Rarick describes a similar experience at Oahu's Haleiwa Theater in the 1980s. 'The place sat about a thousand people ... Guys would show up with a case of beer under their arm. Everybody's getting stoned. Of course, [the screening] would never start on time. A half-hour late, easy. The moment the lights went down, this blue-haze smoke just filled the air. Beer cans and bottles started rollin' down the aisles, the people would just be hooting. I mean, the sight of that first wave on the screen just brought the house down' (quoted in Jenkins 1988–89: 65).

On one level, such varieties of audience reception form part of a process of subcultural identity and community formation through an appeal to, and reinforcement of, subcultural affect and knowledges. Mike Featherstone has noted the operations and boundaries of such a process by observing that 'strong affectual bonds' persist and are maintained when 'people come together in constellations with fluid boundaries to experience the multiple attractions, sensations, sensibilities and vitalism of an extra-logical community' (1995: 47). According to Featherstone, such a meeting embodies a 'sense of being together ... [a] common feeling generated by common emotional adherence to a sign which is recognisable by others' (ibid.).

The construction of a community around and through viewing positions of surf film corresponds to processes which informed the reception of early film. A film screening in the formative days of cinema became 'a public event in the emphatic sense and a collective horizon in which industrially processed experience could be reappropriated by the experiencing subjects' (Hansen 1994: 137). Within this process the 'problems posed by [early] cinema's availability to ... socially unruly audiences in turn prompted the elaboration of classical modes of narration and spectator positioning' (ibid.). Surf film eschews classical fictional and documentary narration with the result that its 'unruly audiences' actively resist the forms of spectator positioning associated with classical (fictional and nonfictional) filmic forms. The subjective engagement with surf film results from the replacement of classical narration with strategies derived from the documentary avant-gardist discourse of delirium. The reception of surf film points to central aspects of this discourse, in particular a form of spectacle that impacts on and works through the senses. In this way the unruly, unrestrained and uninhibited reception of surf film is an expression of the pleasure of spectacular display.[2]

In contrast to the communal experience of watching a surf film in a public space, video reception is a (semi)private act of consumption that takes place primarily in the domestic sphere. Within this space viewing often takes the form of repeated screenings. In his study of participation in surfing, Mark Stranger noted that surfers in his survey 'watched 10.3 *different videos* (an indeterminate number of times)' during the year (1999: 272; emphasis in original). Videos were watched 'repeatedly, either as whole programmes or in fragmented snippets, as viewers searched for their favourite sequences or watch[ed] segments' according to whim or opportunity (ibid.). Stranger points out that despite being 'fragmented, these viewing patterns usually involve[d] an intense degree of concentration' in a way that suggests an 'aesthetic identity' between spectator and subject similar to that found among audiences of surf film (ibid.). Further implicated in this process is the fact that repeated viewing of fragments of surf videos disrupts any sense of a continuous narrative. In this case, 'timeshift' viewing habits reduce viewing to a fast-forward search for spectacular imagery (see Cubitt 1991). As with surf film, spectacle is highlighted by and foregrounded for the viewing audience of surf videos as a central element of the discourse of delirium. An analysis of selected surf films and surf videos emphasises the particular visual and aural practices and styles of the discourses of delirium. Such an analysis reveals that the melding of documentary and avant-garde approaches in the discourse of delirium reproduces an effective and affective mode of documentary representation.

A new wave: surf film

An important scene within Julian Schnabel's film *Basquiat* (1996), a portrait of the artist Jean-Michel Basquiat, depicts the painter frozen in place on a New York street as he looks to the skyline at an enormous wave poised to encroach upon the city. The tsunami functions as a metaphor for the commercial and personal forces which will soon 'swamp' Basquiat and result in his death at an early age. The metaphor is extended in the understanding that the approaching wave will impact on the New York avant-garde art world, imposing its presence on that scene.

The inverse of this position – the recognition of the artistic avant-garde by members of the surf community – was posed in the techniques of a number of surf films of the late 1960s, most notably Alby Falzon's *Morning of the Earth*. The film proclaims its links to the avant-garde, in this case the New American Cinema, by opening with a quotation by one of the leading artists of the movement, Jonas Mekas: 'We are the measure of all things. And the beauty of our creation, of our art, is proportional to the beauty of ourselves, of our souls'.[3] The title of the film, it has been suggested, derives from Nehru's description of Bali, one of the locations for the film (see Lewis 1998: 66). An alternative and, given Falzon's knowledge of Mekas and his work, equally valid source of the title are scenes Mekas filmed the day after his attempt to invade the Flaherty seminar (subsequently included in his film from 1976, *Lost, Lost, Lost*). The sequence is accompanied by a voice-over by Mekas declaring that on this occasion 'he felt close to the earth and at one with the morning' (see James 1989: 112). Mekas's references to an awakening intimate his 'reconciliation with the natural world and the emergence of a new day of cinema' (ibid.).[4] The perception applies equally to *Morning of the Earth*, which documents surfers in the natural world (the film is devoid of imagery of industrialisation) in a form referred to as pure surf film, a term used to refer to a mode of production and a particular content. Independently produced and exhibited and shot on 8 mm and later 16 mm film, pure surf films documented wave riding styles and trends, the evolution of surfboard design, and the lifestyles of 'soul surfers' who eschewed the competitive ethos of the rising professional surfing circuit as part of their search for alternatives to aspects of capitalist culture.[5]

Made with the assistance of a loan of $20,000 from the newly established Australian Film Development Corporation (AFDC), it was expected that *Morning of the Earth* would be profitable; in fact the AFDC used the prospect of commercial success as the prime criterion in deciding to support the project. Though the film did prove to be popular, its market prospects were not necessarily 'safe', as Susan Dermody and Elizabeth Jacka claim (1987: 75). The commercial success of surf films was far from assured. In its innovations, *Morning of the Earth* ran the risk of alienating an audience accustomed to certain styles and content. The film's success attests, in part, to its ability to effectively document the emergent soul surfing lifestyle in a 'psychedelic' mode, thereby fusing documentary and avant-gardist techniques characteristic of the discourse of delirium. While replicating the travelogue ('surfari') format of a number of earlier surf films, *Morning of the Earth* ignores conventions already firmly established in the surf film tradition, including hackneyed big wave sequences, and multiple scenes of wipeouts (frequently reproduced with a puerile comedic voice-over since transferred to the 'Funniest Home Video' format). Further, the film, unlike travelogue documentaries, avoids use of a voice-over, replacing it with a music soundtrack that serves to integrate the episodic narrative structured around surfing in various locations, principally Australia and Indonesia.[6] Independent avant-garde filmmaker Albie Thoms assisted Falzon with editing, during which phase lap dissolves and slow-motion sequences were added to the raw footage shot on location. Thoms has noted that the editing of the film involved what were at the time, in the context of such a work, innovatory techniques such as the step printing of numerous sequences. Thoms comments that Falzon 'shot most of the surfing at 48 or 72 frames a second which is extreme slow motion, but when we printed it, we step-printed it 3 or 4 times slower than that, we slowed it down enormously, and really gave the audience a chance to see the smallest changes in the waves and how they were being ridden' (quoted in Fisher 1999).

In its incorporation of multiple innovations in form and content, *Morning of the Earth* set a new standard for documentary surf films. Within its representation of communal, 'back to earth' lifestyles, indulgence of soft drugs, and an abandonment of commercialism, *Morning of the Earth* explores many themes prominent in underground film which 'emancipated itself from Hollywood by reproducing in the filmic the properties of the aberrant or proscribed ... practices that preoccupied the profilmic' (James 1996: 216). The connections to underground film are extended stylistically in the film. The opening imagery of a sunrise shot on infra-red film stock informs a work which includes a variety of optical effects in addition to slow motion and lap dissolves. The latter techniques, as Thoms points out, 'convey the simultaneous awareness that is necessary for a surfer's survival', and the film's parallel cutting 'reveals the significance of specific aspects of surfboard shaping to the eventual performance in the water' (1978: 128). The result of the deployment of a range of visual effects is a spectacular representation 'capable of revealing truths about life that we otherwise overlook or take for granted' (Thoms 1978: 125). The revelation of 'truth', and the stylistics which relate *Morning of the Earth* to the concerns and practices of underground and experimental cinema, intersect in a delirious discourse of formal excess and documentary realism.[7]

Like *Morning of the Earth*, George Greenough's film *The Innermost Limits of Pure Fun*, which was lauded by the Sydney filmmaking underground on its release, mixes an intense focus on the reality of surfing, here pushed to the point where it approximates an instructional film, with innovative and spectacular shots from inside the breaking wave. Certain scenes, filmed with a hand-held camera, evoke the practices of direct cinema in a way which suggests, to quote film theorist Paul Arthur out of context, the 'liberating marks of rawness as avant-garde work, the crucial distinction [is] not in theme or narrative approach but in the ability of unfettered technique to register a passionate, subjective confrontation with reality' (1992: 39).[8] Such a confrontation reaches its zenith in the final 'Coming of the

Dawn' sequence which begins before sunrise at Lennox Head, New South Wales, with waves illuminated by lights attached to the camera rig. As the sun rises the shots are slowed as Greenough, camera strapped to his back pointing backwards as he rides the waves on a kneeboard, films the interior of a tubing wave.

Greenough's perspective inside the wave inaugurated the point of view of a surfer on or in a wave. Prior to this sequence, surf films had been shot from the beach, a position which, even with a telephoto lens, distanced the spectator from the surfing action. Greenough stated that he 'wanted to get the feel of surfing ... not just what it looked like from the beach. The shot looking out of the tube really pushed the envelope of what a surf movie could be, but for raw action, my favourite angle was looking back at the board's track' (quoted in Gross 1999: 81). Surf film producer John Witzig called the 'Coming of the Dawn' sequence 'an astonishing achievement' and argued that if 'a great film is one that records the lifestyle of a group of people while allowing the personal view, selection and interpretation of the filmmaker, then perhaps it is [a great film]' (quoted in Thoms 2000: 112). Witzig's emphasis on the film as a documentary record which draws upon a personal artistic statement was repeated by Albie Thoms who argued that Greenough's work, which was 'more than a surf movie', articulated a 'personal purity of vision' and that the significance of the final sequence 'lies in the fact that it is the first record from inside the waves' (1978: 124; emphasis in original).[9] Thoms added that the scenes provide 'information of scientific and social importance, information that might help us understand better the quality of life in Australia, how our environment has shaped our characters, what our environment has to offer that might be used to improve our lives' (ibid.). Tinged with a rhetoric that exposes the particular sort of environmentalism of the early 1970s, when the comment was made, Thoms' observation emphasises the potential of the film to recast within its visual spectacle John Grierson's insistence on documentary representation as functional, instructional and educative.

Greenough replicated the 'Coming of the Dawn' sequence in the final segment of the film *Crystal Voyager*, which begins as a biography of Greenough shot by Alby Falzon and culminates in Greenough's own 23-minute film-within-a-film, 'Echoes', a segment which was originally planned as a short film to support the re-release of *Morning of the Earth*. Produced by David Elfick and co-ordinated by Alby Falzon (the team that made *Morning of the Earth*) *Crystal Voyager* examines the multiple talents of George Greenough, surfboard designer, boat builder, filmmaker and philosopher. The focus on a single figure for the entirety of a surf film was in itself an innovation that superseded a popular narrative structure based on the actions of a troupe of surfers filmed in multiple locations. The documentary portrait of Greenough, in which he explains his surfboard designs, boat-building projects and his philosophy of surfing, complements the film's climactic sequence which actualises and represents the philosophies and positions documented in the early parts of the film.

The final sequence replaces the voice-over of Griersonian documentary with a musical composition, 'Echoes', by Pink Floyd. Members of the band had seen and been impressed by Greenough's *The Innermost Limits of Pure Fun* and agreed to donate their music to the film. The eclectic and ethereal music is a perfect accompaniment for the 'ultimate investigation of the breaking wave' (Thoms 1978: 177). The power of the endlessly tubing wave (the working title of the segment was *The More the Power Grinds Over Your Head, the Less That Lands on Top of You*) is demonstrated in the continuous progression of the surfer through the wave. One critic compared the mesmerising sequence to the final scene of Kubrick's *2001: A Space Odyssey* (1968), emphasising the effectiveness of *Crystal Voyager*'s (documentary) approach: '*Crystal Voyager* creates the same feeling [as the end of 2001] using totally real effects: Kubrick constructed the whole thing, but Greenough has filmed the inside of waves and has created something of astounding beauty cinematically' (quoted in Thoms 2000: 121).[10]

Appropriately, Greenough's significant document reworks the long take in an intimate representation of features of the natural world. The 'Echoes' segment – shot at ten times normal speed, a practice which compresses the multiple long takes which Greenough seamlessly joins together into a continuous flow – captures minute details, such as droplets of water on the lens, in its depiction of the surging wave.[11] Such close attention to the natural world suggests the 'imagistic' films of Bert Haanstra, for example, whose *Panta Rhei* (*Everything Flows*, 1951) uses slowed and accelerated shots to document aspects of nature, including clouds, birds, patterns left on a beach by surf, and flowers blooming. The poetic approach to nature of Haanstra and Greenough is continued in Godfrey Reggio's *Koyaanisqatsi* (1983) and his *Powaqqatsi* (1988), Ron Fricke's *Baraka* (1992) and Luc Besson's *Atlantis* (1998), in ways which merge techniques derived from documentary and avant-garde representational approaches. Alby Falzon's work since *Morning of the Earth* extends this field. His films *Same As It Ever Was* (1982), shot in northern India, effectively deploys numerous editorial techniques; and *Globus* (2000), made with Jeff Hornbaker, is a collection of visually stunning images filmed in various locations worldwide: both films open documentary to a variety of filmic styles and actions. In a similar way the 'Echoes' sequence of *Crystal Voyager* elevates the film above the standard form of nonfiction 'surf movie' – stylistically unadorned representations of surfing – within a discourse of delirium which informs a documentary record of surfing with varieties of spectacle aligned with avant-garde and experimental filmmaking. The resultant 'visual and aural overload … induces an absorbed, trance-like condition' which exceeds, revises and replaces the techniques and effects of documentary modes of sobriety (Flaus 1974: 277).

Textual offensiveness: surf video

The shift from film to video as the preferred medium for the majority of surf texts, operating as part of a movement away from film to video in a variety of contexts in the early to mid-1970s, corresponded with changes in surfing styles.[12] Whereas the so-called soul surfing style and accompanying cultural dispositions had dominated the late 1960s, subsequent decades saw the rise of a form of surfing known as power surfing. Power surfing developed in the early 1980s as a style that involves aggressive manoeuvres on the wave, made possible by the introduction of shorter surfboards, including the tri-fin 'thruster'. Power surfing became popular during the 1980s and 1990s, with some commentators claiming that the introduction of the style marked a new era in surfing (see Young & McGregor 1984: 160). The influence of the style is felt in various ways within surf culture and has resulted in the insistence that 'style [and] power' are the definitive features of good surfing (Gane 1996: 73).

The rise of this new surfing style was in many ways endorsed by the simultaneous emergence of surf videos devoted to documenting it. During this period a number of surf video directors defined their work against the production values of the surf films which characterised the soul surfing era. Reflecting this change in form not all videographers were concerned with producing a visual image that 'hold[s] colour, depth and detail the way film does' (Warshaw 1999: 20). A number of surf videos, by making a virtue of low production values, are situated in opposition to the production values of surf films such as *Morning of the Earth* and the formats and standards of television, which occasionally programmes surf videos of broadcast quality. However, like certain independent surf films, surf videos are structured through a discourse of delirium in which formal experimentation and expressive, uncontrolled and primitivist filming and production practices are incorporated into documentary depictions of power surfing and the associated 'hardcore' surf lifestyle.

Synonymous with power surfing, the term hardcore refers to an essentially aggressive surfing style, and intersects with the musical genre used for the soundtrack of many power surf videos.[13] A descendant of punk, with links to thrash, hardcore music is fast, loud, simplistic and lyrically furious – anger derived from opposition to dominant middle-class culture and its celebration in much rock and pop music. Hardcore music 'mounted a self-consciously anachronistic attempt to sustain early punk's negativity ... The entirely recalcitrant music provided a besieged subculture with the basis for defensive rituals [based in] sonic and other forms of violence, and an obstinate antiprofessionalism' (James 1996: 224). The antisocial stance of hardcore music informs a disaffected lifestyle adopted by certain surfers, which one unidentified writer for the 'hardcore' surf magazine *Underground*

Surf summarised in terms of opposition and difference: 'We [should] encourage surfing to be publicly damned ... People don't have to fear us – they just have to NOT WANT TO BE US, not want to identify with a label that spells sick, perverted, deviant' (quoted in Stedman 1997: 81). Just as pure surf films represented aspects of the soul surfing way of life, so independent power surf videos feature elements of the hardcore lifestyle. While power surfing and a hardcore soundtrack are the most obvious points of reference to the hardcore attitude within the videos, other aspects of such an attitude, including shaven heads and styles of body adornment (notably tattooing and body piercing), are featured. The fact that in most cases it is the male body which is the subject of attention reinforces what is essentially an overtly masculinist basis to the filmed activities in ways which rewrite the object of the gaze of those practices also known as hardcore: contemporary pornography.

In places, the purposeful crudity of the production techniques of hardcore surf video informs the documentary mode in ways not achieved in other forms of documentary. In contrast to a smooth tracking shot in which a subject remains in frame, the surfing subject in surf videos may disappear offscreen before again being reframed. The constant recognition of offscreen space implicit in the unanticipated shot effectively reveals not reality, composed through textual systems, but the real which lies beyond the frame, outside systems of representation. Here, as with surf film, the real is further actualised through reference to varieties of spectacular visual styles which inform the structuring discourse of delirium as the basis of display. The spectacular style of surf video is grounded in an aesthetic of motion and speed, produced predominantly through rapid editing. Such a technique is frequently employed by US videographer Taylor Steele, the 'Andy Warhol of surfing' (Thoms 2000: 189) who, in many ways, pioneered the independent tradition of surfing videos. Steele's early videos captured rising Californian surf stars, including Kelly Slater, Rob Machado and Shane Dorian, in a 'brash "slash and burn" visual style' (Thoms 2000: 188). In his early videos, *Momentum* (1992) and *Momentum II* (1993), Steele made a virtue of the inability of his unsophisticated home video equipment to film in slow motion and taped in real time the aggressive and innovatory manoeuvres which characterised the new surfing styles he documented. As Thoms notes, 'eschewing the somewhat romantic slow-motion effects that had been standard in surfmovies for four decades, his footage seemed fresh ... and was assembled with disregard for continuity and the niceties of establishing a scene' (ibid.).

Australian variants of the style followed, among them Glen Winton's *Rad Movez, Volume One* (1993), Justin Gane's *Unleashed* (1994), Chris Stroh's *Intake* and *Stoke* (both 1996), Matt Gye's *Mystery Bag* (1997) and Dylan Longbottom's *Drive* (1997), and innumerable 'underground' videos. The latter works, typically produced anonymously, consist of rough cuts shot at professional surfing contests which are released immediately after the contests, thus pre-empting and subverting corporate-sponsored productions dealing with the same events. The majority of these named and anonymous works mobilise a 'non-stop visual assault style' in representations which correspond with the style of power surfing, the subject of virtually all contemporary surf videos (Dunne 1993: 26). The aesthetic of immediacy and crudeness which informs such works is comparable to, and in many cases derived from, the 'aggressive primitiveness' and 'textual offensiveness' of early 1980s video documentations of punk music performances which, in turn, borrowed from the experimental and documentary impulses of 1960s underground film (see Boddy 1981: 27; James 1996: 217). Mirroring and extending these formative traditions, it is not unusual for independent power surf videos to be distributed personally by the producer/director, often via mail order from a home address. In many cases the artwork for the video cover is simplistic, often little more than a black and white photocopy of a list of contents. As with low-end punk music videos, accessible practices of production and distribution determine that independent surf videos remain 'within the subculture as its autonomous self-representation and self-expression. Produced and consumed entirely within the subculture, [such works promote] a radically amateur aesthetic that refuses the industrial distinction between artist and market' (James 1996: 225).

The real McCoy

The effect of such a *video brut* aesthetic is suggestive of the domestic mode of film and video production, the home movie, and its intimations that anyone can make a film or video, a position celebrated by surf videographers as a feature of the liberating difference between 'hardcore' and commercially-sponsored surf videos. Manufacturers of surfboards and wetsuits and surf clothing companies such as Billabong, Quiksilver, Gotcha and Rip Curl were able to adopt and adapt newly-introduced video technology for the purposes of advertising a company's products. The links between an expanding surf industry and video technology contributed to the rise of corporate-backed and heavily commercialised surf videos that reflect the connections in their content and form. The content of the majority of sponsored surf videos is dominated by reportage of the professional surfing circuit, itself a result of the intervention of the same corporate sponsorship responsible for the production of commercial surf videos.

Sponsorship may also impact formally on the surf text via the imposition of advertisements into the texts in formats which range from the overt placement of advertisements between segments, to practices of product placement, such as the inclusion in obvious ways of particular brands of surfboards or surf wear. In many cases the 'commodity aesthetic' dominates and sublimates any sense of a textual aesthetic beyond that which is produced by or through sponsorship (see Haug 1986). For example, Gorilla Grip, maker of a non-slip footpad for surfboards, commissioned videographers Tim Bonython and Jason Muir to produce an annual series featuring the Hawaiian professional surfing titles. Beginning with *Hawaiian Nine-O* (1990), each instalment of the series features twelve surfing segments, many of which are accompanied by a voice-over narration, with advertisements between the segments which, in their placement and alignment with the voice-over, are frequently difficult to distinguish from the surfing content.

Sponsorship inflects the content and form of the surf text in multiple ways, including in certain cases a veto on the inclusion of any suggestion of drug taking or styles of filming suggestive of drug-induced states, and an abandonment of commissioned music scores in favour of deals between the sponsor and record companies to secure rights to the latest music 'hits' (see Thoms 2000: 158). The sexism that permeates the majority of surf videos is also linked to the practices of commercialism which here, as elsewhere, routinely reproduce reactionary images of gender. Sponsored videos trace equally predictable patterns in other ways. Rip Curl, for example, created *The Search* (1992–99), a series of videos which follow professional surfers around the world in a format which reinvents the cliché of the surfari popularised in Bruce Brown's *The Endless Summer*. Stylistically, such films and videos, with rare exceptions, avoid the risks of experimentation which 'could result in footage that [does not] serve the sponsor's best interests' (ibid.).

Sponsored surf videos, like other surf texts, constitute a form of documentary which has been ignored by a documentary film theory concerned with 'sober' canonical texts. However, sponsorship and sponsored documentary generally have been confronted and incorporated within documentary theory; the work of Robert Flaherty, notably *Nanook of the North*, produced for the fur company Revillon Frères, and *Louisiana Story* (1948), made for Standard Oil, is exemplary here. Study of Flaherty's work points to the fact that sponsorship does not necessarily result in textual impoverishment. Similarly, certain sponsored surf videos are stylistically and formally complex. Alby Falzon's *Can't Step Twice on the Same Piece of Water* (1992) is a sponsored work which overcomes the limitations often evident in the practice. Similarly, and more particularly, sponsored works produced by the contemporary director Jack McCoy transcend formal limitations associated with the sponsorship of surfing. McCoy, 'widely regarded as the sport's premier cinematographer' who 'set the standard of quality' of contemporary nonfiction surf video (Warshaw 2003: 374), utilises commercial sponsorship in the production of a formally innovative, deliriously 'non-sober', avant-gardist documentary display of surfing and the surfing lifestyle (see Falzon & Hoole 1998: 39).

In doing so McCoy's work mediates both the production standards and formal approaches of earlier soul surf film and the expressive practices of power surf video. The relationship of the two forms is exemplified, on the one hand, through McCoy's personal association with Alby Falzon, who acted as an advisor to McCoy's first film *Tubular Swells* (a.k.a. *In Search of Tubular Swells*, 1975), and on the other hand, via his mentorship of Taylor Steele, director of a series of power surf videos. The mediation of the two forms is extended in the fact that McCoy's *Blue Horizon* (2004) depicts the surfing styles of both well-known soul surfer Dave ('Rasta') Rastovich and professional power surfer Andy Irons, in a work which itself combines formal elements of surf film (long takes and vivid colour footage, for example) and the quick editorial cuts and thrash music of independent surf videos. McCoy's work also bridges the two forms in terms of exhibition practices. Whereas soul surf film was typically exhibited in local halls rented for the occasion, and power surf videos were produced for home exhibition, McCoy has experimented with both methods, renting local theatres and halls and advertising screenings via handbills and posters, and, alternatively, transferring all of his films to DVD for domestic exhibition. The mixture of various formal styles and exhibition practices has been a factor which has contributed to McCoy's lengthy career and extensive filmography.

McCoy has produced in excess of 25 films and videos, including *Storm Riders* (1982), *Bunyip Dreaming* (1990), *The Green Iguana* (1992), *Sik Joy* (1994), *Psychedelic Desert Groove* (1996) and *To' Day of Days* (2002). McCoy began his career during the 1960s in Hawaii assisting surf filmmakers Jim Freeman and Greg MacGillivray exhibit surf films, an experience that permitted McCoy to see the work of foundational surf film directors such as Bruce Brown, Bud Browne and John Severson.[14] McCoy migrated to Australia in 1970 and in association with local surf photographer Dick Hoole formed a partnership to exhibit surf films and produce surf photographs for the newly burgeoning surf press. The release of *Tubular Swells*, the first film from the McCoy/Hoole partnership, marked McCoy's move into surf film production. *Tubular Swells* was inspired by the landmark film *Morning of the Earth*, but broadened its image of surfing via the inclusion of contemporary leading surfers filmed in various global locations, particularly Australia, Hawaii and Indonesia. The film was released the same year as the inauguration of a professional international surfing circuit (in December 1975), a coincidence that was to mark the content of later McCoy films, with their focus on the 'stars' of international professional surfing competitions. The new style of surf film was expressed by *Storm Riders*, which features a number of professional surfers on Queensland's Gold Coast and Nias in Indonesia in a mixture of surf film and surf video aesthetics. According to Tim Baker *Storm Riders* 'set a benchmark for surf movies at the time' (Bartholomew with Baker 1996: 247).

In 1990 McCoy was hired by the Australian-based surf wear company Billabong to produce a series of videos which came to define his career. McCoy has extended his collaborative relationship with his sponsor through the Billabong Jack McCoy Surf Film Festival that promotes a variety of surf films at international screenings. McCoy also hosts a short surf film competition, sponsored by the electronics company Panasonic. Further to his own directorial credits McCoy has shot footage for a number of widely-received surf films and videos, including Bruce Brown's *The Endless Summer II* (1994), and the closing footage of Stacy Peralta's *Riding Giants* (2004). As this outline of his career suggests, McCoy's work is largely concerned with documenting the styles of professional surfers in the context of professional surfing competitions. With this focus McCoy has, with corporate backing, been instrumental in revising the structure of surfing competitions, with a resultant impact on his work. Whereas the world championship surf competition is based on numerous rounds in different international locations (the 'circuit') and spread across months, McCoy, supported by Billabong, has instituted the Billabong Challenge, a series of week-long surf events in remote locations attended by professional and other surfers. Surf film director Alby Falzon has said of the practice: 'The surfers come from all over the world; there's money for them and it's an expression of their creativity and talent that offers them and others a perspective [on] surfing' (quoted in Thornley 1999: 56). The result, a speciality event and experimental contest format which constitutes a unique gathering of surfing talent, has been called the 'waveriding Woodstock' (Thornley 1999: 58).

In turn, these events are filmed by McCoy as the basis of many of his best-known works. *Psychedelic Desert Groove*, for example, documents the 1995 Billabong Challenge and typifies the form of McCoy's work in its mixture of surfing footage (which in this case was shot with a crew that included Taylor Steele) and a loose, often semi-fictionalised narrative concerning the exploits and travails of professional surfer Mark ('Occy') Occhilupo. McCoy has worked extensively with Occhilupo, a collaboration that began in Western Australia, which resulted in a sequence in *Bunyip Dreaming*, continued with *The Green Iguana* and other works, and culminated in *Occy* (1998), a survey of the surfer's career. In contrast to the proliferating 'profile a pro' format of many surf videos, which rely on a succession of sequences featuring a professional surfer in various locations, McCoy's portraits combine surfing sequences with set-piece fictionalised scenes and an array of visual effects (see Slater 1999: 68).[15] The sobriety traditionally associated with documentary is rigorously assaulted in such works through a humour which while sometimes sophomoric (*Occy* is subtitled 'The Occumentary'), at other times effectively reflects the relaxed lifestyles and 'good times' available to those in the surfing subculture. The humorous and subversive approach is also found in *Free as a Dog* (2005), McCoy's portrait of professional surfer Joel Parkinson, which is narrated by Parkinson's dog, in a witty translation of the 'voice of God' narration.

Such techniques are complemented by McCoy's attention to the musical soundtrack. McCoy's films frequently eschew the soundtracks – and the relationship of music and image – characteristic of 1980s and 1990s power surf videos in which thrash music is played over footage of surfing sequences, each of which is cut to the style of MTV-inflected jump cuts. In contrast, McCoy employs what he calls 'sound design', in which the image and the music reflect on, and inform, each other. Rather than layer music over images in the editing process, McCoy commences each new film with the music in mind. The idea for his film *The Green Iguana*, for example, originated with a piece of music by that name, which he used to accompany the opening sequence of the film. While the music deployed in this way in each film is not necessarily derived from the generic form favoured by power surf videos, he does apply music by contemporary bands, among them the Australian band Powderfinger.[16] According to McCoy, 'when I'm making a film it's 50 per cent vision and 50 per cent sound. Music is the emotion and I always try to make both mediums very positive. When I choose a soundtrack I always go for a positive message' (quoted in Thornley 1999: 56). He has added that there is 'something missing' from the 'slash-and-burn, wave-after-wave surf action' of many surf videos produced in the 1990s (quoted in George 2003). While he refuses to condemn the approaches of such videos he insists that 'there's an opportunity to take things a little deeper' in terms of a representation of the sport and lifestyle in which sound is used to complement, inform and, at times, narrativise images in ways which are at variance with the relationship of sound and image in numerous surf videos (quoted in ibid.). A McCoy film integrates sound into a documentary display that deploys various visual elements in the scope of its array of aesthetic techniques.

The display operates in part through a style that emphasises shots of surfers taken by McCoy while swimming among them, camera in hand. McCoy combines the point-of-view shot within the tubing wave perfected by Greenough with images derived from hours of in-the-water footage shot on 16mm film, which invests the image with a marked clarity. He applies a range of techniques for such shots, including pole-cam photography, in which cameras mounted on poles of up to eight feet in length are used to replicate the vantage point of the surfer. Like Greenough, McCoy also incorporates a 'split-wave' photography which simultaneously provides a view above and below the water line. Filming from a jet-ski is another variant of the practices deployed by McCoy. The technique permits a perspective from a wave behind or below the surfer. Water shots of this kind are abetted by an intimacy with the surfers and their surfing styles which allows him to be effectively positioned with his camera. The result, according to one assessment, is 'the absolute gold standard in slow motion water photography' (Thornley 1999: 56). Shots taken from the sea, however, do not always provide a perspective of the size of the waves, an important feature of surf films generally and the recent 'big wave' genre in particular (as demonstrated by Peralta's *Riding Giants* and Mc-Coy's *To' Day of Days*). Simple though effective techniques provide perspective on wave size, as in McCoy's documentation of the 1998 Billabong Challenge which was shot in part from the shoreline to include features of the foreground: 'as the cameras tracked with the wave, there was land; a tree, a rock, the line of a point. The effect was to frame the big right [-hand wave], intriguing the eye and giving the shot depth' (Carroll 1999: 12). McCoy acknowledges that the sequence is not complex, 'a tree, a rock, but it's all you need' to bring wave size into relief (quoted in Carroll 1999: 12).

Elsewhere, McCoy's comments on the techniques of filming big wave surfing intimate that the process of filming and framing is complicated by the sheer mass of the wave. Referring to a sequence included in *To' Day of Days* (the first word of the title is a contraction of Teahupoo, the film's location on Fiji), and subsequently used as the finale for *Riding Giants* which features big-waver surfer Laird Hamilton, McCoy has said:

> I turned the high speed camera on. I was using a new lens, larger than normal that would require exact framing. Since there is no viewfinder on my water cameras, I have to sight the shot with my right eye straight down the top of the camera and with the other eye I've trained myself to watch what is happening. As the wave raised to a giant wall of water ... I needed to see this with both eyes and for one second I took my right eye off its camera job and looked at what I thought I was seeing ... Here was a man racing a wall of water ... a wave that with one slight error could have spelt death ... It's a high speed shot, 200 frames per second, 8 times slower than normal ... When Laird is at a very critical moment, the camera moves down slightly, only for a second. That's when I took my eye off the action. The shot shortly thereafter comes back to perfect framing. (2004)

Captivating and enthralling views of this kind inform a documentary display which applies a host of techniques across various works, including brief fantasy segments, animation and comedic action in a way which expands the visual language of observation that underpins the surf genre. Special effects achieved in the editing and printing of the film and its transference to video further extend the display in ways which approximate what John Caldwell calls the 'painterly effects' of 'videographics' (1995: 138). As Caldwell explains, the 'painterly mode [as] used by manufacturers, directors, and designers, describes images that appear worked over graphically, as if by hand. The overt reference here, of course, is to painting with a brush, but since no brushes are actually used in an electronic post-production environment (styluses, track balls, and digitisers are), the term has taken on a broader meaning' (1995: 139). In one of its manifestations the painterly refers to a reworking of images within the frame. 'Instead of transferring scenes correctable only as whole *takes* or *scenes*, new [digital editing] devices ... allow for extreme precision and manipulation *inside* the *visual fields*. Field footage and un-folding takes are no longer considered the given, or basic, unit. Pixels in a vide-ographic landscape are considered the basic building blocks. The artists' control now is seen as wide-ranging and residing over the visual geography of the frame' (1995: 140; emphasis in original). McCoy utilises components of this palette of techniques. For example, certain images in his work have been manipulated via 'painterly deformations' such as a pronounced image plasticity in the form of im-ages from one frame transferred to and wrapped around images in another frame. For Caldwell the 'painterly, aggressive method itself becomes a sign – a feigned reference to a rebellious attitude and avant-gardism' (1995: 142).

The product of the meeting of such avant-gardism within the context of Mc-Coy's observational documentary representations is an expressive display that revels in its anti-sobriety. As the title of *Psychedelic Desert Groove* suggests, images in the video are mutated within psychedelic effects of enhanced colours and im-age plasticity. Similar effects are structured into *The Green Iguana*. Here the sound-track includes a song which contains lyrics which refer to a rainbow and a win-dow, and McCoy includes shots of his son walking on a beach over which are digitally superimposed images of a technicolour rainbow and an open window. In the same sequence words from the song are inscribed on the image, in a way reminiscent of printed text in a comic book speech balloon. The reworking of documentary modes within McCoy's work constitutes a notable example of the forms of representation here referred to as display. The multiple revisions of, and within, an observationalism that is the structural basis of McCoy's work, and the surf genre generally, extends the strict formulations and encompassing 'sobri-ety' characteristic of certain documentary texts. McCoy's productions, which have been described as the 'single greatest body of work by a surf filmmaker',[17] and the incorporation of aspects of earlier soul surf film and power surf video, marks current developments within this area of filmmaking and through it constitutes a significant aspect of the practices and processes of documentary display.

McCoy's work, as with the resistive styles of hardcore power surf videos, in their delirious mixing of documentary and *video brut* practices, and the innovative practices of certain pure surf film, confront and enlarge those practices referred to as documentary. Michael Renov's observation of the current condition of doc-umentary film theory – 'too many practices get excluded; too many theoretical questions remain unanswered' (1999: 323) – points to a core issue in this analysis: unanswered questions and excluded practices suggest a theory that is restricted by its basic tenets. To date documentary theory has, even in the presence of proliferating varieties of practice (among them, so-called reality television), continued to predicate itself dominantly on forms of communication and representation which construct the world in terms of earnestness and solemnity and which are wary of representational practices that disrupt or reject traditional modes. Attention to popular forms such as surf texts shifts the theoretical foundations of documentary towards an acceptance of delirious display.

In this way, the various surf texts analysed here challenge theoretical assumptions that inform the study of documentary by revealing practices which, while claiming to represent the actual as opposed to a fictional world, do so in ways that have been categorised as experimental and documentary. The joining of the two traditions of nonfiction – the documentary and the avant-garde – in a resultant discourse of delirium and associated act of display, and its positioning of surf film and surf video as avant-gardist documentaries, forces a reassessment of documentary practices and theoretical approaches to documentary texts which construct them solely in terms of a discourse of sobriety. The productive outcome of such a reassessment is the opening of a space for surf film and surf video, among other texts, to be recognised and included within the previously exclusionary realm of documentary.

chapter six

Natural Science Film: From Microcinema to IMAX

To repeat, the image is first and foremost an object in the world, with physical characteristics, just like any other object, that make it perceptible. Among these characteristics is one that is especially important for the apparatus: the size of the image.

— Jacques Aumont (1997: 102)

According to Gaston Bachelard, the 'destiny of every image is magnification' (quoted in Virilio 2002: 109). For Walter Benjamin image magnification and enlargement result in new forms of cognition and understanding. Benjamin argued that 'by focusing on hidden details of familiar objects [and] ... commonplace milieux [the camera] extends our comprehension of the necessities which rule our lives' (2005: 116). Béla Belász reinforced the importance of the cinematic practice of magnification within an account of the origin of cinema, which he described in terms of documentary images of nature. 'The first new world', he said, 'discovered by the film camera in the days of the silent film was the world of very small things visible only from very short distances, the hidden life of little things. By this the camera showed us ... hitherto unknown objects and events: the adventures of beetles in a wilderness of blades of grass ... the erotic battles of flowers and the poetry of miniature landscapes' (1972: 54). Jean Epstein reinforced the imbrication of camera, image enlargement and nature when in his manifesto on the magnification of the film image – which he typically equated to the close-up – he wrote that just as 'a stroller leans down to get a better look at a plant, an insect, or a pebble, the lens must include in a sequence describing a field, close-ups of a flower, a fruit, or an animal: living nature' (1977: 11). If, then, as Bachelard claims, magnification is the fate of the image, 'only [magnified] images of nature', as Belász insists, 'bear the convincing stamp of unquestionable authentic reality' (1972: 172).

The connections between magnification and such a documentary reality are integral to the microcinema of Jean Painlevé and the enlarged documentary images of IMAX cinema. Painlevé's combination of Surrealism and science, the familiar and the exotic, entertainment and edification – within magnified images of various species, particularly marine organisms – and the views of natural science subjects so prevalent in the enlargements of IMAX cinema, contribute to the construction of a documentary display understood as an expansion of the realm of the visible. The basis of such a display is, in Painlevé's microscopic film practice and the visually-enhanced images of IMAX, the representation of the normally unseen, resulting in what Yuri Tsivian calls a 'penetrating vision' (1996: 82) and what Jane Goodall calls a 'secret eye' (1999: 116).

However, the natural science subjects displayed in this way have largely been excluded from the field of documentary representation. The position is reinforced in the critical assessment that natural science films are not part of the documentary tradition. As Scott Macdonald notes, 'probably no substantial dimension of film history that is so widely admired by a public audience and so frequently utilised in academic contexts has been so thoroughly ignored by film critics, historians, and theorists as the nature film' (2006: 4). The basis of such exclusion is in many respects traceable to Grierson, who, in the essay 'First Principles of Documentary', consigned nature films with travelogues and newsreels to the 'lower categories' beyond the domain of documentary representation (1998a: 82).[1] Grierson's exclusions were also related to his emphasis on an educative function for documentary and his desire to construct documentary in opposition to Hollywood's mode of production. Such positions have functioned to limit understandings of documentary's capacities to entertain.

This chapter challenges Griersonian emphases and exclusions within a focus on the documentary display of certain 'nature films' and through an analysis of the connections between scopic technology (microcinema and IMAX), an expanded visual regime (and with it new forms of delivering information), and films which are in various permutations humorous, shocking, pleasurable and entertaining. In this way the connections, and the resultant documentary display exemplified in Painlevé's microcinema and the large-screen cinema of IMAX, offer – via a focus on magnified images of aquatic nature – new ways to theorise modernist and contemporary documentary.

Painlevé and the unseen

The magnified image, the basis of microphotography and so-called microcinema, is capable of producing, in a practical and direct way, images of objects that would otherwise be beyond the capacity of the unaided eye. As such, microcinema partakes of a tradition from the eighteenth to the twenty-first centuries which includes new technologies which expand the visual realm, among them X-rays, telescopes, microscopes, photography, digital modelling and cinema itself. Within the context of science, such techniques constitute an expansion of the realm of the visible within and through what are, with each technology, new ways of seeing directed towards measurement and calibration of physical phenomena. Painlevé's microcinema can be situated within such a scientific framework; indeed Painlevé was aware that his filmic practice was conducted within a line of inquiry established by check Jules-Etienne Marey in which cinema was deployed in the service of science.[2]

Microcinema can also be understood within the context of curiosity as the basis of a pleasurable desire 'to know through seeing what cannot normally be seen' (Cowie 1999: 28). The desire to see what is normally hidden or forbidden has a dual effect: 'what may be desired in this coming to know of the hidden is the familiar, the already known, as in the repeated viewing of the now-familiar but still forbidden body of the woman/mother of voyeurism' (ibid.). Alternatively, 'there is the pleasure and wish to see/be shown the unfamiliar. In documentary films the unfamiliar of the seen has been associated with its sensationalism, as a "cinema of attractions", presenting the exotic and the horrific, as well as the bizarre and unusual' (ibid.). Painlevé's microcinema and microphotography are similarly constructed as forms of (scientific) revelation of previously unseen or hidden natural phenomena and, in another way, as forms which dispel sober scientific methods and approaches within entertaining and frequently sensationalised views. It is via a combination of both approaches that Painlevé's filmic practice becomes a documentary display understood to be a positive and constructive expansion of visuality coupled with a productive banishment of sobriety within an entertaining and informative spectacle.

In its presentation of entertaining views, Painlevé's microcinema draws on and is informed by the long history of 'theatrical' uses of microscopy and microcinema, which complements and does not necessarily contradict the application of microscopy within scientific experimentation. Barbara Stafford's book *Body Criticism* (1993) exposes these trends and their connections within a history of Enlightenment microscopy. Stafford examines the ways in which early uses of microscopy played on and exploited phantasm, ruse, visual reconstruction and manipulation. In the eighteenth and nineteenth centuries microscopic studies of protozoa and marine life were 'nothing short of "microscopic theatre", a "spectacle très rejouissant", in which condensed lights revealed astonishing underwater comedy. The hieroglyphic acrobatics ... of "the harlequin, or insect [found in] muddy water", reminded one amateur scientist of lusty springing in the *commedia dell' arte*' (Elkins 1992: 35). Thierry Lefevbre has noted the ways in which filmed microscopic studies replicated dominant genres of drama and comedy (quoted in Tsivian 1996: 84). Tsivian draws together references to *commedia dell' arte*, comedy and drama in his argument that 'scientific films shot through the lens of the microscope were perceived through the prism of Grand Guignol aesthetics' (1996: 86).

However, the early twentieth century also saw the abandonment of a 'theatrical' tradition of microcinema in favour of a more rigorous integration of microscopy, film and science. The latter emphasis was pronounced in the work of Jean Comandon, an early twentieth-century scientist trained in the use of time-lapse microcinematography. Comandon applied his medical background to biological research while simultaneously working for the film production company Pathé Frères. Painlevé praised Comandon as the 'real pioneer of microcinematography' and the 'archetype of the researcher using film', whose work was a sophisticated development of the research conducted by Marey who, in 1893, made cinematic photographs of infusoria under the microscope.[3] Comandon masterfully mediated both science and cinema, using film to popularise his research on the lecture circuit.

Following Comandon, an aspect of Painlevé's genius was his ability to successfully negotiate the separate demands of the scientific community and a general audience. In certain cases this practice was achieved via different prints of the same film. As Painlevé outlined in an interview later in his life: 'A film dealing with scientific subjects always risks being too sophisticated for one audience and too superficial for another. The scientist knows his subject matter and is protective of it' (quoted in Hazéra & Leglu 2000: 179). In contrast, 'an ordinary moviegoer can't always rise to that level ... So with my films, I made one version for scientists, a second for universities, and a third, which was shorter and set to music, for general audiences' (ibid.). Elsewhere Painlevé eschewed the rigours of a strict scientific method – claiming 'science is fiction' – and merged 'science' and the 'popular' in a single film (see McDougall 2000: xiv). Despite the label 'science film' often attached to his works, the resultant films mixed avant-gardist and documentary forms as the basis of an entertaining documentary display that melded innovative sonic elements with the scopic dimensions of a revealing microcinema.

Documents and microphotography

Painlevé's career as a filmmaker brought him into contact with a number of figures prominent in twentieth century avant-garde cinema. His colleagues and acquaintances included Jean Vigo, Joris Ivens, and the Surrealists Luis Buñuel, Man Ray and Georges Franju, with whom he collaborated on *Le Sang des bêtes*. Such a network of influences informed Painlevé's work with a set of ideas and practices characteristic of a large segment of the avant-garde at the time, a tradition which Grierson excluded from the realm of English-language documentary filmmaking.[4] As Raymond Durgnat says, 'Painlevé's micro-masterpieces reconcile attitudes usually kept stiffly apart (Surrealism + science, modernism + ultra-realism). They belong with a French documentary spirit, or movement (Epstein, Storck, Vigo, Franju, Resnais...) which, compared to the English, was less directly sociable, more open to material structures. It also explored "indifferent nature" as Vertov's kino-eye never did' (1996: 81). Painlevé's connections with the avant-garde, specifically that strand marked by Surrealism, were inaugurated in his association with a publishing project launched by Georges Bataille. The practices among the Surrealists of schism and excommunication produced many Surrealisms, including the distinctions between the Surrealism conducted by André Breton and his followers and that undertaken by Bataille (banished by Breton) and the contributors, including Painlevé, to his journal *Documents*.

Among the Surrealist journals of the 1930s (including *Minotaure*, *La Révolution surréaliste*, *Surréalisme*, and *Acéphale*) *Documents* holds a privileged place, emphasised by Annette Michelson when she states that its 'role in the intellectual history of [the twentieth century] must now be seen as one of a seminal, prophetic intervention' (1999: 72).[5] Published between 1929 and 1931, the 17 issues applied in certain ways the title of the journal within an emphasis on the 'documentary aspect' of content (Richardson 1994: 50), a point reinforced by James Clifford who, in an extended analysis of the journal, highlights 'its subversive, nearly anarchic, documentary attitude' (1988: 553). Such latter-day assessments of the journal cannot necessarily be justified in that the word 'documentary' was not at the time, at least within non-English language speaking countries, understood in any Griersonian way. Nevertheless, a similar attitude to the journal's analyses of cultural products not as aesthetic objects but as documents in the sense of transcriptions of representations of physical existence was to be adopted in coterminous developments within documentary film.

The presence of traces of a 'real' world does not contradict the journal's emphasis on the surreal, which emerged within and through the contradictions and disjunctions produced within a collagist alignment of texts from 'high' culture and the popular domain. The subtitle of *Documents* – 'Archéologie, Beaux Arts, Ethnographie, Variétiés' (the latter replacing the word 'Doctrines' after the first three issues) – points to the disparate bases that contributors drew upon for the journal. The result was a striking juxtaposition of previously unrelated material, including essays on Hollywood, Cuban music, jazz, comics and the occult which were aligned with ethnographic analyses and interpretations of contemporary art. Michelson highlights the place of popular cultural texts and their role within the ideological thrust of the Surrealism of *Documents* when she notes that:

As a pioneering venture in the field of cultural studies, the interest and the particularly intriguing quality – one might say, the intellectual charm – of the journal derive partly from its intensifying juxtaposition of essays on forms and issues of popular culture with those of the fine arts, past and recent. The scholars and philosophers of the group, including Bataille himself, are of course among the most distinguished of a generation that brought both a sense of elation and theoretical sophistication to their appreciation of popular culture – American, in particular. Their work initiated and maintained a questioning of cultural canons, of the hierarchisation involved in the categories of 'high' and 'low'. In so doing – and this is crucial to an understanding of their project – they spearheaded a renewal of the siege against the ideology of an international bourgeoisie and its local, French variant. (1999: 73)

Within the collagist approach that was the journal's basic method, the juxtaposition of text and image, notably photographs, was a pronounced feature of the journal's layout as an expression of Surrealist ideas (see Clifford 1988: 551). Indeed, photography occupied a definitive place in the style and intent of the journal. Clifford notes that in Documents, 'the juxtaposition of the contributions, and especially of their photographic illustrations, was designed to provoke ... defamiliarisation' (1988: 552). He underlines this point when he adds that 'Documents, particularly in its use of photography, creates the order of an unfinished collage rather than that of a unified organism' (ibid.). Rosalind Krauss extends Clifford's point in her argument that photography is 'absolutely central – definitive one might say' to Surrealism (1981: 17). In the essay 'The Photographic Conditions of Surrealism', Krauss (1981) applies this thesis within an examination of the work of Man Ray, Hans Bellmer and Jacques-André Boiffard, among other photographers.

Boiffard's photography included images for Breton's novel Nadja (1928) and the numerous images he contributed to Documents, among them the ones made for Bataille's 1929 essay on an unlikely body part, the big toe (see Bataille 1985). On the one hand, if that is the right expression here, Bataille interpreted the big toe as the epitome of the human – the appendage that literally grounds us – and in another way, the big toe signifies baseness through its contact with the mud and excrement underfoot in the world (see Tythacott 2003: 216). The photograph of a big toe by Boiffard – a colleague of Painlevé at the Sorbonne – published with Bataille's essay, is in one sense 'banal', as Rosalind Krauss claims. Krauss argues that Boiffard's image is a 'straight' photograph, and contrasts it with the 'great range of processes used to manipulate the image' in Surrealist photography, of which Man Ray's solarisations come to mind (1981: 17). However, while Boiffard's photograph does not involve the chemical and light effects which contributed to making Man Ray's photography so captivating, the image of a big toe is manipulated – it is a dramatically enlarged (and in this sense, magnified) image of the subject. In another way the photograph of a single big toe disassociated from the other toes and the foot itself, produces an eerie, uncanny effect. A comparable effect, compounded by shock, is produced in the photograph by Eli Lotar, an assistant and collaborator on a number of Painlevé's films from the late 1920s, of rows of dismembered cow trotters lined up against a wall at La Villette abattoir which was used in *Documents* to accompany an article by Bataille.

In similar ways Painlevé's photographs for *Documents* are, as with Bioffard's depiction of a big toe, magnified images and, as with Lotar's slaughterhouse images, capable of shock effects. What has been called the 'most paradigmatic Surrealist image' (Russell 2006), Painlevé's photograph *Lobster Claw* (1927), is an enlarged image shot almost front on, which evokes shock and the uncanny within the fact that it takes on the appearance of an alien face with eye and jaws and hooked nose. Microphotography for Painlevé was a technology capable of revealing nature as another world, a different reality beyond known experience. In images such as *Sea Urchin Pedicels* (1928), *Sea Anemone* (1930) and *The Seahorse* (1934), Painlevé's microphotography intimately depicted features of marine organisms which in the process of magnification exhibit or display intriguing, if sometimes grotesque, aspects of the natural world.

Painlevé's microcinema and other close-ups on nature

Extending his photographic practice, Painlevé's films apply microscopy to images of aquatic nature in a way which led André Bazin to claim that 'Jean Painlevé occupies a singular and privileged place in French cinema' (2000: 147). This unique position rests, in part, on the production of films which can appropriately be labelled Surrealist documentaries. There is nothing paradoxical about the notion of Surrealist documentary, a point made by Robert Short (2003: 157). As Ramona Fotiade comments, documentary could be made to serve the Surrealists' aim 'to explode realist boundaries from within, by infiltrating an accurate account of phenomena with a sense of the inexplicable and the absurd' (1998: 119). Fotiade notes that: 'The pitiless immobility of the camera in front of horrifying images achieves the "shock of the eye" theorised by surrealist writings on film, while pushing the documentary genre far beyond conventional limits' (ibid.). Robert Short argues that the 'joint action of what Walter Benjamin was to call "the optical unconscious" of the camera and the desiring unconscious of the spectator would be sufficient to bring about the transmutation of mundane reality that the surrealists sought … You could say that film's proper vocation for surrealists was documentary, not fiction or artifice' (2003: 15). While the term 'Surrealist documentary' has been applied to a work such as Buñuel's *Las Hurdes*, there was a broader documentary strand within Surrealist film. The opening documentary footage of scorpions in Buñuel's L'Age d'or (The Golden Age, 1930) is one example, a sequence which frames the remaining footage within the context of 'nature film' (Short 2003: 11). Man Ray's use of Painlevé's footage of starfish in his 1928 film of the same name is another example of documentary footage of nature within a Surrealist film.

The Surrealist emphasis on seeing things 'close up' placed a premium on image enlargement and magnification. Louis Aragon, following Breton, stressed the important ability of the close-up and magnification to enhance particular information and meanings. For Aragon: 'objects that were a few moments ago sticks of furniture or books of cloakroom tickets are transformed [on the screen] to the point where they take on menacing or enigmatic meanings' (quoted in Short 2003: 14). In Painlevé's films, as in his photography, magnification combined with his own sense of the surreal as factors in an expressionistic representation. Each Painlevé film tends to focus on a single organism, usually a sea creature. Each film presents, clearly and concisely, the crucial moments in the life cycle of the chosen organism. Painlevé's films were generally eight to 15 minutes long and characterised by low production budgets. Bazin remarked that the limits of Painlevé's film practice were as loose as those of 'documentary film', and that what mattered was not defining but making the films (2000: 147). Painlevé used the unglamorous and restrictive term 'science film' for his own work, as a sub-genre of the general classification of documentary film, devoid of any notions of experimental or avant-garde tendencies (ibid.). Painlevé's attempt to separate his films from the avant-garde was undertaken to legitimate his work in the eyes of the scientific community, and indeed certain of his films were produced solely for this audience. However, Painlevé also sought to reach a general audience. His attempt to negotiate both audiences resulted in works which, despite the label 'science film', mixed avant-garde and documentary forms and practices as the basis of the works' documentary display.

After he stopped using intertitles in the early 1930s Painlevé added voice-overs to his short films, in addition to music. The narration, typically spoken by Painlevé himself, frames organisms within an anthropomorphism that infuses each film. The ironic and sardonic voice-over that Painlevé wrote for Franju's Le Sang des bêtes informs his own work to a marked degree, as in The Seahorse, one of the first films to use location footage shot underwater. This underwater material was edited with footage shot in enormous aquariums where Painlevé and his assistants waited for days to film the birth of a seahorse. Painlevé's narration for this remarkable footage describes the creature's 'slightly affected air of dignity' and the way its pouting lower lip 'gives it a slightly embarrassed air, transformed into anxiety by the highly mobile eyes'. Such anthropomorphism is hardly in the vein developed much later by Walt Disney's so-called live-action nature films, which continued a long literary tradition of unproblematically projecting human values onto nature. For Painlevé, anthropomorphism is a tool that subverts the narcissistic self-portraits so readily imposed on nature. Frequently Painlevé focuses on grotesqueries, as if testing the ability or willingness of audience members to identify with the subject. On one level the voice-overs function as amusing interludes to break up the scientific accounts of animals' biology, but they also serve to create an uncanny effect as they prompt a viewer to reconcile the irreconcilable: the utterly strange appearance of such creatures with human mannerisms.

Within its scopic dimension Painlevé's microcinematography reveals hitherto unseen aquatic worlds. His films include the best known *The Seahorse*, and, among others, *Hyas and Stenorhynchus* (1929), *Freshwater Assassins* (1947) and *Sea Urchins* (1954), a remake in colour of his 1929 film *The Sea Urchins*. As with other Painlevé films produced for a general audience, *Sea Urchins* features an avant-garde score, a homage to his friend Edgar Varèse, composed of the sounds produced by children 'playing' pots and pans, which Painlevé referred to as 'organised noise' (quoted in Berg 2000: 41). The magnified images of the film examine various aspects of the creature's physiognomy and skeleton. According to Ralph Rugoff, Painlevé's cinematography is 'extraordinarily beautiful, boasting images so elegantly composed and strikingly lit that they seem more appropriate to art films than to documentaries and lend his films an aesthetic self-consciousness that vies with their apparent educational function' (2000: 49).

The language of such an assessment suggests descriptions of documentaries produced between the 1920s and 1950s in which the key critical term is 'poetic'. Films such as Ivens' *Rain* (1929) and Humphrey Jennings' war-time films are frequently described in the critical literature as poetic. In these films the scopic realm is maximised beyond a mere capacity to provide information within and through rhetorical strategies, and moves towards a form of representation characterised by images selected dominantly or exclusively for their aesthetic appeal. Jim Leach in an essay on Jennings' *Listen to Britain* (1942) attempts to pin down what it means to call the film 'poetic'. In contrast to what Andrew Higson terms the 'public gaze' of documentary (1995: 192), Leach argues that the 'poetic effect of Jennings' war-time films is associated with what might be called the introduction of a "private eye"' (1998: 158), and in this relation approvingly quotes Lindsay Anderson's estimation that Jennings developed a 'style based on a peculiar intimacy of observation' in which the 'commonplace' is made significant (ibid.). A similar effect is achieved within Painlevé's microcinema in which intimate observation is melded to the 'poetry' of Painlevé's representation of natural phenomena.

In another way the word 'poet' has consistently been applied by critics to Flaherty's films and, according to Grierson, Flaherty was too much the 'poet' to be an effective ('proper') documentarian (1998a: 84–5). In the booklet *The Odyssey of* a *Film-Maker* (1984), Frances Hubbard Flaherty refers, in the context of a discussion of the 'poetic' qualities of her late husband's films, to 'movement' as a fact of life and as the basis of visual 'poetry'. She illustrates the point through mention of a visually 'beautiful film' – *Seifriz on Protoplasm* (1955) by William Seifriz and J. Churchill – which 'shows us under the microscope the rhythmic flow, the measured movement, in protoplasm, the primordial stuff of which we are all made ... The beauty of this film is its simple and profound approach to the rhythmic mystery, taking us on the one hand into physics and chemistry, and on the other hand into the realm of philosophy, religion, poetry' (1984: 57). The basis, then, of this poetically observed reality is its ability to capture 'movement' – the 'rhythmic mystery' of the 'dance of life' – which, according to Flaherty's widow, can 'take us into a new dimension of seeing', which is, in this particular example, only achievable via microcinematography (1984: 56; 58).

The close observations of the movements of microscopic subjects – the basis in this account of visual poetry within the context of a new dimension of seeing – were also traceable in another documentarian, the Australian filmmaker Noel Monkman, a contemporary of Painlevé. Monkman came to underwater photography from his interest in microscopy and throughout the 1920s he filmed on the Great Barrier Reef off the coast of Queensland. Like Painlevé, Monkman built his own subaquatic motion cameras and specially-designed diving equipment. Monkman's first film, *Monkman Microscopics: Strange Monsters in a Drop of Water* (1922), was a study of the microscopic life found in pond water. Monkman, like Painlevé in certain of his films, openly mixed scientific observation and entertainment values, with the stress on the latter developed through the voice-over. 'What is this?' asks the male voice-over in *Monkman Microscopics*, 'A sea serpent, or a Chinese dragon?' The subject in question is the larva of a mosquito, magnified 10,000 times. Throughout his career Monkman produced 28 films, many made in partnership with his wife Kitty and his colleague Bruce Cummings, a radiographer turned naturalist. Monkman's last film, *Invisible Wonders of the Great Barrier Reef* (1961), applies underwater microcinematography to the coral life of the reef and thereby extends a strain of documentaries that create stunning, and often previously unseen, images of aquatic environments which, through an amalgamation of scientific or pseudo-scientific study and magnified images, stress the entertainment value of such footage.[6]

Jacques Cousteau, though he rarely used microphotography, was one of the better-known filmmakers to exploit the potential appeal of such an approach, and detailed attention to spectacular aquatic nature informs *Atlantis* (1991) by Luc Besson. An obvious legacy of Painlevé's microcinema is found in the practices and popularity of *Microcosmos* (1996), a 'day in the life' of insects living in a French meadow. The film, by Claude Nuridsany and Marie Perennou, uses the special effects of time-lapse microcinematography to construct an 'alternative reality' derived from an aesthetic of magnification, close observation and dramatic intervention. More particularly, Painlevé's Surrealist-tinged microcinema is echoed in *The Hellstrom Chronicle* (1971), a documentary which, in its magnified images of the natural world, wittily combines a science fiction-like narrative within a parody of scientific claims to universal knowledge.

Natural science topics, notably those focused on aquatic life forms, constitute a perennial and popular form of programming on numerous television outlets. Science and nature genres regularly appear on the schedules of cable television stations such as Nova, National Geographic and The Discovery Channel, which extend the practices of microcinema in the routine use of 'critter cams' to 'eavesdrop on the hidden world of animals' (Hogarth 2006: 112). More particularly, 'blue chip' productions have extended the practice of close attention to terrestrial and aquatic nature. Within this vein the BBC's Natural History Unit in Bristol is a global leader in natural science television programming. The Unit, which employs up to 300 people, produces around one thousand hours of footage per year and maintains what is, arguably, the largest archive of natural science footage in the world (see Cottle 2004: 89). Established in 1957, the Unit has developed an international reputation for the production of blue chip programmes.

The term 'blue chip nature programming', according to one interpretation, typically refers to 'programmes devoted to observing "spectacular" animal behaviour displayed within "timeless" natural habitats ... [such scenes are] relatively "untainted" by human intervention, whether presenters in front of the camera, producers and animal trainers behind them, or humans interacting with, or on, the "pristine" animal habitats depicted' (Cottle 2004: 88). Such a description, with its emphasis on the minimal presence of a presenter, does not recognise the role within blue chip programmes of a 'personality' such as the ubiquitous David Attenborough, who has figured either before the camera of in voice-over in numerous programmes produced by the BBC's Natural History Unit and other sources, among them *Life on Earth* (1979), *The Living Planet* (1984), *The First Eden* (1987), *Life in the Freezer* (1993), *Attenborough in Paradise* (1996), *State of the Planet* (2001) and *Planet Earth* (2006). More succinctly, and aptly, the term blue chip is used to denote 'big-budget programmes with high production values, perhaps best represented by [the Natural History Unit/Discovery television series] *Blue Planet*' (Kilborn 2006). The series, which deals with the life of the world's oceans, took five years to produce and cost £850,000 per programme, a total of nearly £7 million for the series of eight 50-minute episodes (Cottle 2004: 88). This important series, which was broadcast in the UK in 2001–02, proved popular with viewers and performed 'a function over and above the generation of large ratings. The BBC, though intimately bound up in the changing international production ecology of natural history programmes, also occupies a unique programming space. Symbolically, programmes such as *Blue Planet* can ... help to promote the "public service value" of the BBC' (Cottle 2004: 90).[7] In this relation, Keith Scholey, one-time head of the Natural History Unit, commented that:

> We need to be distinctive, we need to be public service, and we need to claw in larger audiences. And the BBC gets rewarded in all sorts of ways for productions like *Blue Planet* which is important in audience terms and is very, very important in terms of overall BBC public perception; that we are there to provide and to inform, educate and entertain. (Quoted in ibid.)

Scholey's emphasis on a form of natural science programming that simultaneously informs, educates and entertains reflects a shift in the definition of documentary.[8]

Where once, notably within Griersonianism, information and education were stressed as the object of (public service) documentary, the demands of contemporary television programming (and the specific features of natural science programmes), among other forces, results in a situation in which the long-banished notion of entertainment enters into discussions and definitions of 'documentary'. In certain recent forms of natural science programming – namely reconstructions of prehistoric life in shows such as *Walking with Dinosaurs* (1999) and *Walking with Beasts* (2001) – entertainment values are enhanced by, or operate through, spectacular computer generated imagery (see Kilborn 2006). Similarly, in the blue chip *Blue Planet* entertainment (and information) is produced via a visual spectacle reliant on a range of (non-CGI) techniques. The high production values of *Blue Planet* include a music soundtrack by composer George Fenton especially commissioned for the series, and painstakingly set up and edited time-lapse photography. The majority of the 7,000 hours of footage produced for the series was shot on film stock to give a clearer screen image than is achieved with video, though video was used to enhance certain shots. As the series co-director Alastair Fothergill notes, 'video works better [than film] underwater. For *Blue Planet*, being able to film in murky conditions was important ... Video is very good in lowlight [such as] infrared and high-sensitivity conditions' (quoted in Goldsmith 2003: 39).

In particular, the series used close-ups and image magnification to provide access to previously unseen nature. Fothergill underlines the expressive and spectacular characteristics of enlarged shots of aquatic nature when he notes the arresting effect of 'big images' (quoted in ibid.). When footage from *Blue Planet*, originally broadcast on the small screen of television, was projected onto a cinema screen it produced another level of visual effect. Fothergill points to this when he describes a screening of *Blue Planet* in London's Royal Festival Hall, with an orchestra accompanying the projection on a massive cinema screen. 'It was a total wow!' (quoted in ibid.).[9]

Such a 'wow' factor is an integral element of the magnified images in Painlevé's films. In yet another way, the bases of Painlevé's works, particularly his use of an ironic and humorous voice-over and his magnified close-ups of grotesque nature to produce uncanny effects, are variously replicated in the documentary *Cane Toads* (1987), a study of the biology, ecology and environmental impact associated with the introduction of the species to the sugar cane fields of northern Queensland. *Cane Toads* is a rare work which uses humour to depict an environmental disaster in a way that does not detract from the full weight of the situation. The video sleeve notes indicate the film's mix of comedy, ecological information and critique of scientific rationality:

> Australia is being rapidly taken over by a fat ugly creature [that] sees its sole purpose in life as being the pursuit of sexual gratification. *Bufo Marinus* – the cane toad – was imported into Queensland from Hawaii in 1935 for a specific reason – to combat the grey-back beetle that was destroying the sugar crop. The mission failed: the beetle could fly and the cane toad couldn't. Oblivious of its failure the cane toad adapted to its new surroundings and proceeded to breed so rapidly that it has now become a pest of plague proportions ... Could it be that the total conquest of Australia is just a hop, step and a jump away? (Quoted in McKie 1994: 101)

Given the topic – environmental degradation, scientific and bureaucratic mismanagement of the environment, and the rapid ability of the pest to reproduce and further encroach on the habitats of indigenous flora and fauna – a stentorian and preachy narration could have been deemed an appropriate mode of address. Instead, *Cane Toads* (which is subtitled 'An Unnatural History') playfully combines shots from the point of view of a toad, humorous asides concerning toads as pets, and ecological data, presented in a whimsical voice-over. The film mixes comedy, gothic, thriller and horror genres within the context of a documentary that uses 'stereotypical "national" music in the worst travelogue tradition accompanying every different overseas location [in the film], and a children's choir version of "All Things Bright and Beautiful" counterpoints unflattering close-ups of amphibians. *Cane Toads* foregrounds the extremely strange and self-contradictory behaviour of the human species, which ranges from love to unrestricted violence towards the toads' (McKie 1994: 102).

In these and other ways *Cane Toads* meets, if not exceeds, Painlevé's demands for a documentary that encompasses the 'unexpected, the usual, and lyrical' (Painlevé 2000a: 152). In his polemical essay 'The Castration of the Documentary', published in *Les Cahiers du cinéma* in 1953, Painlevé criticises the 'glut' of 'mediocre documentaries' that are 'banal and uninspired' and neither 'challenging' or innovative (2000a: 150). Painlevé's response to such a situation came in the form of instructions to filmmakers published in another polemic, 'The Ten Commandments', which appeared as the notes for a programme of films he organised in 1948 around the title 'Poets of the Documentary'. The list of points includes the admonitions: 'You will not show monotonous sequences without perfect justification', and 'You will abandon every special effect that is not justified' (2000b: 159), a position that incorporates microcinematography, the basis of an aesthetic which he elsewhere justified by labelling the practice a 'cinematic eye' (2000a: 156).

Painlevé's attack on a form of documentary stereotyped as unemotional, lacking 'lyricism', humourless and devoid of expressive imagery, could be read in other contexts as a critique of Griersonian forms bound by expository conventions and in the service of a notion of public 'betterment'. By reacting to a documentary genre which had been reduced to formal sterility, Painlevé set an agenda for an anti-Griersonian mode of documentary, one enacted in *Cane Toads*, an innovative film that in many ways is in direct succession to Painlevé's work. Brian Winston proposes the film as an example of what he calls post-Griersonian documentary (1995: 255), a phrase suggestive of the fact that *Cane Toads*, together with the Surrealist-inflected documentary display of the magnified vision of Painlevé's micro-cinema, constitute productive alternatives to the traditional emphasis on Griersonian forms in English-language documentary film theory.

IMAX and the aquatic

The mixture of natural science, entertainment and magnification within the documentary display of Painlevé's films is reconfigured and reworked within the meeting of natural science subjects, spectatorial attraction and the enlarged image of IMAX technology. As numerous commentators have noted, IMAX is the new cinema of attractions, drawing audiences, as did the original cinematic attractions, to see cinematic wonders and to witness the technology that projects such images (see Gunning 1990: 58). IMAX technology – which projects two- and three-dimensional 70mm images onto large format screens, 21 metres wide and 28 metres high[10] – may be the basis of audience appeal, though the new technology results in a specific outcome, what Paul Arthur has called 'the primacy of the visual' (1996: 79). Informing this point, Charles Acland, a scholar of the technology and economics of IMAX, notes that by drawing upon 'the particularities of nineteenth-century bourgeois perception, IMAX continues to insist upon spectatorial primacy as a form of knowledge' (1998: 434). The various factors implicated here – technology, the visual as spectacle and as a mode of knowledge and entertainment – coalesce in the observation that 'IMAX is about the spectacle of seeing and the technological excess necessary to maintain the spectacle' (Acland 1997: 304).

The emphasis on the dialectic of seeing and technology found in such assessments, while necessarily foregrounding the visual in the form of technologically-enhanced display, typically tends to ignore or deny the referent of the IMAX image. Summarising this position, Acland says of IMAX that the 'actual subject of the film is superfluous' (ibid.). If such were the literal case IMAX films would range across numerous and varied subjects, when in practice the determination of the technology and 'spectatorial primacy' restrict the content of IMAX films to a limited range of topics, notably those which treat natural science or natural history subjects. Films such as *Beavers* (1988) and *Mountain Gorilla* (1991), with their mixture of earnest environmentalism and animal antics, and films about the oceans and their inhabitants (for example, *Nomads of the Deep* (1979), *The Deepest Garden* (1988), *Into the Deep* (1995) and *Deep Sea 3D* (2006)), dominate IMAX production. In these terms, an excessive visual technology is dominantly applied to the representation of natural science subjects, thereby constructing the resultant spectacle as a form of documentary display. The production of such a display within and through IMAX technology implicates the aesthetics and economics, and their connections, of magnification as image enlargement.

'Not so much to mean as to reveal': enlarging 'total cinema'

The theoretical writings of André Bazin frequently form the basis of critical analyses of large-screen visual technology, and Bazin's essay 'The Myth of Total Cinema' (1946) has become a crucial reference in this relation. In this essay Bazin subscribes to the notion of linear causality in history in which, as he argues elsewhere, 'idea' or thought necessitates or directs 'technical means' in the development of cinema. Bazin is not a technological determinist, though his historical schema is teleological, wherein each stage in the development of cinema (sound, colour, depth of field shot and widescreen, for example) presaged and led inevitably to the next phase. The 'myth' of cinema – a concept that Bazin does not necessarily endorse, though numerous critics have interpreted his essay as evidence of an extremely naïve positivism on his part – is, according to Bazin, the notion inspired by cinema's inventors that cinema is ruled by its own 'integral realism' (1967: 17). Such realism drives the technological perfection of the cinematic apparatus towards a 'perfect illusion of the outside world' (1967: 20). According to Bazin, the 'perfect illusion' of reality (an illusion which historically becomes reality) constitutes the premise or 'idea' that cinema's progressive evolutionary stages of development have worked to implement. Such stages, as Bazin points out in his essay, include widescreen technology.

Jean-Louis Comolli is not the only critic to reject Bazin's teleology and to argue that a variety of factors – particularly technology, ideology and the basic consideration of economics – as opposed to any 'idealistic phenomenon', determine the development of the cinematic apparatus.[11] Nevertheless, Bazin's further observations on widescreen cinema, notably in his 1953 essay 'Will Cinemascope Save the Film Industry?' (see 1997), demonstrate that he was not unaware of the role of economic factors in the emergence of widescreen technology. Bazin's essay opens with an acknowledgement that the introduction of CinemaScope and 3-D technology was attended by economic circumstances. However, his analysis then abandons the economy 'since the economy does not determine the essence of the new process, but only provides the occasion for its appearance' (quoted in Spellerberg 1985: 28). Bazin praises CinemaScope's angle of vision as, he argues, approximating a natural one. For Bazin, the productive and positive 'fact' of CinemaScope is implicated with an 'optics of cinema ... defined not only by the proportions of the image, but also by what one can introduce into the frame' (1997: 82). Bazin adds that:

> Unlike the eye, which has a single optical system, the camera has at its disposal a wide variety of lenses covering more or less unlimited angles. In the case of wide angles, the use of short focal lengths partly compensates for the narrowness of the screen. This system has its drawbacks, though, for the more one moves away from the physical properties of the eye, the more obvious are the distortions in perspective. The indisputable advantage of [the anamorphic lens] is its multiplication by two of the angle of its specially developed lens, without modifying the lens's other optical characteristics. What happens when the image is projected onto a wide screen, then, is not only that the viewer's angle of vision gets widened – an angle, moreover, that depends on where he is seated in the theatre – but also that the depth of his perception of photographed reality is genuinely increased. (1997: 83)

In these terms, a 'genuine increase' in the 'perception of reality' (Bazin 1997: 83) results in a closer approximation to reality than that achieved in earlier stages of cinematic development. Such an approximation is nearer to the thing itself – reality. The 'myth' of cinema is never far away for Bazin.

Bazin anticipated the resultant critiques of his stance by materialists such as Comolli when, in his essay, he acknowledged that the 'aesthetic destiny' of cinema does not, 'from a materialistic point of view ... [take] precedence over ... materialistic or commercial [considerations]' (1997: 86). In another way, 'where Bazin found artifice and more reality, the materialists found more hidden illusion and less reality [of the cinema]' (Spellerberg 1985: 29). The arguments of both Bazin and the materialists concerning cinema and reality are complicated by the fact that both positions are based on conceptions of realism operative in fiction film, particularly through reference to the realistic effects of deep focus and the representation of depth of field. Having mentioned that numerous CinemaScope films are documentaries, Bazin immediately returns to an analysis of fiction film and its relationship to CinemaScope. However, Bazin's recognition of documentary points to his inclusion of the form within his all-encompassing term 'film'. Certainly, the conclusion to his essay encapsulates a position that echoes in theories of both documentary and fiction film. Film, Bazin concludes, 'will get even nearer to its profound vocation, which is to show before it expresses, or, more accurately, to express through the evidence of the real. Put yet another way: the cinema's ultimate aim should not be so much to mean as to reveal' (1997: 90–1).

Within his oblique and fleeting references to documentary film, Bazin offers a useful summary of the mode of representation referred to here as documentary display. In Bazin's terms, documentary display can be described as a representation of 'the real' that privileges 'showing' or revelation over the imposition of didactic meaning, or more appropriately, that constructs meaning within and through a form of revelatory display. Such a practice – showing before telling, or a telling through showing – implicates forms of observationalism, a point taken up by Comolli through reference to direct cinema. Writing at a time when direct cinema techniques were dominantly applied within forms of television reportage, Comolli notes that direct cinema stylistics have been applied in both fiction and documentary film and as such the term cannot be restricted (or reduced) to a 'strict reportage' (1980a: 225).

Rather than a presumed objective record of profilmic reality as claimed by its adherents, Comolli notes the *manipulation*, as he put it, of reality within direct cinema. Such a situation, and its associated shift from commentary to reflection, results in a productive approach to reality: 'The movement which takes [direct cinema] across the threshold where it begins to be affected by fiction provokes a contrast effect such that the film-document, even as it takes on an overlay of fiction and is thereby slightly denatured, immediately gains a new value on another level' (1980a: 227). For Comolli, observational '[direct cinema] responds to the flight from reality with a new lease of meaning and coherence and emerges from the dialectic endowed with perhaps greater conviction, its truth reinforced by and because of this detour though the "fictitious"' (ibid.). Comolli confirms that direct cinema – through its manipulations, as opposed to any claim to direct '"contact" with "reality"' – is capable of representing experience (1980a: 243). Comolli argues that:

In *direct cinema* ... the filmed event does not pre-exist the film and the filming, but is produced by it. It is not therefore possible to speak of a 'reality' alien to the film of which the film would be the image, but only of material shot which is all the reality the film will have anything to do with. Editing begins with the material shot, just as the shooting script of a classical film starts from the 'reality' it deals with. *Direct cinema* rejects all a priori form or signification, and all pre-determination and aims, not to reproduce things 'as they are' (as they are intended by the scenario of the film or of 'life' – i.e. of ideology), but positively to transform them, to take them from an unformed, uncinematic stage to the stage of cinematic form. As such, direct cinema emerges in the best instances, not as a model, but as a practice of cinema. (Ibid.; emphasis in original)

The best ends of such a practice, according to Comolli, do not merely 'capture' reality – an approach that opens itself to the reproduction of ideologically-coded existing meanings – but reworks objects and experience through a process of representation which always acknowledges 'the inevitable difference between the filmed image of the object and the object itself' (1980a: 224). In these terms a refusal of (the reproduction of ideologically-laden) meaning results in productive (in the sense of manipulated and revelatory) representations of reality. Ironically, such a conclusion echoes and in some senses parallels the conclusion expressed by Bazin, albeit in a language which is devoid of references to ideology: 'not so much to mean as to reveal'. Such a film practice (in Comolli's emphasis) when applied to nonfictional content is the basis of a documentary display which, among its other forms, is (extending Bazin's analysis of CinemaScope) implicated with the magnified or enlarged images of IMAX.

A certain tendency of the IMAX cinema

Charles Acland evokes Bazin in a summary of IMAX that highlights the capacity of the technology to provide an enhanced illusion of the real. As Acland notes,

IMAX ... takes us another step towards Bazin's objective. Barring the various critiques of Bazin, and of realism as the 'essence' of motion pictures, IMAX is unambiguously a film technology and form designed to create the experience of being there, or getting there, for spectators. Its goal is one of simulation, or hyper-realism, of producing images so real that they offer an illusion of material presence, and of creating the sensation of movement for spectators. This leads IMAX to continue technological development to improve upon the illusion. The conventions of film realism, cinéma vérité and continuity editing are never part of the IMAX promotional material; instead, it refers to the technological innovations in screen size, film stock, film speed, screen curvature, 3-D and architecture. In the end, this becomes its own best argument for investment in its technology; only IMAX film systems can create IMAX film realism. (1998: 431).

Acland's emphasis on the illusion of realism within IMAX points to one component of its revelatory capacity – its emphasis on showing over telling (or telling through showing). Following a line of argument posed by Comolli's materialism, any assessment of the practice and capabilities of cinema must also involve economic factors. In this way both aesthetics and economics are considered within the following analysis of the documentary display of IMAX. The relationship between aesthetics, economics and documentary display is exemplified through reference to the output of MacGillivray Freeman Films, one of the largest and most prolific producers of IMAX films.

MacGillivray Freeman Films was co-founded in 1965 by Greg MacGillivray and his partner, the late Jim Freeman, for the production of nonfictional surf films. After producing numerous works in the genre they turned to the making of large-screen films. The company inaugurated its large-screen work with the 70mm film *To Fly!* (1976), one of the earliest IMAX productions, which made over $100 million at the box office (see Griffiths 2006: 252). The returns were outmatched by the company's *Everest* (1998), produced on a budget of $4.5 million. The film made over $120 million by January 2003, making it the highest-grossing documentary and large-screen film of its time, and the 15th highest-grossing film in the US in 1998 (see ibid.), despite the fact that it appeared on only 32 (large-format) screens that year (see McQuire 2000: 54). Though the productions of MacGillivray Freeman Films encompass a variety of subjects, as exemplified in the aeronautic adventure of *To Fly!* and the variation of a travelogue that is *Everest*, there is, as with IMAX films generally, a marked emphasis on aquatic themes within the company's output, including *The Living Sea* (1995), *Dolphins* (2000) and *Coral Reef Adventure* (2003).

While the films referred to here have all returned healthy profits, based on a ratio of production costs to box office receipts, such a calculation masks the expenses associated with the production and exhibition of IMAX films, notably the fact that the costly filmmaking apparatus requires its own expensive theatre. IMAX producer Stephen Low notes that the costs of producing a 3-D IMAX film are extremely high: 'stock costs are twenty times Hollywood's, and you may get three shots a day, not 50. Even a 30-million-dollar film is difficult when there's only a couple of hundred theatres, once a distributor gets less than 20 per cent of the gate' (quoted in Wolff 1999). The level of returns to distributors was addressed during 2001 in a study funded by the Giant Screen Theater Association that recom-

mended increased efforts to lower film print costs. In comparison to conventional exhibition, where distributors pay the costs of prints, the exhibitors of large-
screen films generally must meet print costs, which, in 2001, ran at $25,000 for a
2-D large-format print and $50,000 for a 3-D print, which at the time were ten to
twenty times the costs of conventional film prints (see DiOrio 2001: 15).

The rising costs associated with IMAX production, distribution and exhibition – evident in part in the 'inflated ticket prices' (Acland 1997: 290) – had led to
reconsiderations of IMAX film exhibition. In 1998 Greg MacGillivray believed that
IMAX films would revive the practice of 'films as road shows' with megasize films
rotating among one hundred or so theatres and attracting residents from a broad
geographic radius. According to MacGillivray at the time: 'I think you will see
[IMAX films] in every city with more than 300,000 people and in some cities with
fewer than that. With nonfiction stories in spectacular settings, it will work really
well' (quoted in Booth 1998: 49). While the optimistic prognosis of numerous local IMAX theatres has not eventuated, the basic economic factors associated with
IMAX – appropriately summarisable in terms of 'money on the screen' (Maltby
& Craven 1995: 24)[12] – have resulted in an emphasis on the practices and effects
of documentary display – 'nonfiction stories in spectacular settings' in MacGillivray's words – as the basic aesthetic and economic strategy of IMAX.

The aesthetics of the IMAX text, which implicate both the sonic and visual
domains, have drawn on, and 'enlarged', many existing features of documentary
film. Following a trend in documentary production wherein celebrity voices are
used to provide narration, the films of MacGillivray and Freeman rely on recognised actors for voice-over narration, for example Liam Neeson for Everest and
Meryl Streep for The Living Sea and Hurricane on the Bayou (2006). Earlier deployment of the practice in works such as the 1987 Dear America: Letters Home from Vietnam (which includes narration by a parade of well-known actors) and, notably,
Ken Burns' The Civil War (1990), and recent expressions of the practice in Penguins
(2005), narrated by Morgan Freeman, and the IMAX Deep Sea 3D, which is narrated
by both Johnny Depp and Kate Winslet, rework an unmodulated, stentorian and
authoritarian 'voice of God' narration. In place of this traditional mode of voice-
over, star-driven narration legitimates content within a process wherein the veracity of information is vouchsafed by the familiar and intimate, and in these terms
trustworthy, celebrity voice.

Just as the sonic realm of narration is revised in such a practice as it is applied
to IMAX films, the visual domain is also vigorously reworked as the central component of the IMAX documentary aesthetic. In this way, for example, the visual
grammar of IMAX exploits the potential of the long take. Greg MacGillivray explains that the 'screen size requires a number of separate eye fixations, so shots
need to be longer to allow the audience to take in the entire image. Quick cuts can

be too jarring' (quoted in Griffiths 2006: 256). The resultant long takes in IMAX filming emphasise an observational 'showing', which within IMAX's 'gigantism', overcomes what David MacDougall (1992–93) has called the problem of the long take, specifically the potential of the shot to result in spectator ennui. The IMAX long take actively involves spectators in an observational image in which they are given the opportunity to linger over objects in the large frame, scanning the enlarged image as they are simultaneously immersed in it.

Reinforcing the visual capacities of IMAX, Paul Virilio describes the technology as a form of 'cataract surgery' wherein the screen is metaphorically transplanted on to the eyes of spectators (1990: 169). Charles Acland provides a number of ways in which this process operates in practice. According to him:

> The Living Sea ... is notable less for its eco-friendly message than for the schools of multicoloured fish, edited and composed in contrasting fashion so that their fluid movements are like watching a firework display. Other images compete for the educational theme of The Living Sea, especially IMAX's stock point of view travelling camera shots, here used to fly over ocean islands, to swim through underwater seascapes, and to participate in a coastguard practice rescue mission. This is not to suggest that these powerful images are incompatible with Meryl Streep's gentle narration about the interconnectedness of oceanic life; rather, through the size and clarity of the image emerges a kind of postcard environmentalism, in which grand vistas of landscapes and animal life appear to be literally brought before you. As the audience learns about 'the living sea', they also experience the pleasure of spectatorial centrality, finding that the power of the IMAX gaze is a mastery over the film subject. (1998: 430)

A slight revision of Acland's conclusion highlights the operation of display implicit in the process he describes, within which an audience learns about the sea through the pleasures of spectatorial activity.

Central to the function of display in this case is, as Acland notes, the point of view shot, which in The Living Sea for example, is used to simulate motion. Within the IMAX point of view shot inquiry, or understanding, is achieved within a visual display that promotes a sense of 'being there' in a physical, almost haptic way that verges on the experience of a theme ride. An almost complete absence in IMAX films of fictional narrative based on characters, a condition stemming from technological restrictions associated with the format, means that the IMAX point of view shot is not deployed in the construction of spectator identification with characters. Instead, it promotes movement, simultaneity and visceral effect (IMAX publicity proclaims that the 'IMAX experience' is the 'next best thing to being there') which results in a vibrant, kinetic display. The IMAX image positions audiences seemingly to move into the image itself. 'The format represents the real so extraordinarily that its effect marries the imperative to the conditional. Just look! ... This is what it *would be like if* you were really there!' (Wollen 1993: 28; emphasis in original).

The continuous immersion of the spectator in the image begs the question of whether the expressive characteristics of the IMAX display changes a spectator's interpretative focus. Certain analyses of CinemaScope have pointed to such an effect in the suggestion that the format opened 'new sights for new ways of thinking' (Charles Barr quoted in Wollen 1993: 29). Within this process the documentary display of IMAX (in a similar way to CinemaScope) leads to, or opens a path for, new or different forms of cognition. The conclusion reinforces the basic operations of Painlevé's microcinema of marine life and IMAX's enlarged images of aquatic nature: a pronounced emphasis on the visual – a technologically-enhanced revelatory 'showing'. The resultant display operative through the enlarged images of Painlevé's microcinema and IMAX cinema reveals previously unseen worlds, and in this way image enlargement and enhancement function as a mode of cognition and understanding. Together, the magnified images of marine life in Painlevé's microcinema and in the expanded screens of IMAX produce a documentary display which radically enhances the basic premise of documentary as a mediation of the real world capable of generating knowledge and understanding.

afterword

Documentary Display: Re-Viewing Nonfiction Film and Video is a study of the expressive, evocative, entertaining and pleasurable capacities of documentary film and video. As such, the book contributes to a new way of seeing – or re-viewing – documentary images, and revises features of theoretical approaches to such imagery, including the tradition in which documentary representation has been confined. Against a Griersonian tradition dominated by 'sober' expository forms, documentary display advances and productively exploits a lineage which, as chapter one explains, was inaugurated by the early cinema of attractions and its connections to avant-gardist representational forms. Reference to documentary display denotes a fertile field of documentary forms and styles and an inclusive theory of the genre of documentary itself. Such a revision of documentary theory and reconsideration of assessments of documentary practice is informed in this book by reference to a range of cases and effects, including the modernist avant-garde and its influences on 'city symphonies' and the city film; direct cinema and rockumentary; varieties of image polysemy, as expressed in found-footage film; a late-twentieth century independent avant-garde and its impact on surf film and video; and the technologies of microcinema and IMAX and their reconfiguration of documentary images of nature.

Display contributes in a positive way to what recent commentators have labelled a 'post-documentary' culture. Brian Winston's use of the term, quoted in the last chapter, evokes a post-Griersonian documentary devoid of the authoritarian, expository positions which underpin the truth claims of Griersonian documentary. John Corner uses the phrase post-documentary in reference to a decisive shift, mainly manifested in the arena of television, towards so-called popular factual entertainment and its formats such as docusoaps and gamedocs. In a similar way, one feature of the new productions – 'a performative, playful element' – is evident in rockumentary, for example, in which, to apply aspects of Corner's analysis of popular factual entertainment, 'self-display is no longer viewable as an attempt to feign natural behaviour but is taken as a performative opportunity in its own right' (2000a).[1] Corner characterises the emergent performative space of popular factual entertainment as 'documentary as diversion' and argues that doc-usoaps and other formats in this category, together with an 'extensive borrowing of the "documentary look" by other kinds of [television] programme [contribute] to a weakening of documentary status' (2000a), the latter a reference to what has traditionally been constructed as the core feature of documentary – its claims on the real.[2]

Contrasting with such an inference, 'diversion' can be seen to constitute one component of a display which productively informs documentary practices in a post- (traditional) documentary culture. Recast in this way, the diversionary aspects of documentary display include, among other features, the corporeal presence as spectacle in city film, rockumentary's intense focus on the bodily performance of rock music, the collagist jump cuts of found-footage film as pleasurable shock, the avant-gardist and affective representational practices of surf film and surf video, and the magnification of nature as arresting attraction. The combination of such moments within documentary display adds weight to Corner's perceptive argument that the 'terms of "seeing others" and "seeing things" on the screen today are very different from those of the defining moments of documentary history [based on] an expository realism' (2000a).

In another way, the potential of display to force a revision of critical assessments of the field of documentary representation is linked to practices which are predicated on entertainment, fun and pleasure, and which rework the ways in which documentary addresses its audiences. Whereas the Griersonian documentary constructed the audience in terms of 'the public' to be educated (or less generously, indoctrinated), documentary display variously positions audiences as rowdy and unrestrained (as in surf film and rockumentary), as seeking adventure and previously unavailable sights (as in the magnification of aquatic nature), as travellers and ethnographers (as in the new global city film), and all of these characteristics in contemporary found-footage film. In each case the 'status of documentary' is affirmed in the sense that display also positions the viewer as an inquiring subject seeking to understand specific social acts and a range of social, historical and natural science topics. The outcome is that informational or knowledge effects are often attenuated though not erased within the pleasures audiences derive from the kinetic movement within the frame and between frames, the meditative stare of the extended long take, the presence of the performative body, and varieties of image enlargement, among other stylistic capacities of display. Historically, the ability of documentary to impart information and to 'educate' has been pursued through expository forms in which the viewer was informed or told of experiences via a voice-over, onscreen presenter, or titles. In place of such a 'telling', documentary display emphasises 'showing' – the capacities and attractions and symbolic properties of the image and its contents. A heavy-handed exposition 'tells' us something about the world; the 'showing' of display represents experience within an aesthetic that is capable of being vibrant, affective and expressive, and which can in places embody the visually 'excessive' in terms of image manipulation and visual effects.

Visual excess – the excessive – refers to moments which are not contained by narrative; moments of spectacle which 'break out' of, or away from, the narrative. An example of this process is the song and dance routine of the musical film genre, wherein the narrative is held in suspension in the presence of the spectacle of singing and dancing. Richard Dyer refers to the qualities of such sequences in terms of 'colour, texture, movement, rhythm, melody, camerawork' which jointly create within the musical an impression of utopian abundance and energy (Dyer 1985: 224). Such moments are enjoyed for their effects or impact separate from any dominant narrative arrangements. As Bill Nichols insists, such sequences and moments are not aberrant, and the 'notion that what is excess lacks organisation or pattern is disreputable. It may be better to say that in narrative films excess is what does not fit into a given analytic scheme; it is [what remains] when we agree upon limits for what will pass as information' (1991: 141). In this way, Charles Altman argues that 'the more a static notion of dominance [within a text] leads us to concentrate on a specific definition of textual unity, the more elements there are that fall outside the bounds of that unity ... Unless we recognise the possibility that excess – defined as such because of its refusal to adhere to a system – may itself be organised as a system, then we will hear only the official language and forever miss the text's dialect, and dialectic' (1989: 347). Display attends to dialect and dialectic. In its connections to spectacle, a rich and productive documentary display functions in excess to documentary's narrativised argumentative drive.

Such a condition marks the continuing links between documentary display and the early cinema of attractions with which it shares a number of features. The earliest films, those of the Lumière brothers, demonstrate certain characteristics of the attractions that were developed in so-called primitive cinema. The 'documentary' effect of the Lumières' *actualités* was available in attempts by the brothers to catch life *sur le vif* and was present in the films' demotic and everyday subject matter: feeding a baby, rowing a boat out of a coastal harbour, tearing down a brick wall. Apart from the novelty of the new technological apparatus of cinema and its moving images, early audiences derived other pleasures from the first screenings. It has been noted that with *Le déjeuner de bébé* (*Baby's Breakfast*, 1895) 'spectators were transfixed, not by the animated figures themselves, but by the rustling leaves in the background. Similarly in *Barque sortant du port* [*Boat Leaving a Harbour*, 1896] it was the random movement of the waves which attracted attention, and in *Démolition d'un mur* [*Demolishing a Wall*, 1896] a free-floating brickdust that filled the air' (Macdonald & Cousins 1996a: 4).[3] While the short films showed life, and constructed mini-narratives from everyday experience, it was the 'excessive' that captivated audiences – those moments of rustling leaves, waves on the sea and dust in the air that exceed the slight narratives and any accompanying truth claims. In a related way, documentary display's representation of reality exceeds or transcends narrative and argument to present captivating visual images of a world which itself constantly refuses all representation. In this sense all visual representation is evanescent, a lingering image of uncontainable experience. Documentary display is the hint of the magnitude of this experience.

notes

introduction

1 Nichols describes exposition as the 'dominant mode' of documentary in 'Documentary and the Coming of Sound' (1995). Brian Winston critiques the dominance of Griersonianism in his book *Claiming the Real: The Documentary Film Revisited* (1995).

2 The histories of these forms are examined in Beattie (2004).

3 Jonathan Bignall discusses the 'end of documentary' claim in *Big Brother: Reality TV in the Twenty-First Century* (2005: 26).

4 Laura Mulvey discusses 'stillness' in the moving images of film and video in *Death 24X a Second: Stillness and the Moving Image* (2006).

5 In many ways this argument is a legacy of Grierson's insistence on documentary as a form of publicly shared knowledge and a tool for citizenship.

chapter one

1 Grierson used the phrase in 'The Documentary Producer', a paper written for *Cinema Quarterly* in 1933. See Higson (1995: 191).

2 This point is discussed in Beattie (2004: chapter 2).

3 The crux of Anstey's review of *Listen to Britain*, as Andrew Higson points out, is that it was 'good art, but bad propaganda!' (1984: 24).

4 Brian Winston convincingly makes this case in *Claiming the Real: The Documentary Film Revisited* (1995: part 3).

5 Jeffrey Youdelman has made this point, which, in his support of exposition, he insists is misguided. He is quoted in Bruzzi (2000: 46).

6 This assessment is a paraphrase of Bill Nichols' observation in *Representing Reality: Issues and Concepts in Documentary* (1991: 109).

7 A productive starting point for an analysis of the sonic pleasures derivable from documentary film is the music soundtrack accompanying foundational works of documentary film. Hanns Eisler's music for Joris Ivens' film *The 400 Million* (1939) and Hum-

phrey Jennings' sonic innovations in *Listen to Britain* (1942) offer useful examples for such an analysis. The expansion of the sonic realm within the Hollywood text, and the notion of sonic 'shock', are recent developments in this field. On the former see Sergi (2001), and on the latter see Chion (1994).

8   Gunning together with André Gaudreault first used the term 'cinema of attractions' at the 1985 Colloquium on Film History at Cerisy. The paper was published as 'Le cinema des premier temps: un defi a histoire du film?' (in Aumont, Gaudreault & Marie 1989). Gunning has refined and further defined the term in 'The Cinema of Attractions: Early Film, its Spectator and the Avant-Garde' (1990); 'An Aesthetic of Astonishment: Early Film and the (In)Credulous Spectator' (1994); and '"Now You See it, Now You Don't": The Temporality of the Cinema of Attractions' (2004).

9   See the undated facsimile of the 1812 edition of *On the Sublime and the Beautiful*. Scott MacDonald, for example, refers extensively to the 'visual sublimity' of the film's imagery in *The Garden in the Machine: A Field Guide to Independent Films about Place* (2001).

10 This interpretation of the Burkean sublime is indebted to an analysis of Burke's ideas by Novak (1980).

11 The concept of the sublime in relation to film is examined in Freeland (1999).

12 A selection of such criticism is quoted in Erickson (2005: 14).

chapter two

1   Scott Bukatman elaborates various perspectives on 'kaleidoscopic' visuality in a range of texts, including city films, in 'Kaleidoscopic Perceptions' (2003). On 'rhythm' in the city symphony see, for example, Kolaja & Foster (1965); Medhurst & Benson (1981); and Schobert (2003). The metaphor of 'rhythm' was, perhaps inevitably, implicated with descriptions of 1920s city films as 'city symphonies'. The word 'symphony' was a common part of avant-garde film production in Weimar Germany. Viking Eggerling's experiments in 'revolving pictures' resulted in his *Diagonal Sinfonie* in 1924. His collaborator Hans Richter extended the musical metaphor in the title of his films *Ryththmus 21* (1921) and *Rhythmus 23* (1923). Prior to his *Berlin: Symphony of a Great City* Ruttmann made four abstract films informed by music: *Opus I-IV* (1919–23). The 'symphony' popularised by *Berlin* led to further experiments in 'visual music', among them Richter's *Renn-symphonie* (*Racing Symphony*, 1928–29) and *São Paulo, Symphonie d'un métropole* by Rudolph Rex and Adalberto Kemeny (1929). Soon after the completion of his *Chelovek s kino-apparatom* (*The Man with a Movie Camera*, 1929) Dziga Vertov published a statement in which he argued that his film is constructed in the 'form of a visual symphony'. The statement is reprinted in Michelson (1984).

Tracing a lineage for the city symphonies of the 1920s to avant-garde formalist experiments raises the question of origins of the city symphony form, a point which has attracted a degree of critical attention. Most critics concerned with this question propose Cavalcanti's *Rien que les heures*, a film completed before *Berlin*, though not premiered until after the release of Ruttmann's film, as a precursor. Annette Michelson presents a more cogent answer to the question of origin when she notes that in 1926 Mikhail Kaufman made the documentary *Moscow, a day in the life of the city*, a structure which, it seems, influenced both *Berlin* and *The Man with a Movie Camera* (see 1984: xxiv).

2 The absence of people within analyses of the city film is exemplified in Paul Arthur's study of the form in terms of 'categories' and 'inventories' of architectural adornment (see 2005a: 45–60). A similar analysis is undertaken by Scott MacDonald in 'The City as Motion Picture', in his *The Garden in the Machine: A Field Guide to Independent Films about Place* (2001).

3 Vertov, in return, reserved his 'sharpest and most aggressive polemic attacks ... for the "art film", that compromised product of aesthetic Menshevism represented most dangerously, in his view, by Eisenstein's work' (Michelson 1979: 32).

4 With reference to film theory of the 1970s and 1980s, Laura Mulvey's influential paper from 1975 on the look in fictional cinema ignores the look back.

5 Grierson made this comment in 1935. A number of documentary films produced within the context of the British Documentary Movement around that time depicted mine work, among them Jack Holmes' *The Mine* (1935) and Cavalcanti's *Coal Face* (1936). More particularly Grierson was most likely reflecting on *Industrial Britain* (1931–32), a film that he co-directed with Flaherty, which includes a sequence on coal mining.

6 Siegfried Kracauer identifies a cycle of 'cross section' films in his *From Caligari to Hitler: A Psychological History of the German Film* (1947: 187).

7 The paraphrase is of a statement by William Uricchio quoted in MacDonald (2001: 153).

8 Susan Buck-Morss (1986) argues that male authors have consistently interpreted women in the modern urban context in terms of the figure of the prostitute. Janet Wolff (1985) maintains that male authors have generally failed to recognise the ways in which women experience modernity. Patrice Petro (1989) addresses both the absence and the stereotyping of women in Weimar film and its criticism.

9 Gleber refers to an unpublished manuscript by Hake as the source of her comments. Hake's argument was subsequently published as 'Urban Spectacle in Walter Ruttmann's *Berlin, Symphony of the Big City*' (1994).

10 Kracauer's references to cinema, particularly the Weimar cinema of Ruttmann's *Berlin*, as a 'mass ornament' that exploits visual pleasures over cognition constitutes a criticism of the narrative of Ruttmann's film. See Kracauer (1947). In *Theory of Film* Kracauer decries what he sees as the lack of (narrative) 'content' in Ruttmann's film (1960: 207).

11 Malcolm Turvey discusses Vertov's representation of machinery in 'Can the Camera See? Mimesis in "Man with a Movie Camera"' (1999).

12 In many cases charges of fascism against Ruttmann are related to the fact that he stayed in Germany during Hitler's rise to power and was recruited to contribute films to Hitler's propaganda projects. Biography is used *ex post facto* as a way of maintaining that Ruttmann's early films reflect fascist concerns. Biography or the mechanical visual metaphor are not as persuasive as clues to an emerging fascism in Ruttmann's work as is *Berlin*'s satirical and scathing critique of the Weimar Republic's liberalism and modernity.

13 Barber states that the camera was concealed in a suitcase. Helmut Weihsmann comments that the camera was camouflaged in a box which was wheeled along the streets and boulevards (1997: 22).

14 Emerging rights to privacy and the deployment of cameras at the turn of the twentieth century are discussed in Gunning (1995) and (1999: 56); and Mensel (1999).

15 Nicole Brenez's remarkably informative and important essay 'À Propos de Nice and the Extremely Necessary, Permanent Invention of the Cinematic Pamphlet' assesses Vigo's film in relation to subsequent and recent city films, including a number of city films focused on the Middle East, the subject of the latter part of this chapter. The essay, translated from the French by Adrian Martin, appears in the valuable source Rouge (no. 6, 2005), an online journal co-edited by Martin. See http://www.rouge.com.au/.

16 The evocative phrase 'performance of the real' comes from John Corner in his discussion of televisual popular factual entertainment (2002).

17 Hansen notes that a central feature of the early so-called cinema of attractions was 'above all, an openly exhibitionist tendency epitomized by the recurring looks of actors at the camera' (1987: 180). The return look in New York City film is a core characteristic of the genre's nonfictional cinema of attractions, and what is referred to here as documentary display.

18 In most cases critical attention to Thompson's film has focused on the use of trick photography to provide 'visual interest' and, consequently, the place of the corporeal within the film is denied (see, for example, MacDonald 2001: 163). Such an approach echoes Kracauer's description (and denunciation) of Ruttmann's Berlin, a point carried in MacDonald's characterisation of N.Y., N.Y as a film which 'is as detached from particular lives as Ruttmann's Berlin: A Symphony of a Big City' (ibid.). Contrary to such claims, just as Ruttmann's film is structured around the actions of the (female) inhabitants of Berlin, so too the visual capacity of Thompson's film is built around the presence of the corporeal. The opening segments, for example, depicting the beginning of the day, are evoked by a man stretching after a night's sleep, followed by a close-up of teeth being brushed, and the accelerating pace of the day is constructed within images of pedestrian traffic in Manhattan, while the start of the day's work is signalled by shots of hands at a typewriter. Thompson's film lacks the open look at the camera which is deployed as a structural device in the films of Rudy Burkhardt and Weegee though it does rally forms of embodiment as a central component of the visual organisation of the city film.

19 The reference to a 'fractured travelog' is from Arthur (2005a: 52).

20 Richard Barsam (1992) puts the production date at 1950, Scott MacDonald (2001) puts it at 1952.

21 The phrase 'descriptive poetics' is from Wilkinson, 'Hasta la victoria siempre', Senses of Cinema, at http://sensesofcinema.com/contents/01/17/cteq/hasta.

22 The Griersonian representation of the 'victim' is discussed in Winston (1988).

23 The phrase 'cognitive mapping' is by Fredric Jameson (1991).

24 British urban planning films are discussed in Gold and Ward (1994) and Bullock (1997).

25 Fredric Jameson discusses the concept of what he calls national allegory in 'Third-World Literature in the Era of Multinational Capitalism' (1986).

26 The French publisher Gallimard has recently published Malle's notebooks from his

trip to India, wherein Malle expands on his observations on *Calcutta* (see Malle 2005).

27 Ostor, Gardner's collaborator on the film, refers to the individuals featured in the film as 'characters' (see 1994). His essay provides a detailed explication of the film's sequences.

28 Brakhage (2003) pays particular attention to the film's skein of metaphorical allusions.

29 The debate for and against *Forest of Bliss*, which took place mainly in the pages of the SVA (*Society for Visual Anthropology*) *Newsletter* in the late 1980s and sporadically throughout the 1990s in the *Newsletter*'s successor, the *Visual Anthropology Review*, is set out in Mac-Dougall (2001: 69) and Merman (1997: 50).

30 Marcus Banks' observations on the interpretative strategies applied by ethnographic scientists to ethnographic film exposes the unsophisticated position implicit in the comments by Ruby and Moore: 'In my own experience of watching films with other social scientists I have noticed a pronounced desire to read film as a sequence of animated photographs, each accompanied by explanatory narration. When this desire cannot be fulfilled, as in *Forest of Bliss*, the tendency seems to be a retreat into incomprehension' (2001: 22–3).

31 Nichols casts the distinction in terms of 'social science canons of evaluation and cultural theory modes of interpretation' and argues that the 'adoption of reflexive, text-centered strategies in many cross-cultural forms of representation has yet to be matched by a comparable adoption of cultural theory in ethnographic film criticism' (1994: 80).

32 Ruby tempered his assessment of the place of the 'artistic' within ethnographic film-making – though not his criticisms of Gardner's work – in his essays collected as *Picturing Culture: Explorations of Film and Anthropology* (2000). The argument that *Forest of Bliss* resists categorisation as 'ethnographic film' has been made by Peter Loizos in his book *Innovation in Ethnographic Film: From Innocence to Self-Consciousness, 1955–1985* (1993: 162). Loizos presented a variation of the same argument in an earlier work, 'Admissible Evidence? Film in Anthropology' (1992).

33 Reflecting on Charles Baudelaire's writings, Benjamin drew a parallel between city strolling and watching film in terms of a series of 'shocks' registered by the spectator during both experiences (1983: 132). According to Benjamin in his 'Artwork' essay, cinema irrupts within urban life, producing its own version of shock, notably in relation to the visual impact of montage. Benjamin's notion of the cinematic shock-effect is discussed in Hansen (1987) and Buck-Morss (1992).

34 The term 'sensory reports' is by Laura Marks (2000), quoted by Naficy (2001: 28).

chapter three

1 'Rockumentary' as it is conceived here primarily refers to nonfictional works based on a concert performance by a rock performer or rock band(s), or those which mix concert performances by a rock musician or bands with scenes of the musician(s) off-stage. This loose description is intended to distinguish 'rockumentary' from numerous closely aligned works, especially those which have been spawned by the rise of DVD as

the major home format for visual entertainment. As one reviewer of music DVDs notes, 'DVD always runs the risk of turning into a dustbin for live [music] shows' (Sweeting 2004: 134). Rockumentary is distinguishable from outtakes of performances (frequently culled from 'live' television shows, so-called television music specials). Further, the description of rockumentary employed here sets the form apart from promotional videos such as those produced for MTV, analyses of the music industry or musicology, and histories of musical genres such as rock or the blues.

Rock music is not the exclusive musical form enacted in 'rockumentary', though for the sake of convenience the popular form of music referred to as rock is appropriated to serve as the label for various popular contemporary music styles represented in observational documentary forms and variants.

2   Although Scorsese has become best known for his fictional films, he began his filmmaking career working on nonfictional rock films. He was an assistant director and principal editor on *Woodstock* (1970), and in 1971 he was associate producer of *Medicine Ball Caravan*, a film of a US tour undertaken by assorted rock bands, among them The Youngbloods. In 1972 he was an advisor to the production *Elvis on Tour*. In 2005 he released *No Direction Home*, a biographical study of Bob Dylan which heavily utilises footage shot by D.A. Pennebaker. Scorsese's recent work includes a documentary on the Rolling Stones (*Shine a Light*, 2008).

3   In the infrequent instances when rockumentary is mentioned in film and television history it is interpreted as a moment within the broader history of American direct cinema. In this way the film historians David Bordwell and Kristin Thompson have argued that rockumentary is the 'most widespread use of Direct Cinema' (1997: 668), and Brian Winston has noted that direct cinema 'made the rock performance/tour movie into the most popular and commercially viable documentary form thus far' (1995: 52).

4   Pennebaker's study of Bob Dylan during his 1965 tour of England was released as *Dont Look Back* (no apostrophe).

5   The putative distinctions between American direct cinema and French *cinéma vérité* are analysed in Beattie (2004: chapter 5).

6   Dick Fontaine of Granada Television's *World in Action* (1963–99) commissioned the Maysles brothers to the make the film. Fontaine's own film of the Beatles in the US – *Yeah, Yeah, Yeah!* (1964) – was, according to Stummer, 'the first *cinéma vérité*-style documentary ... on British TV' (2004: 12).

7   As Steve Neale points out, *Seven Brides for Seven Brothers* (1954) and *Oklahoma!* (1955) can also be considered as musicals and westerns (2000: 166). However, these films more rigorously integrate components of the musical genre than is the case in *Paint Your Wagon*, with its ill-conceived inclusion of Lee Marvin singing, among other blunders.

8   Barsam pointed to arguments concerning direct cinema's failure to contextualise historical conditions when he noted that 'some viewers [of direct cinema] recognized it as art while they still seemed to yearn for the Griersonian interpretative viewpoint against which direct cinema developed' (1992: 333).

9   Nichols has stated that 'I use "social actor" to stress the degree to which individuals represent themselves to others; this can be construed as performance' (1991: 42).

10 Forms of popular factual entertainment such as docusoaps and gamedocs are analysed in Beattie (2004). Henry Bial notes that 'performative' and 'performativity' are frequently used in critical analyses 'to describe a performance without the connotations of artificiality or superficiality that accompany the world "theatrical"' (2004: 145). Bial's description of performativity is heuristic, and lacks, for example, the theoretical sophistication of reformulations by Jacques Derrida and Judith Butler of John Austin's arguments concerning the performative. Nevertheless, Bial's description grounds disparate usages of the term 'performative' as used here and is thus a useful way to understand the concept.

11 Dylan's parody of his own stage persona is continued in the fictional film *Masked and Anonymous* (2003), in which he plays an ageing rock star, Jack Fate. The title of the film is a reference to the impossibility of knowing the Fate character and, by extension, to the elusiveness of the Dylan persona. This elusiveness is extended in Todd Haynes' film *I'm Not There* (2007).

12 Albert Maysles' association with the Rolling Stones continues in the current era. He is a cameraman on *Shine a Light*, Martin Scorsese's documentary on the Rolling Stones.

13 In Robert Frank's *Cocksucker Blues* (1973), another rockumentary involving the Rolling Stones, the notion of uncontrolled cinema and performance is pushed in another direction. In the film Frank, not a professed practitioner of direct cinema, produced an uncontrolled and unfettered representation of the Stones' riotous 1972 tour of the US. Through an absence of directorial intervention in the profilmic scene, the film documents various illicit backstage antics. Frank's ability to 'open' backstage actions to the type of attention typically given in the rockumentary to onstage performance produces a revelatory insight into censorious events. The effectiveness of this representation was demonstrated in the fact that the film was embargoed by the band and has rarely been publicly screened.

14 The historian Milton Viorst places the events at the Altamont concert within what he describes as 'the days of death' (1979: 523).

15 Aspects of Kael's criticisms are echoed in Albert Goldman's review of the film (1970) for the *New York Times* (see 1992).

16 Kenneth Anger's film *Scorpio Rising* is analysed in this volume within chapter 4.

17 Such questions in effect motivated Kael's review, 'Beyond Pirandello' (1970).

18 In this case a voice-over commentary, as opposed to interviews, may have provided a clearer exposition. Scorsese's own commentary on American cinema for the BFI series on national cinemas (*A Personal Journey with Martin Scorsese through American Cinema*, 1995) and for his documentary series *My Voyage to Italy* (2001) are, in contrast to his interview technique in *The Last Waltz*, erudite and engaging.

19 'Backstage' rehearsals are a central component of non-direct cinema approaches. Jean-Luc Godard's *One Plus One* (1968) uses scenes of the Rolling Stones rehearsing their song 'Sympathy for the Devil' as the film's central structuring device.

20 The emphasis on the visual over the sonic in *Don't Look Back* results in the fact that the film rarely includes a complete version of a song.

21 Andrew Goodwin reinforces the point when he states with reference to MTV that 'It is clear that the visuals often remain subordinate to the rhythm of the music, thus re-

versing the conventional cinematic relations between visual narrative and "illustrative" soundtrack' (1987: 41).

22 The formal characteristics of punk cinema are discussed in Buchsbaum (1981); Sargeant (1995); Thompson (2004); and, most importantly, James (1996).

23 Other documentations of punk music and the punk subculture in the US include Amos Poe's *Night Lunch* (1975) and *Blank Generation* (1976); Lech Kowalski's *D.O.A* (1981); Penelope Spheeris's *The Decline of Western Civilization 1* (1981), *The Decline of Western Civilization 2: The Metal Years* (1988), *The Decline of Western Civilization 3* (1998); and Dirk Dirksen's *Dead Kennedys* (1984).

24 Despite the absence of media exposure, Fugazi sold over 200,000 copies of its albums through its own music label.

25 This is according to Jem Cohen (October 1998) in an untitled and unpaginated booklet accompanying the DVD version of *Instrument* (Dischord Records, Washington, DC, 1999 and 2001).

26 Stephen Mamber first used the term in his analysis of the narrative structures of direct cinema (1974: 115).

27 See Berlinger (2004) for a discussion of this issue.

chapter four

1 Arthur (2005a: 45–60) is typical of this critical practice.

2 For a dismissive reaction to the film see Powers (1988), and for an approving critique of the film see Dempsey (1988–89).

3 Marks also discusses the Flaherty session elsewhere (see 1996).

4 The point is recognised in Skoller (2005).

5 Recently Arthur revised his impression of easy access to sources. 'Greater emphasis on intellectual property rights ... has created obstacles for continued easy access to archival materials', he has noted (2005b: 24).

6 Nichols makes the suggestion in relation to the function of 'realist' segments in collage films (1996: 57).

7 Recontextualisation shares certain aspects of the method the Situationists called detournement, the 'undoing' or 'turning away' – the reconfiguration – of images circulated by corporate culture. In 'Methods of Detournement', Guy Debord and Gil Wolman argue that the practice is 'not limited to correcting a work or to integrating diverse fragments of out-of-date works into a new one; one can also alter the meaning of those fragments in any appropriate way' (1981: 9).

8 John Fiske (1986; 1987) has celebrated the 'open' (in Eco's terms), polysemic, character of television and its ability to produce subversive or resistant readings. Posing his arguments against critical positions forged within British cultural studies, he admits that the potential for such interpretations are contained by the limitations of preferred readings. Ambiguity does not here refer to the 'open' text; it is a form of polysemy constituted through the construction of histories from source footage which simultaneously critique the sources used in their construction.

9 Historical context reinforced Baldwin's criticism of history as conspiracy. *Tribulation 99* was released a few months before Oliver Stone's *JFK* (1991), thereby capitalising on and critiquing cinematic conspiracy theories in general and those surrounding the Kennedy Administration in particular.

10 Conner has, in turn, noted his debt to Joseph Cornell. Cornell's *Rose Hobart* (1936–39) was seminal in the development of found-footage filmmaking as an avant-gardist documentary practice. See Sitney (1990) for an examination of Cornell's films.

11 Raymond Durgnat describes *Scorpio Rising* as 'sometimes a documentary, sometimes an apprehension of occult correspondences and connections' (1989: 33).

12 As a child Anger acted alongside Mickey Rooney in the version of *A Midsummer Night's Dream* extracted in *Scorpio Rising*.

13 Released between Anger's *Cosmic Ray* and *Scorpio Rising*, Jack Smith's *Flaming Creatures* (1962–63) also used 'found' songs – taken from film soundtracks – as an ironic accompaniment and counterpoint to his images.

14 The scene is replicated in Paul Schrader's *American Gigolo* (1980) in which the central male character, a 'gigolo', lays out a suit of expensive attire and slowly and fastidiously dresses in the clothes. The scene is accompanied by the heavy-handed theme song 'Call Me', a love song which is also a pun on the life of the 'call girl/boy'.

chapter five

1 Certain connections between surf texts and the counterculture are analysed in Booth (1994; 1996).

2 In this case the experience is more a form of 'jouissance' than 'plaisir'. As John Corner defines Roland Barthes' use of the term, the sensual pleasure which is jouissance is 'intense ... generating emotions which are at least temporarily out of control' (1999: 100). Such emotions are manifest in an uncontrollable, unruly, audience.

3 Chuck Kleinhaus discusses the New American Cinema as a 'movement [that] ranged from short, visually complex experimental works through *cinéma-vérité* documentary to unique dramatic features' (1998: 313). Curiously, he includes Bruce Brown's *The Endless Summer* (1964) within the New American Cinema, a film that does not sit easily with the categories he has outlined.

4 James applies this description within an analysis of punk videos and pornographic videos. As the analysis here makes clear, the production and distribution of such works in many ways parallels the production and distributive practices of independent surf videographers.

5 A number of critiques have sought to identify and clarify surfing and the surfing lifestyle as a politically adversarial activity. Arguably, the boldest attempt to frame surfing as a textually and politically subversive practice is found in Fiske, Hodge and Turner (1987). The question 'Can surfing be genuinely transgressive, an alternative to hegemonic capitalist processes?' is addressed in Lewis (1998).

6 Though comprised of music from a variety of bands the soundtrack is integrated through a commonality of themes expressed in various song titles: 'Sure Feels Good'; 'Open Up

Your Heart'; 'Making it on Your Own'; 'I'm Alive'; 'Come with Me'. The emphasis in the titles on an unfettered personal utopianism reflects and extends the film's content.

7   Another of Falzon's films is *Metaphysical* (1996), a record of the Quiksilver Pro 1996 surf contest in East Java. Falzon's work is examined in Collins (1995); Kidman (n.d; in a magazine published in association with the release of the video by the same name); and Falzon's *Morning of the Earth*, a colour magazine devoted to the film (n.d).

8   In its original context Arthur is talking of the films of Jonas Mekas.

9   Thoms' review originally appeared in the underground press in Australia in 1972.

10 Kubrick is said to have requested a personal print of *Crystal Voyager* (see Shearer 1999: 20).

11 Greenough's career is surveyed in Holmes (1976); Gross (1999); Shearer (1999); and McMillen (2005).

12 Fredric Jameson sees video during this period as an emergent 'cultural dominant' and privileged form (1991: 67).

13 The connections between power surf videos and hardcore punk music extends to ex-tra-textual situations. It is becoming increasingly common for power surf videos to be screened at hardcore music concerts; for example, the films of Taylor Steele are often screened prior to concerts by the bands Frenzal Rhomb and Pennywise, and Tim Bony-thon's *Biggest Wednesday: Condition Black* (1998) screened in support of performances by the band Midnight Oil.

14 Freeman and MacGillivray later formed MacGillivray Freeman Films to produce IMAX films, as analysed in chapter 6 of this volume.

15 McCoy has also profiled professional surfer Wayne Lynch, in *A Day in the Life of Wayne Lynch* (1977), which was edited by David Lourie, an American avant-garde filmmaker then residing in Australia. According to Nat Young's autobiography, *A Day in the Life of Wayne Lynch* incorporates footage shot by McCoy for a film Young made in association with Lourie, *Fall Line* (1977). McCoy's film was released before *Fall Line*, and thus, according to Young, eclipsed the content of his film (Young 1998: 313–14).

16 The band Powderfinger, in turn, included a Jack McCoy surf film as an extra feature of the DVD *These Days* (2004) of the band's concert footage.

17 Quoted in volume four of *50 Years of Surfing on Film* (1996), a series of productions produced by the *Surfer's Journal* and screened in the US on the Outdoor Life Network.

chapter six

1   However, certain subsequent definitional processes of documentary were more inclusive. Nature films clearly fall within the description of documentary devised in 1947 by the World Union of Documentary Filmmakers (WUDF), an organisation created in Brussels by Henri Langlois which (ironically) included Grierson in its membership. According to the WUDF, a documentary is 'any film that documents real phenomena or their honest and justified reconstruction in order to consciously increase human knowledge through rational or emotional means and to expose problems and offer solutions from an economic, social or cultural point of view' (quoted in Painlevé 2000 a: 149).

2   Configurations of science and cinema, and the aesthetics of science film, are also evident in the work of Dutch filmmaker Jan Cornelis Mol, a contemporary of Painlevé (see Wahlberg 2006).

3   See Painlevé (1932; 1967).

4   Connections between documentary and the international avant-garde in the twentieth century are examined by Nichols (2001).

5   The most extensive analysis of *Documents* is the recent book *Undercover Surrealism: Georges Bataille and DOCUMENTS* (Ades & Baker 2006). Important essays on the journal include Clifford (1988) and Hollier and Ollman (1992).

6   Monkman's films and his career are discussed in Love (2000).

7   The popularity of the series is demonstrated in the fact that it was watched in the UK by 13 million viewers, making it the most watched series on British television after the long-running soap operas *Coronation Street* (1960–) and *EastEnders* (1985–) (Goldsmith 2003: 42).

8   Changing definitions of documentary resulting from the proliferation of nature programming such as *Blue Planet* have been reflected in a (renewed) critical anxiety over whether nature and so-called wildlife programmes 'are really documentaries'. See Bousé (1998) for a discussion of the question. The point is also raised in Aldridge and Dingwall (2003) and in Macdonald (2006). Just as representations of nature, or 'wildlife', have been situated within specific slots in film production and TV programming, so, too, have various critical responses to such work tended to locate it as a form which, while grounded in 'traditional documentary', is a category of nonfiction representation with specific features, notably a high degree of 'entertainment value'. See Mitman (1999); Bousé (2000); and Burt (2002).

9   Footage shot for *Blue Planet* was subsequently re-edited and released for the cinema screen in the form of the film *Deep Blue* (2005).

10 The dimensions of a 35mm screen are 4.6 metres by 8.6 metres. An IMAX 70mm screen in Jakarta, Indonesia is 21.5 metres by 28.3 metres.

11 Comolli presented his arguments in various French publications in the early 1970s. One of the most accessible sources for his ideas in English is Comolli (1980b).

12 Maltby and Craven use the phrase to refer to the economic practices of Hollywood though it is clear that it is also an apt paraphrase of the economic directives of IMAX.

afterword

1   See Corner (2000a) for an elaboration of the notion of a 'post-documentary' culture.

2   The core of documentary as [Griersonian] 'claims on the real' and the limitations of this concept are extensively and persuasively critiqued by Brian Winston (1995).

3   According to Macdonald and Cousins it was the future filmmaker Georges Méliès who made these comments on the Lumières' audience. Siegfried Kracauer suggests that it was 'the contemporaries of Lumière' who noted audience reactions to seeming incidentals in the image (1960: ix).

bibliography

Acland, C. (1997) 'IMAX in Canadian Cinema: Geographic Transformation and Discourses of Nationhood', *Studies in Cultures, Organizations, and Societies*, 3, 289–305.

_____ (1998) 'IMAX Technology and the Tourist Gaze', *Cultural Studies*, 12, 3, 429–45.

Adams, A. (1999) 'Behind the Screens', *The City Paper* (Philadelphia), 29 April–6 May, 5.

Ades, D. and S. Baker (2006) *Undercover Surrealism: Georges Bataille and DOCUMENTS*. Cambridge, MA: MIT.

Aldgate, T. (1979) *Cinema and History: British Newsreels and the Spanish Civil War*. London: Scolar Press.

Aldridge, M. and R. Dingwall (2003) 'Teleology on Television? Implicit Models of Evolution in Broadcast Wildlife and Nature Programmes', *European Journal of Communication*, 18, 4, 435–53.

Altman, C. (1989) 'Dickens, Griffith, and Film', *South Atlantic Quarterly*, 88, 2, Spring, 321–59.

Andersen, R. (1995) *Consumer Culture and TV Programming*. Boulder: Westview Press.

Anderson, K. T. (2003) 'Toward an Anarchy of Imagery: Questioning the Categorization of Films as "Ethnographic"', *Journal of Film and Video*, 55, 2–3, Summer/Fall, 73–87.

Anon. (2001) 'The Man with the Mini-Camera', *The Economist*, 36, 8242, 10 June, 79.

Anstey, E. (1942) 'Review of *Listen to Britain*', *The Spectator*, 3 March, 8.

Armes, R. (1978) *A Critical History of the British Cinema*. London: Secker and Warburg.

Arthur, P. (1992) 'Routines of Emancipation: Alternative Cinema in the Ideology and Politics of the Sixties', in D. James (ed.) *To Free the Cinema: Jonas Mekas and the New York Underground*. Princeton: Princeton University Press, 17–48.

_____ (1993) 'Jargons of Authenticity (Three American Moments)', in M. Renov (ed.) *Theorizing Documentary*. New York: Routledge, 108–34.

_____ (1996) 'In the Realm of the Senses: IMAX 3D and the Myth of Total Cinema', *Film Comment*, 32, 1, 78–81.

_____ (1998) 'On the Virtues and Limitations of Collage', *Documentary Box*, 11, 31 January. Available at http://www.yamagata.yamagata.jp/yidff/docbox/11/box1-1-e.html (accessed 23 September 2005).

_____ (2003) 'Essay Questions', Film Comment, 39, 1, 58–62.

_____ (2005a) A Line of Sight: American Avant-Garde Film Since 1965. Minneapolis: University of Minnesota Press.

_____ (2005b) 'Extreme Makeover: The Changing Face of Documentary', Cineaste, 30, 3, Summer, 18–24.

Aumont, J. (1997) The Image. London: British Film Institute.

Banks, M. (2001) Visual Methods in Social Research. London: Sage.

Barbash, I. and L. Taylor (2001) 'Radically Empirical Documentary: An Interview with David and Judith MacDougall', Film Quarterly, 52, Winter, 2, 2–14.

Barber, S. (2002) Projected Cities. London: Reaktion Books.

Barnouw, E. (1983) Documentary: A History of the Non-Fiction Film. Oxford: Oxford University Press.

Barr, C. (1992) Widescreen Cinema. Cambridge, MA: Harvard University Press.

Barsam, R. (1992) Nonfiction Film: A Critical History. Bloomington: Indiana University Press.

Barthes, R. (2004 [1957]) 'The Face of Garbo', in L. Braudy and M. Cohen (eds) Film Theory and Criticism: Introductory Readings, sixth edition. New York: Oxford University Press, 589–91.

Bartholomew, W. with T. Baker (1996) Bustin' Down the Door. Sydney: HarperSports.

Bataille, G. (1985 [1929]) 'The Big Toe', in Visions of Excess: Selected Writings 1927–1939 Minneapolis: University of Minnesota Press, 20–1.

Bauldrie, J. (1990) 'Looking Back: D.A. Pennebaker Interviewed', in J. Bauldrie (ed.) Wanted Man: In Search of Bob Dylan. London: Black Springs Press, 44–54.

Bazin, A. (1967 [1946]) 'The Myth of Total Cinema', in What is Cinema?, vol. 1. Berkeley: University of California Press, 17–22.

_____ (1971) What is Cinema?, vol. 2. Berkeley: University of California Press.

_____ (1997 [1953]) 'Will Cinemascope Save the Film Industry', in B. Cardullo (ed.) Bazin at Work: Major Essays and Reviews from the Forties and Fifties. New York: Routledge, 77–92.

_____ (2000 [1947]) 'Science Film: Accidental Beauty', in A. Bellows, M. McDougall and B. Berg (eds) Science is Fiction: The Films of Jean Painlevé. San Francisco: Brico Press, 145–7.

Beattie, K. (2004) Documentary Screens: Non-fiction Film and Television. Houndmills, Basingstoke: Palgrave Macmillan.

Belász, B. (1972 [1952]) Theory of the Film (Character and Growth of a New Art). New York: Arno Press.

Bell, D. (1999) 'Final Cut, Final Battle', in D. Bell (ed.) Woodstock: An Inside Look at the Movie that Shook Up the World and Defined a Generation. Los Angeles: Michael Wise Productions, 228–32.

Benjamin, W. (1983 [1939]) 'On Some Motifs in Baudelaire', in Charles Baudelaire. London: Verso, 107–54.

_____ (2005 [1937]) 'The Work of Art in the Age of Mechanical Reproduction', in A. Utterson (ed.) Technology and Culture: The Film Reader. London: Routledge, 105–26.

Berg, B. (2000) 'Contradictory Forces: Jean Painlevé, 1902–1989', in A. Bellows, M. McDonald and B. Berg (eds) Science is Fiction: The Films of Jean Painlevé. San Francisco: Brico Press, 12–47.

Berlinger, J. with G. Milner (2004) *Metallica: This Monster Lives: The Inside Story of Some Kind of Monster*. New York: Robson Books.

Bial, H. (2004) 'Performativity', in H. Bial (ed.) *The Performance Studies Reader*. London: Routledge, 145–6.

Bignall, J. (2005) *Big Brother: Reality TV in the Twenty-First Century*. Houndmills, Basingstoke: Palgrave Macmillan.

Blum-Reid, S. (2003) *East-West Encounters: Franco-Asian Cinema and Literature*. London: Wallflower Press.

Boddy, W. (1981) 'New York City Confidential: An Interview with Eric Mitchell', *Millennium Film Journal*, 7, 9, 27–36.

Booth, C. (1998) 'IMAX Gets Bigger (By Getting Smaller)', *Time* (Australia), 20 July, 48–9.

Booth, D. (1994) 'Surfing 60s: A Case Study in the History of Pleasure and Discipline', *Australian Historical Studies*, 103, 262–79.

_____ (1996) 'Surfing Films and Videos: Adolescent Fun, Alternative Lifestyle, Adventure Industry', *Journal of Sport History*, 23, 3, 313–27.

Bordwell, D. and K. Thompson (1997) *Film Art: An Introduction*, fifth edition. New York: McGraw-Hill.

Bousé, D. (1998) 'Are Wildlife Films Really "Nature Documentaries"?', *Critical Studies in Mass Communication*, 15, 116–40.

_____ (2000) *Wildlife Films*. Philadelphia: University of Pennsylvania Press.

Brakhage, S. (1976 [1963]) *Metaphors on Vision*. New York: Anthology Film Archives.

_____ (1989) *Film at Wit's End: Eight Avant-Garde Filmmakers*. Edinburgh: Polygon.

_____ (2003) *Telling Time: Essays of a Visionary Filmmaker*. New York: Documentext.

Brenez, N. (2005) '*A propos de Nice* and the Extremely Necessary, Permanent Invention of the Cinematic Pamphlet', *Rouge*, 6. Available at http://www.rouge.com.au/ (accessed 19 February 2006).

Brennan, P. (2002) 'Cutting through Narcissism: Queer Visibility in *Scorpio Rising*', *Genders Online Journal*, 36. Available at http://www.genders.org/g36/g36_brennan.html (accessed 8 May 2005).

Brenton, S. and R. Cohen (2003) *Shooting People: Adventures in Reality TV*. London: Verso.

Brunner, R. (2004) 'Interview: Metallica's "Monster" a Demon of its Own Making', *U-Wire*. Available at http://www.uwire.com/ (accessed 14 September 2005).

Bruzzi, S. (2000) *New Documentary: A Critical Introduction*. London: Routledge.

Buchsbaum, J. (1981) 'A La Recherche des Punks Perdus', *Film Comment*, 17, 3, 43–6.

Buck-Morss, S. (1986) 'The Flâneur, The Sandwichman and the Whore: The Politics of Loitering', *New German Critique*, 39, Fall, 99–140.

_____ (1992) 'Aesthetics and Anaesthetics: Walter Benjamin's Artwork Essay Reconsidered', *October*, 62, Fall, 3–41.

Bukatman, S. (2003) *Matters of Gravity: Special Effects and Supermen in the 20th Century*. Durham: Duke University Press.

Bullock, N. (1997) 'Imagining the Post-War World: Architecture, Reconstruction and the British Documentary Film Movement', in F. Penz and M. Thomas (eds) *Cinema and Architecture: Méliès, Mallet-Stevens, Multimedia*. London: British Film Institute, 52–61.

Burke, E. (n.d.) *On the Sublime and the Beautiful*. Charlottesville: Ibis.

Burt, J. (2002) *Animals on Film*. London: Reaktion Press.

Buskirk, M. (1992) 'Commodification as Censor: Copyrights and Fair Use', *October*, 60, Spring, 82–109.

Caldwell, J. T. (1995) *Televisuality: Style, Crisis, and Authority in American Television*. New Brunswick: Rutgers University Press.

Calvino, I. (1985) *Mr. Palomar*. New York: Harcourt, Brace, Jovanovich.

Carroll, N. (1999) 'Jack's Jack...', *Deep* (Australia), 4, 3, 12–14.

Chapman, J. (1979) 'Two Aspects of the City: Cavalcanti and Ruttmann', in L. Jacobs (ed.) *The Documentary Tradition*. New York: Norton, 37–42.

Chion, M. (1994) *Audio-Vision: Sound on Screen*. New York: Columbia University Press.

Clifford, J. (1988) *The Predicament of Culture: Twentieth-Century Ethnography, Literature, and Art*. Cambridge, MA: Harvard University Press.

Collins, P. (1995) 'Same As it Ever Was: The Journey of Alby Falzon', *Revelation Magazine*, 15, 27–30.

Comolli, J.-L. (1980a [1969]) 'Excerpts from *Cahiers du cinéma* 209 and 211', in C. Williams (ed.) *Realism and the Cinema: A Reader*. London: Routledge and Kegan Paul, 224–53.

_____ (1980b) 'Machines of the Visible', in T. de Laurentis and S. Heath (eds) *The Cinematic Apparatus*. New York: St Martins Press, 121–42.

_____ (1999) 'Documentary Journey to the Land of the Head Shrinkers', *October*, 90, Fall, 36–49.

Corner, J. (1995) *Television Form and Public Address*. London: Edward Arnold.

_____ (1996) *The Art of Record: A Critical Introduction to Documentary*. Manchester: Manchester University Press.

_____ (1999) *Critical Idea in Television Studies*. Oxford: Clarendon Press.

_____ (2000a) 'Documentary in a Post-Documentary Culture? A Note on Forms and their Functions'. Available at http://info.lut.ac.uk/research/changing.media/John%20Corner%paper.htm (accessed 8 April 2005).

_____ (2000b) 'What Can We Say about "Documentary"?', *Media, Culture and Society*, 22, 681–88.

_____ (2002) 'Performing the Real: Documentary Diversions', *Television and New Media*, 3, 3, 255–69.

_____ (2003) 'Television, Documentary and the Category of the Aesthetic', *Screen*, 44, 1, Spring, 92–100.

Cottle, S. (2004) 'Producing Nature(s): On the Changing Production Ecology of Natural History TV', *Media, Culture and Society*, 26, 1, 81–101.

Court, D. (1995) 'Documenting the Nation: A Personal Evaluation of Australia's Documentary Regime', *Metro Magazine*, 104, 58–60.

Cowie, E. (1997) 'Documenting Fictions', *Continuum: The Australian Journal of Media and Culture*, 11, 1, 54–66.

_____ (1999) 'The Spectacle of Actuality', in J. Gaines and M. Renov (eds) *Collecting Visible Evidence*. Minneapolis: University of Minnesota Press, 19–45.

Cox, D. (1998) 'Media Meltdown'. Available at http://sensesofcinema.com/contents/01/13/meltdown.html (accessed 10 October 2005).

Cronin, P. (ed.) *Herzog on Herzog*. London: Faber and Faber.

Crowdus, G. and D. Georgakas (1988) 'History is the Theme of all My Films: An Interview with Emile de Antonio', in A. Rosenthal (ed.) *New Challenges for Documentary*. Berkeley: University of California Press, 165–79.

Cubitt, S. (1991) *Timeshift: On Video Culture*. London: Routledge.

Cunningham, S. (1984) 'A Framework for the Study of Australian Newsreel Production, 1930–1945', in W. Levy, G. Cutts and S. Stockbridge (eds) *The Second Australian History and Film Conference*. Sydney: Australian Film and Television School, 120–5.

Debord, G. and G. Wolman (1981 [1956]) 'Methods of Detournement', in K. Knalb, ed. and trans.*Situationist International Anthology*. Berkeley: Bureau of Public Secrets,8–13.

Dempsey, M. (1988–89) 'Quatsi (sic) Means Life: The Films of Godfrey Reggio', Film Quarterly, 42, 2, Winter, 3–12.

Dermody, S. and E. Jacka, *The Screening of Australia*, Currency Press, Sydney, 1987.

DeRogatis, J. (2002) 'Wilco is Trying to Break Your Heart', *Chicago Sun-Times*, 28 July, NC4.

DiOrio, C. (2001) 'Large-Screen Biz Group Eyes Woes, Remedies', *Variety*, 12 July, 15.

Dixon, W.W. (1995) *It Looks at You: The Returned Gaze of Cinema*. Albany: State University of New York Press.

____ (1998) 'Performativity in 1960s American Experimental Cinema: The Body as Site of Ritual and Display', *Film Criticism*, 23, 1, Fall, 48–52.

Doane, M.A. (1980) 'The Voice in the Cinema: The Articulation of the Body and Space', *Yale French Studies*, 60, 33–50.

____ (2002) *The Emergence of Cinematic Time: Modernity, Contingency, the Archive*. Cambridge, MA: Harvard University Press.

Donald, J. (1995) 'The City, the Cinema: Modern Spaces', in C. Jenks (ed.) *Visual Culture*. London: Routledge, 77–95.

Dunne, G. (1993) 'Video Review', *Tracks*, March, 26.

Durgnat, R. (1989) 'Private Worlds', in J. Pilling and M. O'Pray (eds) *Into the Pleasure Dome: The Films of Kenneth Anger*. London: British Film Institute, 22–9.

____ (1996) 'Jean Painlevé', in K. Macdonald and M. Cousins (eds) *Imagining Reality: The Faber Book of the Documentary*. London: Faber and Faber, 80–1.

Dyer, R. (1985) 'Entertainment and Utopia', in B. Nichols (ed.) *Movies and Methods, vol. 2*. Berkeley: University of California Press, 220–32.

Economy, J. (2000) 'The Death of an Ideal: 1970 Documentary "Gimme Shelter" a Harsh Epitaph for the Woodstock Generation', *Chicago Tribune*, 9 October, Tempo section, 3.

Eisenstein, E. (1957 [1929] 'The Cinematographic Principle and the Ideogram', in *Film Form*. Cleveland: World Publishing, 28–44.

____ (1988 [1923]) 'The Montage of Attractions', in R. Taylor (ed.) *S.M. Eisenstein, Writings, 1922–1934*. London: British Film Institute, 35–50.

Elkins, J. (1992) 'On Visual Desperation and the Bodies of Protozoa', *Representations*, 40, Autumn, 33–56.

Epstein, J. (1977) 'Magnification and Other Writings', *October*, 3, Spring, 9–25.

Erickson, S. (2005) 'Eccentric and Aloft', *Gay City News* (New York), 4, 22, 2–8 June, 14.

Falzon, A. (n.d.) *A Morning of the Earth*. Sydney: Woolloomooloo Picture Company and EMAP Australia.

Falzon, A. and D. Hoole (1998) 'What's On at the Movies?', in M. Thornley and V. Dante (eds) *Surfing Australia*. Hong Kong: Periplus, 36–41.

Featherstone, M. (1995) *Undoing Culture: Globalisation, Postmodernism and Identity*. London: Sage.

Fielding, R. (1972) *The American Newsreel, 1911–1967*. Norman: University of Oklahoma Press.

Fisher, T. (1999) 'Interview [with Albie Thoms]'. Available at http://bonza.rmit.edu.au/essays/text/1999/tim_fisher/Albie_Thoms_Interview.html (accessed 14 February 2005).

Fiske, J. (1986) 'Television and Popular Culture: Reflections on British and Australian Critical Practice', *Critical Studies in Mass Communication*, 3, 200–16.

_____ (1987) *Television Culture*. London: Methuen.

Fiske, J., J. B. Hodge and G. Turner (1987) (eds) *Myths of Oz: Reading Australian Popular Culture*. Sydney: Allen and Unwin.

Flaherty, F. H. (1984) *The Odyssey of a Film-Maker: Robert Flaherty's Story*. Putney, VT: Threshold Books.

Flaus, J. (1974) 'Crystal Voyager', *Cinema Papers*, 2, 277.

Flynn, P. J. (1987) 'Waves of Semiosis: Surfing's Iconic Progression', *American Journal of Semiotics*, 5, 397–418.

Fotiade, R. (1998) 'The Slit Eye, the Scorpion and the Sign of the Cross: Surrealist Film Theory and Practice Revisited', *Screen*, 39, 2, Summer, 109–23.

Freeland, C. (1999) 'The Sublime in Cinema', in C. Plantinga and G. Smith (eds) *Passionate Views: Film, Cognition, and Emotion*. Baltimore: Johns Hopkins University Press, 65–83.

Frith, S., A. Goodwin and L. Grossberg (1993) (eds) *Sound and Vision: The Music Video Reader*. London: Routledge.

Frosh, P. (2003) *The Image Factory: Consumer Culture, Photography and the Visual Content Industry*. Oxford: Berg.

Gaines, J. (1999) 'Political Mimesis', in J. Gaines and M. Renov (eds) *Collecting Visible Evidence*. Minneapolis: University of Minnesota Press, 84–102.

Gamboni, D. (2002) *Potential Images: Ambiguity and Indeterminacy in Modern Art*. London: Reaktion Books.

Gane, J. (1996) 'Videographer: Justin Gane', *Waverider*, 42, 72–6.

Gardner, R. (1996) 'The Impulse to Preserve', in C. Warren (ed.) *Beyond Document: Essays in Nonfiction Film*. Habover: Wesleyan University Press, 169–80.

Gardner, R. and A. Ostor (2001) *Making Forest of Bliss: Intention, Circumstance, and Chance in Nonfiction Film: A Conversation between Robert Gardner + Akos Ostor*. Cambridge, MA: Harvard Film Archive.

Gaughan, M. (2003) 'Ruttmann's Berlin: Filming in a "Hollow Space"', in M. Shiel and T. Fitzmaurice (eds) *Screening the City*. London: Verso, 41–57.

George, S. (2003) 'The Surfer Interview with Jack McCoy', *Surfer Magazine*, 44, 12. Available at http://surfermag.com/magazine/archivedissues/mccoy/index.html (accessed 31 January 2005).

Gitlin, T. (1988) 'Phantom India', in A. Rosenthal (ed.) *New Challenges for Documentary*. Berkeley: University of California Press, 536–41.

Gleber, A. (1997a) 'Female Flanerie and the Symphony of the City', in K. von Ankum (ed.) *Women in the Metropolis: Gender and Modernity in Weimar Culture*. Berkeley: University of California Press, 67–88.

____ (1997b) 'Women on the Screens and Streets of Modernity: In Search of the Female Flâneur', in D. Andrew (ed.) *The Image in Dispute: Art and Cinema in the Age of Photography*. Austin: University of Texas Press, 55–86.

Goehr, L. (1995–96) 'The Perfect Performance of Music and the Perfect Musical Performance', *New Formations*, 27, Winter, 1–22.

Goffman, E. (1969) *The Presentation of Self in Everyday Life*. London: Allen Tate.

____ (2004) 'Performances', in H. Bial (ed.) *The Performance Studies Reader*. London: Routledge, 59–63.

Gold, J. and S. Ward (1994) 'We're Going to Do it Right this Time: Cinematic Representations of Urban Planning and the British New Towns, 1939 to 1951', in S. Aitken and L. Zonn (eds) *Place, Power, Situation, and Spectacle: A Geography of Film*. Lanham, MD: Rowman and Littlefield, 229–58.

Goldman, A. (1992 [1970]) 'Altamont: "A Crime without an Instigator"', in *Sound Bites*. London: Abacus, 167–71.

Goldsmith, D. (2003) *The Documentary Makers: Interviews with 15 of the Best in the Business*. Mies, Switzerland: RotoVision.

Goodall, J. (1999) 'The Nemesis of Natural History', in M. Thomas (ed.) *Uncertain Ground: Essays between Art+Nature*. Sydney: Art Gallery of New South Wales, 106–23.

Goodwin, A. (1987) 'Music Video in the (Post) Modern World', *Screen*, 28, 3, Summer, 36–55.

Green, J. (2005) 'This Reality which is Not One: Flaherty, Buñuel and the Irrealism of Documentary Cinema', in G. Rhodes and J. Springer (eds) *Docufictions: Essays on the Intersection of Documentary and Fictional Filmmaking*. Jefferson, NC: McFarland, 64–87.

Grierson, J. (1979 [1935]) 'Summary and Survey: 1935', in F. Hardy (ed.) *Grierson on Documentary*. London: Faber and Faber, 52–69.

____ (1998a [1932]) 'First Principles of Documentary', in I. Aitken (ed.) *The Documentary Film Movement: An Anthology*. Edinburgh: Edinburgh University Press, 81–92.

____ (1998b [1942]) 'The Documentary Idea', in I. Aitken (ed.) *The Documentary Film Movement: An Anthology*. Edinburgh: Edinburgh University Press, 103–14.

Griffiths, A. (2006) 'Time Traveling IMAX Style: Tales from the Giant Screen', in J. Ruoff (ed.) *Virtual Voyages: Cinema and Travel*. Durham: Duke University Press, 238–58.

Gross, P. (1999) 'Moving Forward: A Greenough Scrapbook, 1960–1970', *The Australian Surfer's Journal*, 2, 2, Autumn, 68–121.

Gundersen, E. (2004) 'Candid Metallica Creates Angst-Filled "Monster"', *USA Today*. Available at http://www.usatoday.com/ (accessed 3 August 2005).

Gunning, T. (1990) 'The Cinema of Attractions: Early Film, its Spectator and the Avant-Garde', in T. Elsaesser (ed.) *Early Cinema: Space, Frame, Narrative*. London: British Film Institute, 56–62.

____ (1994) 'An Aesthetic of Astonishment: Early Film and the (In)Credulous Spectator', in L. Williams (ed.) *Viewing Positions: Ways of Seeing Film*. New Brunswick, NJ: Rutgers University, 114–33.

_____ (1995) 'Tracing the Individual Body: Photography, Detectives, and Early Cinema', in L. Charney and V. Schwartz (eds) *Cinema and the Invention of Modern Life*. Berkeley: University of California Press, 15–45.

_____ (1999) 'Embarrassing Evidence: The Detective Camera and the Documentary Impulse', in J. Gaines and M. Renov (eds) *Collecting Visible Evidence*. Minneapolis: University of Minnesota Press, 46–64.

_____ (2004) '"Now You See it, Now You Don't": The Temporality of the Cinema of Attractions', in L. Grieveson and P. Kramer (eds) *The Silent Cinema Reader*. London: Routledge, 41–50.

Gunning, T. and A. Gaudreault (1989) 'Le cinéma des premier temps: un defi a histoire du film?', in J. Aumont, A. Gaudreault and M. Marie (eds) *Histoire du Cinéma: Nouvelles Approches*. Paris: Publications de la Sorbonne, 49–63.

Hake, S. (1994) 'Urban Spectacle in Walter Ruttmann's *Berlin, Symphony of the Big City*', in T. Kniesche and S. Brockmann (eds) *Dancing on the Volcano: Essays on the Culture of the Weimar Republic*. Columbia, SC: Camden House, 127–37.

Hansen, M. (1987) 'Benjamin, Cinema and Experience: "The Blue Flower in the Land of Technology"', *New German Critique*, 40, Winter, 179–224.

_____ (1991) *Babel and Babylon: Spectatorship in American Silent Film*. Cambridge, MA: Harvard University Press.

_____ (1994) 'Early Cinema, Late Cinema: Transformations of the Public Sphere', in L. Williams (ed.) *Viewing Positions: Ways of Seeing Film*. New Brunswick, NJ: Rutgers University Press, 134–54.

Haug, W. (1986) *Critique of Commodity Aesthetics: Appearance, Sexuality and Advertising in Capitalist Society*. Minneapolis: University of Minnesota Press.

Hazéra, H. and D. Leglu (2000) 'Jean Painlevé Reveals the Invisible', in A. Bellows, M. McDougall and B. Berg (eds) *Science is Fiction: The Films of Jean Painlevé*. San Francisco: Brico Press, 170–9.

Hernandez, R. (2002) 'Phases and Stages', *The Austin Chronicle*, 21 June. Available at http://www.austinchroncile.com/issues/dispatch/2002-06-21/music_phases2.html (accessed 11 October 2005).

Heylin, C. (1991) *Dylan: Behind the Shades*. London: Penguin.

Higonnet, A., M. Higonnet and P. Higonnet (1984) 'Facades: Walter Benjamin's Paris', *Critical Inquiry*, 10, 3, March, 391–419.

Higson, A. (1984) 'Addressing the Nation: Five Films', in G. Hurd (ed.) *National Fictions: World War Two in British Films and Television*. London: British Film Institute, 22–6.

_____ (1995) *Waving the Flag: Constructing a National Cinema in Britain*. Oxford: Clarendon Press.

Hill, A. (2002) 'Big Brother: The Real Audience', *Television and New Media*, 3, 3, 323–40.

_____ (2005) *Reality TV: Audiences and Popular Factual Television*. London: Routledge.

Hogarth, D. (2006) *Realer than Reel: Global Directions in Documentary*. Austin: University of Texas Press.

Hollier, D. and L. Ollman (1992) 'The Use-Value of the Impossible', *October*, 60, Spring, 3–24.

Holmes, P. (1976) 'In Search of Alternative Energy and Power: An Interview with George Greenough', *Tracks*, December, 31–3.

Horak, J.-C. (1995) *Lovers of Cinema: The First American Avant-Garde, 1919–1945*. Madison, WI: University of Wisconsin Press.

James, D. (1989) *Allegories of Cinema: American Film in the Sixties*. Princeton: Princeton University Press.

_____ (1996) *Power Misses: Essays Across (Un)Popular Culture*. London: Verso.

Jameson, F. (1981) *The Political Unconscious: Narrative as a Socially Symbolic Act*. Ithaca: Cornell University Press.

_____ (1986) 'Third-World Literature in the Era of Multinational Capitalism', *Social Text*, 15, 65–88.

_____ (1991) *Postmodernism: Or, The Cultural Logic of Late Capitalism*. Durham: Duke University Press.

Jarratt, P. (1977) *The Wave Game*. Sydney: Soundtracts.

Jenkins, B. (1988–89) 'Mr Clean: The Extraordinary Surfing Life of Randy Rarick', *The Australian Surfer's Journal*, 2, 1, Summer, 54–65.

Jones, S. (2003) 'A Director's Notes on the Making of "I am Trying to Break Your Heart"', (booklet accompanying the DVD). Los Angeles: Plexifilm (unpaginated).

Kael, P. (1970) 'Beyond Pirandello', *New Yorker*, 114, 19 December, 113–14.

Katz, J. (1991) 'From Archive to Archiveology', *Cinematograph*, 4, 96–103.

Kaufman, B. (1979) 'Jean Vigo's *À propos de Nice*', in L. Jacobs (ed.) *The Documentary Tradition*. New York: Norton, 75–8.

Kellner, D. and D. Streible (2000) 'Introduction: Emile de Antonio: Documenting the Life of a Radical Filmmaker', in D. Kellner and D. Streible (eds) *Emile de Antonio: A Reader*. Minneapolis: University of Minnesota Press, 1–86.

Kidman, A (n.d.) 'Albert Falzon', *Litmus: A Surfing Odyssey*. Sydney: The Val Dusty Experiment, 55–62.

Kilborn, R. (2006) 'A Walk on the Wild Side: The Changing Face of TV Wildlife Documentary', *Jump Cut*, 48, Winter. Available at http://www.ejumpcut.org/archive/jc48.2006/AnimalTV/text.html (accessed 29 August 2006).

Klaver, E. (2003) 'Spectatorial Theory in the Age of Media Culture', in P. Auslander (ed.) *Performance: Critical Concepts in Literary and Cultural Studies*, vol. II. London: Routledge, 309–21.

Kleinhaus, C. (1998) 'Independent Features: Hopes and Dreams', in J. Lewis (ed.) *The New American Cinema*. Durham: Duke University Press, 307–27.

Kolaja, J. and A. Foster (1965) 'Berlin, Symphony of a City as a Theme of Visual Rhythm', *Journal of Aesthetics and Art Criticism*, 23, 2, 353–8.

Kracauer, S. (1947) *From Caligari to Hitler: A Psychological History of the German Film*. Princeton: Princeton University Press.

_____ (1960) *Theory of Film: The Redemption of Physical Reality*. Oxford: Oxford University Press.

Krauss, R. (1981) 'The Photographic Conditions of Surrealism', *October*, 19, Winter, 3–34.

Leach, J. (1998) 'The Poetics of Propaganda: Humphrey Jennings and *Listen to Britain*', in B.K. Grant and J. Sloniowski (eds) *Documenting the Documentary: Close Readings of Documentary Film and Video*. Detroit: Wayne State University Press, 154–70.

Levy, D. (1982) 'Reconstituted Newsreels: Re-enactments and the American Narrative Film', in R. Holman (ed.) *Cinema 1900–1906: An Analytical Study*. Brussels: FIAF, 243–60.

Levy, S. (2002) *Ready, Steady, Go! Swinging London and the Invention of Cool*. London: Fourth Estate.

Lewis, A. (2000) 'Stories that Tell Themselves: The Texas Documentary Tour: Meet Albert Maysles', *The Austin Chronicle*, 11 February. Available at http://www.austinchronicle.com/issues/dispatch/2000-02-11/screens_feature.html (accessed 29 January 2005).

Lewis, J. (1998) 'Between the Lines: Surf Texts, Prosthetics, and Everyday Theory', *Social Semiotics*, 8, 1, 55–70.

Leyda, J. (1964) *Films Beget Films: A Study of the Compilation Film*. New York: Hill and Wang.

Loizos, P. (1992) 'Admissible Evidence? Film in Anthropology', in P. Crawford and D. Turton (eds) *Film as Ethnography*. Manchester: Manchester University Press, 50–65.

____ (1993) *Innovation in Ethnographic Film: From Innocence to Self-Consciousness, 1955–1985*. Chicago: University of Chicago Press.

Love, R. (2000) *Reefscape: Reflections on the Great Barrier Reef*. Sydney: Allen and Unwin.

Macdonald, K. and M. Cousins (1996a) 'The Kingdom of Shadows', in *Imagining Reality: The Faber Book of Documentary*. London: Faber and Faber, 3–6.

____ (1996b) 'The Burning Question', in *Imagining Reality: The Faber Book of Documentary*. London: Faber and Faber, 364.

MacDonald, S. (2001) *The Garden in the Machine: A Field Guide to Independent Films about Place*. Berkeley: University of California Press.

____ (2006) 'Up Close and Political: Three Short Ruminations on Ideology in the Nature Film', *Film Quarterly*, 59, 3, Spring, 4–21.

MacDougall, D. (1992–93) 'When Less is Less: The Long Take in Documentary', *Film Quarterly*, 46, 2, Winter, 36–46.

____ (2001) 'Gifts of Circumstance', *Visual Anthropology Review*, 17, 1, Spring/Summer, 68–85.

____ (2006) *The Corporeal Image: Film, Ethnography, and the Senses*. Princeton: Princeton University Press.

McCoy, J. (2004) 'Jack McCoy's Tips and Tricks'. Available at http://www.panasonic.com.au/support/downloads/more_info.cfm?objectID=1672 (accessed 11 October 2005).

McDougall, M. (2000) 'Introduction: Hybrid Roots', in A. Bellows, M. McDougall and B. Berg (eds) *Science is Fiction: The Films of Jean Painlevé*. San Francisco: Brico Press, xiv–xviii.

McKie, D. (1994) 'Telling Stories: Unnatural Histories, Natural Histories, and Biopolitics', *Australian Journal of Communication*, 21, 3, 99–110.

McMillen, J. (2005) 'Five Days North: A Surfing Odyssey', in *Blue Yonder: A Journey into the Heart of Surf Culture*. Sydney: Macmillan, 77–85.

McQuire, S. (2000) 'Impact Aesthetics: Back to the Future in Digital Cinema?: Millennial Fantasies', *Convergence*, 6, 2, Summer, 41–61.

Malle, L. (2005) *L'Inde fantôme: Carnet de voyage*. Paris: Gallimard.

Maltby, R. and I. Craven (1995) *Hollywood Genres: An Introduction*. Oxford: Blackwell.

Mamber, S. (1974) *Cinéma Vérité in America*. Cambridge, MA: MIT.

Mandelbaum, M. (1980) 'The Presuppositions of Metahistory', in G. Nadel (ed.) *Metahistory: Six Critiques*. Middleton, CT: Wesleyan University Press, 39–52.

Marks, L. (1996) 'The Audience is Revolting: Coalition and Transformation at the Flaherty Seminar', in P. Zimmerman and E. Barnouw (eds) *The Flaherty: Four Decades in the Cause of Independent Cinema* (Special issue of *Wide Angle*), 17, 1–4, 277–91.

_____ (2000) *The Skin of the Film: Intercultural Cinema, Embodiment, and the Senses.* Durham: Duke University Press.

_____ (2002) *Touch: Sensuous Theory and Multisensory Media.* Minneapolis: University of Minnesota Press.

Medhurst, M. and T. Benson (1981) 'The City: The Rhetoric of Rhythm', *Communication Monographs*, 48, March, 54–72.

Mensel, R. (1999) '"Kodakers Lying in Wait": Amateur Photography and the Right of Privacy in New York, 1885–1915', *American Quarterly*, 43, 1, March, 24–45.

Merman, E. (1997) 'Being Where? Experiencing Narratives of Ethnographic Film', *Visual Anthropology Review*, 13, 1, Spring, 40–51.

Michelson, A. (1979) 'Dr. Crase and Mr. Clair', *October*, 11, Winter, 30–53.

_____ (1984) *A Kino-Eye: The Writings of Dziga Vertov.* Berkeley: University of California Press.

_____ (1999) 'Eisenstein at 100: Recent Reception and Coming Attractions', *October*, 88, Spring, 69–86.

Miller, J. (1999) *Almost Grown: The Rise of Rock.* London: Heinemann.

Mitman, G. (1999) *Reel Nature: America's Romance with Wildlife on Film.* Cambridge, MA: Harvard University Press.

Moore, A. (1988) 'The Limitations of Imagist Documentary: A Review of Robert Gardner's *Forest of Bliss*', *SVA Newsletter*, Fall, 1–3.

Moritz, W. and B. O'Neill (1978) 'Some Notes on the Films of Bruce Conner', *Film Quarterly*, 31, 4, Summer, 36–42.

Mulvey, L. (1975) 'Visual Pleasure and Narrative Cinema', *Screen*, 16, 3, 6–18.

_____ (2006) *Death 24X a Second: Stillness and the Moving Image.* London: Reaktion Books.

Naficy, H. (2001) *An Accented Cinema: Exilic and Diasporic Filmmaking.* Princeton: Princeton University Press.

Natter, W. (1994) 'The City as Cinematic Space: Modernism and Place in Berlin, *Symphony of a City*', in S. Aitken and L. Zonn (eds) *Power, Place, Situation, and Spectacle: A Geography of Film.* Lanham, MD: Rowman and Littlefield, 203–27.

Neale, S. (1979) '*Triumph of the Will*: Notes on Documentary and Spectacle', *Screen*, 20, 1, 63–86.

_____ (2000 [1990]) 'Questions of Genre', in R. Stam and T. Miller (eds) *Film and Theory: An Anthology.* Oxford: Blackwell, 157–78.

Nichols, B. (1988) 'The Voice of Documentary', in A. Rosenthal (ed.) *New Challenges for Documentary.* Berkeley: University of California Press, 48–63.

_____ (1991) *Representing Reality: Issues and Concepts in Documentary.* Bloomington: Indiana University Press.

_____ (1993) '"Getting to Know You...": Knowledge, Power, and the Body', in M. Renov (ed.) *Theorizing Documentary.* New York: Routledge, 174–92.

_____ (1994) *Blurred Boundaries: Questions of Meaning in Contemporary Culture.* Bloomington: Indiana University Press.

_____ (1995) 'Documentary and the Coming of Sound'. Available at http://www.filmsound. org/film-sound-history/documentary.htm (accessed 7 February 2005).

_____ (1996) 'Historical Consciousness and the Viewer: _Who Killed Vincent Chin?_', in V. Sobchack (ed.) _The Persistence of History: Cinema, Television, and the Modernist Event._ New York: Routledge, 55–68.

_____ (2000) 'Film Theory and the Revolt Against Master Narratives', in C. Gledhill and L. Williams (eds) _Reinventing Film Studies._ London: Arnold, 34–52.

_____ (2001) 'Documentary Film and the Modernist Avant-Garde', _Critical Inquiry_, 27, 4, Summer, 580–610.

Noll, G. and A. Gabbard (1989) _Da Bull: Life over the Edge._ Berkeley: North Atlantic Books.

Novak, B. (1980) _Nature and Culture: American Landscape Painting, 1825–1875._ London: Thames and Hudson.

October (1979) 'An Interview with Mikhail Kaufman', _October_, 11, Winter, 54–76.

O'Toole, L. (1979) 'Werner Herzog Interviewed by Lawrence O'Toole', _Film Comment_, November/December, 34–48.

Ostor, A. (1994) '_Forest of Bliss_: Film and Anthropology', _East-West Film Journal_, 8, 2, 70–104.

Painlevé, J. (1931) 'Cinema in the Service of Science', from the Archives of Jean Painlevé. Available at http://www.lesdoc.com/archives (accessed 23 December 2005).

_____ (1967) 'Remarks on the Work of Dr Comandon', from the Archives of Jean Painlevé. Available at http://www.lesdoc.com/archives (22 December 2005).

_____ (2000a [1953]) 'The Castration of the Documentary', in A. Bellows, M. McDougall and B. Berg (eds) _Science is Fiction: The Films of Jean Painlevé._ San Francisco: Brico Press, 149–56.

_____ (2000b [1948]) 'The Ten Commandments', in A. Bellows, M. McDougall and B. Berg (eds) _Science is Fiction: The Films of Jean Painlevé._ San Francisco: Brico Press, 159.

Pennebaker, D.A. (1971) '_Don't Look Back_ and _Monterey Pop_', in A. Rosenthal (ed.) _The New Documentary in Action: A Casebook in Film Making._ Berkeley: University of California Press, 189–98.

Petrić, V. (1993) _Constructivism in Film: The Man with the Movie Camera: A Cinematic Analysis._ Cambridge: Cambridge University Press.

_____ (1995) 'Vertov, Lenin, and Perestroika: The Cinematic Transposition of Reality', _Historical Journal of Film, Radio and Television_, 15, 1, March, 3–18.

Petro, P. (1989) _Joyless Streets: Women and Melodramatic Representation in Weimar Germany._ Princeton: Princeton University Press.

Pike, A. and R. Cooper (1980) _Australian Film, 1900–1977._ Melbourne: Oxford University Press.

Plantinga, C. (1996) 'Moving Pictures and the Rhetoric of Nonfiction: Two Approaches', in D. Bordwell and N. Carroll (eds) _Post-Theory: Reconstructing Film Studies._ Madison: University of Wisconsin Press, 307–24.

_____ (1997) _Rhetoric and Representation in Nonfiction Film._ Cambridge: Cambridge University Press.

_____ (1999) 'The Scene of Empathy and the Human Face on Film', in C. Plantinga and G. Smith (eds) _Passionate Views: Film, Cognition, and Emotion._ Baltimore: Johns Hopkins University Press, 239–55.

Polan, D. (1986) '"Above All Else to Make You See": Cinema and the Ideology of Spectacle', in J. Arac (ed.) _Postmodernism and Politics._ Minneapolis: University of Minnesota Press, 55–69.

Powers, J. (1988) 'Kitschy Quatsi [sic]', *California*, June, 126.

Pronay, N. (1971) 'British Newsreels in the 1930s. 1. Audience and Producers', *History*, 56, 411–18.

_____ (1972) 'British Newsreels in the 1930s. 2. Their Policies and Impact', *History*, 57, 63–72.

_____ (1976) 'The Newsreels: The Illusion of Actuality', in P. Smith (ed.) *The Historian and Film*. Cambridge: Cambridge University Press, 95–120.

Renan, S. (1967) *Introduction to the American Underground Film*. New York: Dutton.

Renov, M. (1993a) 'Introduction: The Truth about Non-Fiction', in M. Renov (ed.) *Theorizing Documentary*. New York: Routledge, 1–11.

_____ (1993b) 'Toward a Poetics of Documentary', in M. Renov (ed.) *Theorizing Documentary*. New York: Routledge, 12–36.

_____ (1999) 'Documentary Horizons: An Afterward', in J. Gaines and M. Renov (eds) *Collecting Visible Evidence*. Minneapolis: University of Minnesota Press, 313–26.

Richardson, M. (1994) *Georges Bataille*. London: Routledge.

Robins, K. (1996) *Into the Image: Culture and Politics in the Field of Vision*. London: Routledge.

Romney, J. (1995) 'Access All Areas: The Real Space of Rock Documentary', in J. Romney and A. Wootton (eds) *Celluloid Jukebox: Popular Music and the Movies since the 1950s*. London: British Film Institute, 82–93.

Roscoe, J. (2001) 'Real Entertainment: New Factual Hybrid Television', *Media International Australia*, 100, 9–20.

Rosenthal, A. (1980) '*In the Year of the Pig* and *Underground*: Emile de Antonio', in A. Rosenthal (ed.) *The Documentary Conscience*. Berkeley: University of California Press, 205–26.

Rotha, P. (1952 [1935]) *Documentary Film: The Use of the Film Medium to Interpret Creatively and in Social Terms the Life of the People as it Exists in Reality*. New York: Hastings House.

Rothman, W. (1997) *Documentary Film Classics*. New York: Cambridge University Press.

Ruby, J. (1990) 'The Emperor and His Critics', *SVA Newsletter*, Spring, 9–11.

_____ (2000) *Picturing Culture: Explorations of Film and Anthropology*. Chicago: University of Chicago Press.

Rugoff, R. (2000) 'Fluid Mechanics', in A. Bellows, M. McDonald and B. Berg (eds) *Science is Fiction: The Films of Jean Painlevé*. San Francisco: Brico Press, 49–57.

Russell, A. (2006) 'Review of "Undercover Surrealism" exhibition' (May–June 2006, London), *Seen and Heard International*. Available at http://www.musicweb.uk.net (accessed 10 October 2006).

Russell, C. (1999) *Experimental Ethnography: The Work of Film in the Age of Video*. Durham: Duke University Press.

Rutsky, R. and J. Wyatt (1990) 'Serious Pleasures: Cinematic Pleasure and the Notion of Fun', *Cinema Journal*, 30, 1, Fall, 3–19.

Salles Gomes, P. E. (1972) *Jean Vigo*. London: Secker and Warburg.

Sandusky, S. (1992) 'The Archaeology of Redemption: Toward Archival Film', *Millennium Film Journal*, 26, Fall, 3–25.

Sargeant, J. (1995) *Deathtripping: An Illustrated History of the Cinema of Transgression*. London: Creation Books.

_____ (2001) 'No Text/No Truth/Jouissance and Revolution: An Interview with Craig Baldwin'. Available at http://sensesofcinema.com/contents/01/13/baldwin-revolution.html (accessed 4 September 2005).

Savlov, M. (1999) 'Walking the Straight Edge: The Texas Documentary Tour: Jem Cohen and Fugazi', _The Austin Chronicle_. Available at http://www.austinchronicle.com/gyrobase/Issue/stroty?oid=73737 (accessed 3 September 2004).

Schobert, W. (2003) '"Painting in Time" and "Visual Music": On German Avant-Garde Films of the 1920s', in D. Scheunemann (ed.) _Expressionist Film: New Perspectives_. New York: Camden House, 237–50.

Sekula, A. (1993) 'Reading the Archive', in B. Wallis (ed.) _Blasted Allegories: An Anthology of Writings by Contemporary Artists_. Cambridge, MA: MIT, 114–28.

Sennett, R. (1994) _Flesh and Stone: The Body and the City in Western Civilization_. New York: Norton.

Sergi, G. (2001) 'The Sonic Playground: Hollywood Cinema and its Listeners', in M. Stokes and R. Maltby (eds) _Hollywood Spectatorship: Changing Perceptions of Cinema Audiences_. London: British Film Institute, 121–31.

Severn, S. (2002–03) 'Robbie Robertson's Big Break: A Reevaluation of Martin Scorsese's _The Last Waltz_', Film Quarterly, 56, 2, Winter, 25–31.

Shearer, S. (1999) 'Aquaman', _Deep_ (Australia), 4, 3, 18–23.

Short, R. (2003) _The Age of Gold: Surrealist Cinema_. London: Creation Books.

Siegal, M. (1997) 'Documentary that Dare/Not Speak its Name: Jack Smith's _Flaming Creatures_', in C. Holmlund and C. Fuchs (eds) _Between the Sheets, In the Streets: Queer, Lesbian, Gay Documentary_. Minneapolis: University of Minnesota Press, 91–106.

Sitney, P. A. (1979) _Visionary Film: The American Avant-Garde, 1943–1978_, second edition. Oxford: Oxford University Press.

_____ (1990) 'The Cinematic Gaze of Joseph Cornell', in K. McShine (ed.) _Joseph Cornell_. New York: The Museum of Modern Art, 68–89.

Skoller, J. (2005) _Shadows, Specters, Shards: Making History in Avant-Garde Film_. Minneapolis: University of Minnesota Press.

Slater, E. (1999) 'Video Reviews', _Surfer_, 40, 10, 68.

Sontag, S. (1967 [1964]) 'Jack Smith's _Flaming Creatures_', in G. Battcock (ed.) _The New American Cinema: A Critical Anthology_. New York: Dutton, 204–10.

Sounes, H. (2001) _Down the Highway: The Life of Bob Dylan_. New York: Grove Press.

Spellerberg, J. (1985) 'CinemaScope and Ideology', _The Velvet Light Trap_, 21, Summer, 26–33.

Spielmann, Y. (1999) 'Aesthetic Features in Digital Imaging: Collage and Morph', _Wide Angle_, 31, 1, January, 131–48.

Stafford, B. (1993) _Body Criticism: Imaging the Unseen in Enlightenment Art and Medicine_. Cambridge, MA: MIT.

_____ (1994) _Artful Science: Enlightenment Entertainment and the Eclipse of Visual Education_. Cambridge, MA: MIT.

Stedman, L. (1997) 'From Gidget to Gonadman: Surfers, Feminism, and Postmodernism', _Australian and New Zealand Journal of Sociology_, 33, 1, 75–90.

Stranger, M. (1999) 'The Aesthetics of Risk: A Study of Surfing', _International Review for the Sociology of Sport_, 34, 3, 265–76.

Stummer, R. (2004) 'Revealed: Unseen Pictures of The Beatles in America', *Independent on Sunday*, 11 January, 12.

Suarez, J. (1996) *Bike Boys, Drag Queens, and Superstars: Avant-Garde, Mass Culture, and Gay Identities in the 1960s Underground Cinema*. Bloomington: Indiana University Press.

Sussex, E. (1972) 'Grierson on Documentary', *Film Quarterly*, 26, 1, Autumn, 24–30.

Sweeting, A. (2004) 'Break for the Border', *Uncut*, 85, June, 134.

Taussig, M. (1992) 'Tactility and Distraction', in G. Marcus (ed.) *Reading Cultural Anthropology*. Durham, NC: Duke University Press, 8–14.

Thompson, S. (2004) 'Punk Cinema', *Cinema Journal*, 43, 2, Winter, 47–66.

Thoms, A. (1978) *Polemics for a New Cinema*. Sydney: Wild and Woolley.

_____ (2000) *surfmovies* [sic]: *A History of the Surf Film in Australia*. Noosa: Shorething Publishing.

Thornley, M. (1999) 'Surfing's Vibe Tribe', *Underground Surf* (Australia), 18, 52–8.

Tsivian, Y. (1996) 'Media Fantasises and Penetrating Vision: Some Links between X-Rays, the Microscope, and Film', in J. Bowlt and O. Matich (eds) *Laboratory of Dreams: The Russian Avant-Garde and Cultural Experiment*. Stanford, CA: Stanford University Press, 81–99.

Turvey, M. (1999) 'Can the Camera See? Mimesis in "Man with a Movie Camera"', *October*, 89, Summer, 25–50.

Tythacott, L. (2003) *Surrealism and the Exotic*. London: Routledge.

Uricchio, W. (1995) 'Archives and Absences', *Film History*, 7, 256–63.

Van Wert, W. (1974) 'The "Hamlet Complex" or, Performance in the Personality-Profile Documentary', *Journal of Popular Film*, 3, 257–63.

Vernet, M. (1989) 'The Look at the Camera', *Cinema Journal*, 28, 2, Winter, 48–63.

Viorst, M. (1979) *Fire in the Streets: America in the 1960s*. New York: Simon Schuster.

Virilio, P. (1990) 'Cataract Surgery: Cinema in the Year 2000', in A. Kuhn (ed.) *Alien Zone: Cultural Theory and Contemporary Science Fiction Cinema*. London: Verso, 169–74.

_____ (2002) 'The Visual Crash', in T. Levin, U. Frohne and P. Weibel (eds) *CTRL [Space]: Rhetorics of Surveillance from Bentham to Big Brother*. Cambridge, MA: MIT, 108–13.

Wahlberg, M. (2006) 'Wonders of Cinematic Abstraction: J.C. Mol and the Aesthetic Experience of Science Film', *Screen*, 47, 3, 273–89.

Warshaw, M. (1999) 'Rough Cut: Surfing on Film', *The Australian Surfer's Journal*, 2, 2, 10–27.

_____ (2003) *The Encyclopedia of Surfing*. New York: Harcourt.

Waugh, T. (1985) 'Beyond *Vérité*: Emile de Antonio and the New Documentary of the Seventies', in B. Nichols (ed.) *Movies and Methods*, vol. 2. Berkeley: University of California Press, 233–57.

_____ (1990) '"Acting to Play Oneself": Notes on Performance in Documentary', in C. Zucker (ed.) *Making Visible the Invisible: An Anthology of Original Essays on Film Acting*. Metuchen, NJ: Scarecrow Press, 64–91.

Wees, W. (1993) *Recycled Images: The Art and Politics of Found Footage Films*. New York: Anthology Film Archives.

_____ (2000) 'Old Images, New Meanings: Recontexualizing Archival Footage of Nazism and the Holocaust', *Spectator*, 20, 1, Fall/Winter, 70–6.

Weihsmann, H. (1997) 'The City in Twilight: Charting the Genre of the "City Film", 1900–1930', in F. Penz and M. Thomas (eds) *Cinema and Architecture: Méliès, Mallet-Stevens, Multimedia*. London: British Film Institute, 8–27.

Weiner, B. (1971) 'Radical Scavenging: An Interview with Emile de Antonio', *Film Quarterly*, 25, Autumn, 3–15.

White, H. (1987) *The Content of the Form: Narrative, Discourse and Historical Representation*. Baltimore: Johns Hopkins University Press.

Wilkinson, T. (2001) 'Hasta la victoria siempre', *Senses of Cinema*. Available at http://sensesofcinema.com/contents/01/17/cteq/hasta (accessed 2 August 2005).

Williams, L. (1991) 'Film Bodies: Gender, Genre, and Excess', *Film Quarterly*, 44, 4, Summer, 2–13.

____ (2000) 'Discipline and Fun: Psycho and Postmodern Cinema', in C. Gledhill and L. Williams (eds) *Reinventing Film Studies*. London: Arnold, 351–78.

Winston, B. (1988) 'The Tradition of the Victim in Griersonian Documentary', in A. Rosenthal (ed.) *New Challenges for Documentary*. Berkeley: University of California Press, 269–87.

____ (1995) *Claiming the Real: The Documentary Film Revisited*. London: British Film Institute.

____ (1998a) 'Not a Lot of Laughs: Documentary and Public Service', in M. Wayne (ed.) *Dissident Voices: The Politics of Television and Cultural Change*. London: Pluto, 145–58.

____ (1998b) 'Theatrical and Television Documentary: The Sound of One Hand Clapping', in T. Elsaesser and K. Hoffmann (eds) *Cinema Futures: Cain, Abel or Cable? The Screen Arts in the Digital Age*. Amsterdam: Amsterdam University Press, 167–76.

Wolff, E. (1999)'The Big Picture: Filmmakers Assess the State of the Giant Screen', *Millimeter*, 1 May. Available at http://millimeter.com/mag/video_big_picture_filmmakers/ (accessed 2 November 2004).

Wolff, J. (1985) 'The Invisible Flâneuse: Women and the Literature of Modernity', *Theory, Culture and Society*, 2, 3, 37–46.

Wollen, P. (1982) 'The Two Avant-Gardes', in *Readings and Writings: Semiotic Counter-Strategies*. London: Verso, 92–104.

Wollen, T (1993) 'The Bigger the Better: From CinemaScope to Imax', in P. Hayward and T. Wollen (eds) *Future Visions: New Technologies of the Screen*. London: British Film Institute, 148–65.

Young, N. and C. McGregor (1984) *The History of Surfing*, revised edition. Palm Beach: Palm Beach Press.

Young, N. (1998) *Nat's Nat and That's That*. Angourie: Nymboid Press.

Zryd, M. (2003) 'Found Footage Film as Discursive Metahistory: Craig Baldwin's Tribulation 99', *The Moving Image*, 3, 40–61.

index